By the same author

Alone Through China and Tibet

Dancing with the Dead

Looking for George: Love and Death in Romania

Mother Tongues: Travels Through Tribal Europe

HELENA DRYSDALE

Strangerland

A Family at War

PICADOR

First published 2006 by Picador
an imprint of Pan Macmillan Ltd
Pan Macmillan, 20 New Wharf Road, London N1 9RR
Basingstoke and Oxford
Associated companies throughout the world
www.panmacmillan.com

ISBN-13: 978-0-330-41169-1
ISBN-10: 0-330-41169-1

1 3 5 7 9 8 6 4 2

A CIP catalogue record for this book is available from
the British Library.

Phototypeset by Intype London Ltd
Printed and bound in Great Britain by
Mackays of Chatham plc, Chatham, Kent

Author's note

Although the intimate detail in *Strangerland* may often suggest fiction, this is a work of non-fiction, and any reference to actual people either living or dead is in no way coincidental. The story is true, and based on an extraordinary range of surviving documents. The hunt for these, and the detective work involved, is described in the Postscript.

Since the documents were written in the nineteenth century, the names and spellings of those times have been retained. Hence the use of nineteenth-century transliterations of Indian words such as Cawnpore, which is now known as Kanpur, or the Hoogley River, now known as the Hugli, or 'solar topee' instead of the modern 'solar topi'. In New Zealand the Wairau, Poverty Bay and White Cliffs Massacres have now been tactfully downgraded to 'incidents', while with an eye on racial sensitivities the Maori Wars have today become 'the New Zealand Land Wars'.

Acknowledgements

I would like to thank the following for their help in the writing of *Strangerland*. I am deeply grateful to all of them. They are:

Tim Boyer, Anthony Chamier, Peter Coxon, Sir Edward Dashwood, Merida Drysdale, Adam Fergusson, Geordie Fergusson, Bamber Gascoigne, Andrew Luff, Cathy McGregor, Gregory Morris, Constance Miller, Gascoyne (Jim) Miller, Peter Newman, Denys Oldham, Dr Rosalind Ramsay, Ronald Seymour Shove, and Coralie Smith, all of whom provided crucial pictures, books, diaries, letters, and other material and help. Tim Bates, Tim Boyer, Emma Craigie, Peter Coxon, Bamber Gascoigne, Gavin McLean, Gregory Morris and Richard Pomeroy, who read parts or all of the typescript and suggested valuable improvements. The staff at Picador, in particular Nicholas Blake, Editorial Manager, and Editor Sam Humphreys for tireless and skilful editing. My agent Derek Johns for unstinting support. Sir Robin and Lady Campbell, the Hickley family, Georgie and Ben Lutyens, and the Miller and McGregor families for hospitality in New Zealand. The Marquess of Salisbury, and Sir Geoffrey Newman and Lady Ann Newman for allowing me to browse their archives.

Thanks also to the willing and friendly staff of the following libraries: the Library of the British Empire & Commonwealth Museum, Bristol; the archives at Hatfield House; the Hocken Library, Dunedin; the London Library; Motueka Museum; Nelson Provincial Museum; the Royal Commonwealth Society Collection in Cambridge University Library; the Oriental and India Office Collection at the British Library; John Oxley Library, Queensland; the Public Record Office; Puki Ariki Museum, New Plymouth; Tairawhiti Museum, Gisborne; the Manuscripts and Archives Section in Wellington's Alexander Turnbull Library.

Thanks to the Marquess of Salisbury for permission to quote from letters written by the Gascoyne family and the 2nd and 3rd Marquesses; to Constance Miller for permission to quote from her unpublished book, *The Gascoyne Story*; and to the Alexander Turnbull Library for permission to quote from letters written by Isabella, Charles and Frederick Gascoyne and Donald McLean. Isabella's letters have been slightly edited, substituting full stops where she used hyphens, but otherwise the words are hers.

Thanks to the Society of Authors' K. Blundell Trust for a generous grant to help with research.

Finally, special thanks to Richard, Tallulah and Xanthe Pomeroy for coming with me on this long journey. *Strangerland* is dedicated to them.

Timeline

1805 Surgeon John Campbell marries Eliza Monro in Calcutta.

1806 Charles Gascoyne born in Olveston, Gloucestershire.

1810 Isabella Augusta Eliza Campbell born in Madras.

1811 Eliza Campbell and her children arrive in England on the *Sovereign*.

1814 First missionaries land in New Zealand.

1815 Eliza returns to Madras, leaving Isabella and her brothers in England.

1816 Captain John Campbell dies of cholera in Secunderabad.

1820 Eliza Campbell dies in London.

1826 Charles Gascoyne receives a cadetship for the East India Company's Bengal Cavalry.

1827 Isabella leaves school, aged seventeen.

1834 Charles becomes Interpreter and Quartermaster for the 5th Bengal Light Cavalry. Isabella sails for India on the *Broxbournebury*.

1835 Isabella Campbell marries Charles Gascoyne in Meerut. Isabelle Gascoyne born in Cawnpore.

1836 Archy Campbell marries Emily Payter in Calcutta.

1837 Charles Gascoyne born in Cawnpore.

1838 Frederick Gascoyne born in Cawnpore; baby Charles dies.

1839 Charles joins Lord Auckland's staff. Invasion of Afghanistan.

1840 Mary Gascoyne born in Kurnaul. The Gascoynes sail for England on the *Carnatic*. The Treaty of Waitangi makes New Zealand a British colony. Donald McLean lands in New Zealand.

1841–2 Uprising in Kabul and 1st Afghan War. The New Zealand Company sends out its first shipment of settlers.

1842 Emily [Amy] Gascoyne born in Scotland. Miss Sutherland employed as governess. Nelson founded.

1843 The Gascoynes leave England for Calcutta.

1844 Gascoyne baby girl dies in Muttra.

1845–6 Charlie Gascoyne born in Muttra. 1st Sikh War. Archy Campbell dies. New Zealand's War in the North.

1846 Charlotte Gascoyne born in Meerut.

1849 The Gascoynes move to Lohughat.

1852 Caroline Gascoyne born in Lohughat. New Zealand granted self-government.

1853 Isabella and Charlie sail for England on the *Hindoostan*. The rest of the family lands in Nelson. Donald McLean appointed master-buyer of Maori land.

1854 Isabella and Charlie land in New Zealand. The Gascoynes move to Pangatotara.

1857 Isabella leaves home. The Indian Mutiny. Fred becomes a cadet at Maraekakaho. First Maori king elected.

1858 Charles demands separation for life. Izzy marries John Greenwood and gives birth to their first child.

1859 Isabella returns to Pangatotara.

Timeline

1860   Fred works for John Greenwood at his saw mill. Taranaki War.

1861   Fred starts gold panning near Collingwood.

1863   Fred's gold-mining claim flooded. He joins the Hawke's Bay militia. Invasion of the King Country. Isabella and Charles baptized by Plymouth Brethren.

1864   Bamber Gascoyne lands in New Plymouth. Pai Marire springs up in Taranaki.

1865   Pai Marire and war spread to East Cape.

1866   Te Kooti exiled to Chatham Islands.

1868   Te Kooti escapes from Chatham Islands. Poverty Bay Massacre.

1869   White Cliffs Massacre. Prince Alfred arrives. McLean becomes Minister for Native Affairs and Defence.

1872   Charles dies in Pangatotara. Fred marries Marion Carr in Napier.

1877   Donald McLean dies. Pangatotara destroyed by floods.

1891   Fred becomes Resident Magistrate of the Chatham Islands.

1903   Isabella dies in Nelson.

1926   Fred dies in Hastings.

Contents

New Zealand, North Island

N

0 _____ 120 miles
0 _____ 200km

Golden (Massacre) Bay
Tasman (Blind) Bay
Collingwood
Aorere River
Riwaka
Brooklyn
Motueka
Pangatotara
Baton River
Nelson
Moutere
Arthur Range
Motueka River
Wairau River

NELSON PROVINCE

MARLBOROUGH

Greymouth

Christchurch ● Lyttelton

CANTERBURY PROVINCE

Waimate ●

OTAGO

Chatham Is.

to Chatham ⟶
Waitangi ●

Pitt Is.

New Zealand, South Island

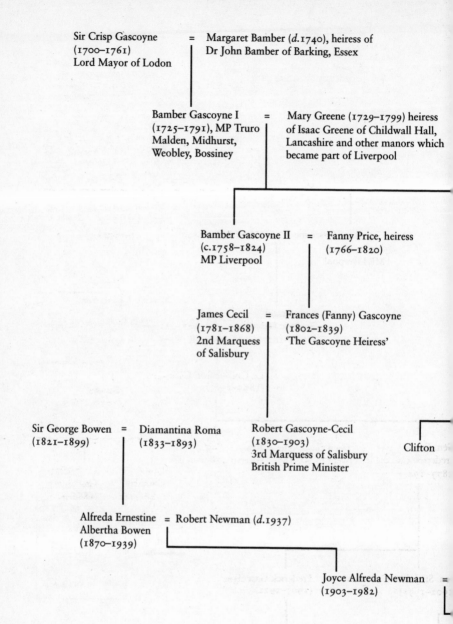

Sir Crisp Gascoyne
(1700–1761)
Lord Mayor of Lodon

= Margaret Bamber (*d.*1740), heiress of
Dr John Bamber of Barking, Essex

Bamber Gascoyne I
(1725–1791), MP Truro
Malden, Midhurst,
Weobley, Bossiney

= Mary Greene (1729–1799) heiress
of Isaac Greene of Childwall Hall,
Lancashire and other manors which
became part of Liverpool

Bamber Gascoyne II
(c.1758–1824)
MP Liverpool

= Fanny Price, heiress
(1766–1820)

James Cecil
(1781–1868)
2nd Marquess
of Salisbury

= Frances (Fanny) Gascoyne
(1802–1839)
'The Gascoyne Heiress'

Sir George Bowen
(1821–1899)

= Diamantina Roma
(1833–1893)

Robert Gascoyne-Cecil
(1830–1903)
3rd Marquess of Salisbury
British Prime Minister

Clifton

Alfreda Ernestine
Albertha Bowen
(1870–1939)

= Robert Newman (*d.*1937)

Joyce Alfreda Newman
(1903–1982)

=

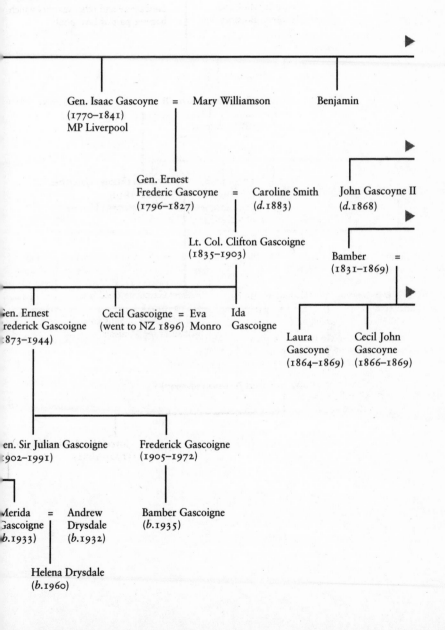

Gen. Isaac Gascoyne = Mary Williamson   Benjamin
(1770–1841)
MP Liverpool

Gen. Ernest
Frederic Gascoigne = Caroline Smith   John Gascoyne II
(1796–1827)   (d.1883)   (d.1868)

Lt. Col. Clifton Gascoigne
(1835–1903)   Bamber   =
                                       (1831–1869)

Gen. Ernest   Cecil Gascoigne = Eva   Ida
Frederick Gascoigne (went to NZ 1896) Monro Gascoyne
(1873–1944)   Laura   Cecil John
                                                   Gascoyne   Gascoyne
                                                   (1864–1869)   (1866–1869)

Gen. Sir Julian Gascoigne   Frederick Gascoigne
(1902–1991)   (1905–1972)

Merida   = Andrew   Bamber Gascoigne
Gascoigne   Drysdale   (b.1935)
(b.1933)   (b.1932)

Helena Drysdale
(b.1960)

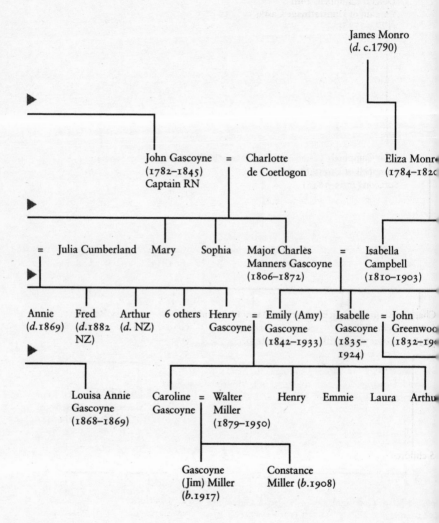

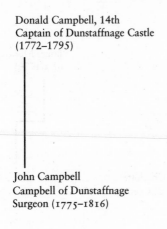

Donald Campbell, 14th
Captain of Dunstaffnage Castle
(1772–1795)

= John Campbell
Campbell of Dunstaffnage
Surgeon (1775–1816)

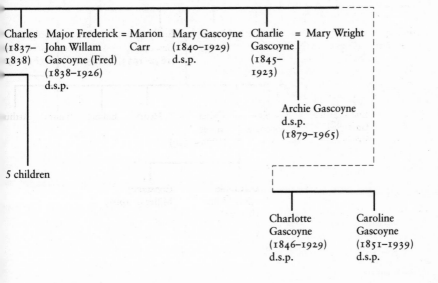

Charles
(1837–
1838)

Major Frederick = Marion
John Willam   Carr
Gascoyne (Fred)
(1838–1926)
d.s.p.

Mary Gascoyne
(1840–1929)
d.s.p.

Charlie   = Mary Wright
Gascoyne
(1845–
1923)

Archie Gascoyne
d.s.p.
(1879–1965)

5 children

Charlotte
Gascoyne
(1846–1929)
d.s.p.

Caroline
Gascoyne
(1851–1939)
d.s.p.

ONE

Isabella

1852

As Isabella Gascoyne was hoisted onto the shoulders of her stocky Kumaoni bearers, she clutched the armrests of her jhampan and braced her back and feet for shock. The four men grunted as they stood, and flung her this way and that until they found their stride. Not an elegant mode of transport, unlike the beloved landau and pair she had been forced to abandon on the plains; more a wooden armchair on poles with nothing except a small cushion for comfort. As it was the only way to reach Lohughat, she would have to suffer this for the next three days.

Jolting past Almorah's new hospital, past the magistrate's whitewashed bungalow in its palm-shaded compound and over the stone flags of the close and filthy streets of the bazaar, she felt newly hatched. Everything she saw seemed to glisten with her own newness. Over the last few years she had stopped noticing things; now she observed the sun sending long morning shadows out of the cantonment and across the deserted parade ground, the bony haunches of a Brahmin bull which blocked her way before squeezing left into a side alley, and the open-fronted shops with their proprietors lurking in the dark interiors who called to the Burra Bibi to come in and buy! Buy! BUY!

There had been moments when Isabella had loathed India. It had killed her father with cholera and her mother with grief. It had killed two of her children and two of her brothers, one with cholera and the other, her favourite, by destroying his liver. But today she loved it. She had been born here; India was in her blood, a part of her. It did not occur to her that this was the last time she would make this journey.

Since she arrived in India twenty years earlier, Isabella's health had been so robust that she had astonished her family and friends. How, they wondered, did she withstand the rigours of the climate – the suffocating heat, the dust-swirling winds of the plains, the fever-filled rainy season, the sometimes bitterly cold frosts up in Kumaon? While other women crinkled and fell like yellowing moths – perhaps the pale-lemon sallow – Isabella fluttered on regardless. Then to everyone's surprise, after Caroline's birth she barely left her bed for weeks. Cocooned in her mosquito net, she shrivelled in the dark. The blinds were dropped, the punkah swayed back and forth, and the older children took turns to sit with her, dabbing her forehead with eau de cologne, while Charles read to her (mainly poetry and his beloved Walter Scott), but nothing could rouse her. The new baby languished.

Dr Pierson was summoned urgently from Almorah. When he arrived two days later he recommended that Isabella should accompany him home so as to be constantly under his care. Caroline was Isabella's ninth baby, and the doctor insisted that at the age of forty-two this should be her last.

Dr Pierson was sympathetic enough to prescribe company

which, while she lodged with him and his wife, he would attempt to provide, but she hated being away from her family. This was the first time she and Charles had been parted for more than a few weeks. Charles wrote to her in Almorah, 'My own dearest Isabella, I would like, believe me, to be by your bedside, my hand in your hand, to nurse you in your illness. You know I never like you to go from home even for an hour and would never have consented to your leaving me save for your health . . .'

Isabella kept all Charles's letters. Later she would need them to remind her of how he once felt, or – if none of his sentiments were true – as proof of his hypocrisy.

Now her strength had returned and she was desperate to get home to Lohughat. After two months of the loquacious Dr Pierson she was even eager to endure her husband's melancholy, and their silent evenings together punctuated only by the deferential padding of bare Indian feet.

The path climbed a rocky hillside, the boulder-strewn bed of the Shooal dwindling below. A bearer stumbled on loose rock, sending pebbles scuttering behind them. They hugged the scree to the left; Isabella dared not look down to the right, down into a tree-tufted chasm that grew steeper by the minute. The acute angle made her skirts drop back and her black button boots bounced on the footboard in front of her. The bearers at the rear bore her full weight, and their muscles bulged with the strain. They had nearly a thousand feet to climb. She would walk a bit, she said, but they ignored her; the Memsahib was too weak and her skirts too cumbersome.

A white diamond glinted in a cleft in the hills then they reached the pass and, as it flattened and opened out, ridge upon

filmy ridge hove into view, shaggy with forest that was silhou-
etted against the sharp points of the highest and most distant
of the Snowy Ranges. Isabella forgot her nervousness to gaze in
awe at the soaring grandeur as if for the first time. She identified
Nanda Devi, its buttressing spurs seeming to prop up the central mass like a cathedral; and there was Pancha-Chuli, a huge
white pyramid supported at each corner by symmetrical peaks.

After crossing a plateau furrowed by ravines and dotted
with outbursts of granitic masses, at last they reached the
longed-for dak bungalow, a ramshackle rest house with a room
furnished with a charpoy, a table and two hard chairs. Isabella's bearers provided water for a wash and a simple dinner. The
night was chilly: they were up at 6,633 feet.*

It was late the next day before they emerged from the
gloomy sal forest and descended to the Lohughat River. They

---

* An exquisite map, the first ever made of Kumaon and British Gurwhal, was
compiled in 1849 in the office of the Surveyor General of India, incorporating
the latest additions from the researches of Captain Henry Strachey and Lieutenant Richard Strachey, engineers. The Stracheys were part of the Great
Trigonometrical Survey, which between 1802 and 1880 for the first time
mapped the entire Indian subcontinent, marking Isabella's route along the high
Mornaula ridge on a scale of eight British miles to one inch. The Stracheys
drew the Himalayan foothills like hairs coiling up the flanks of a knee, or
stretch marks up a breast, a technique that makes it easier to follow Isabella's
ridge than the onion-ring contours used in the versions of the 1860s and 1930s.
Probably to cater for the later map-makers with their troops of bearers lugging
chains and theodolites and telescopes, dak bungalows were built at That and
Dol, but in Isabella's day none are marked until the pilgrimage site at Deo
Dhoora, twenty-nine miles from Almorah. This was too far for one day's journey, so Isabella's baggage coolies must have carried a tent, and erected it for
her. The 1849 map, then only three years old, marks the track as fit only for
camels, but it was a while since a camel had been spotted in the hills, curling
its rubbery lips in disdain.

crossed the last stretch of undulating grassland sprinkled with deodars, then climbed the last precipitous slope towards the Bungalow. Here, finally, was the entrance gate and the avenue of huge apricot trees, their trunks nearly two feet in diameter. Here was the garden with its avenue of horse chestnuts that Isabella loved so much, and then the Bungalow itself, with its pillared roof of stone slabs hanging sullenly overhead and shading its deep veranda. Here was Charles hurrying loose-limbed and elegant down the veranda steps, their children flocking behind. Everyone had come to greet her, including Miss Sutherland, the tall handsome governess with her auburn hair piled on her head. Even the servants came hurrying out to salaam the Memsahib and to exclaim at her marvellous recovery. It was a wonderful homecoming, better than she could have envisaged.

Isabella joyfully observed her offspring. Fred was turning thirteen and becoming almost as handsome as his father, though sturdier. Fifteen-year-old Izzy was as reserved as ever – she was shy after her mother's long absence. Then there was Mary, the stolid but clever one, aged twelve; Amy at eleven becoming the vivacious beauty of the family; Charlie, six; Charlotte, five; and baby Caroline in the arms of her ayah.

Fred shouted that a tiger had paid them a call. He dragged his mother around the garden to show her where it had left its spoor *here* and *here*. He described how Captain Lockett, their only neighbour and a great shikari, had come down from Raikott with his gun as he was afraid that this could be the man-eater who had recently killed the barefoot letter carrier while he was running with the mail from Petoragarh. Captain Lockett had studied the spoor and declared this to be a different tiger, and as there was no sign of injury it was probably still able to kill in the wild, so had no need to kill man. It would not yet have acquired the taste for human flesh. He reassured them that they could sleep safely in their beds.*

That evening while Isabella's ayah was brushing out her dark hair, Charles came in and dismissed the girl. There were things they needed to discuss. Isabella assumed he wanted to talk about plans for the tea garden; recent research had shown that the height and the climate were perfect for it. They had already done well from renting out the shooting to British officers; of their three bungalows, two were used by shikari who ventured up from the plains to hunt deer and tiger. They had also been successful with rare birds that had been stuffed and sold in Almorah. Now the talk was of tea. Captain Lockett was already doing well, and throughout the district revenues from tea were said to be rising. There were hopes that one day, when railway lines criss-crossed India, a station would be built in the foothills to take their tea down to Calcutta, and across the seas to England.

Charles announced abruptly that far from investing in Lohughat, they would be leaving it. Why? Isabella was appalled. The children loved the place, and she was tired of moving. When Charles was still with the cavalry she had enjoyed their peripatetic life, largely because of the companionship of the regiment. She had pitied the wives of Collectors

---

* Almorah was where the famous tiger-hunter Major Jim Corbett later made his name, tracking and shooting man-eaters who were mauling villagers around Lohughat during the 1920s and '30s. He defeated such notorious killers as the Chowgarh, Kanda and Thak man-eaters, and the infamous Bachelor of Powalgarh, but he was also celebrated for his work on the conservation of tigers, and one of India's greatest national parks bears his name.

and other civilians who were deposited on some lonely frontier without a white face for a thousand miles; she was used to the gregarious society of Charles's fellow officers, who were so accomplished when it came to social niceties, and to whiling away long hot afternoons talking about nothing in particular with no sign of fatigue. Now that Charles had left the regiment they would have to start their new lives in some strange part of India on their own.

Charles replied that they would not be moving to another part of India. He had been sent a book that had convinced him of the desirability of moving somewhere a great deal further away. He produced two volumes bound in maroon leather. The book was called *Hursthouse's New Zealand, or, Zealandia, the Britain of the South*.

Charles might as well have said the moon. Fourteen thousand miles or two hundred thousand, it made no difference: they were equally remote from those Isabella loved. All she knew about New Zealand was that it lay at the other end of the earth, and was populated by warring cannibals and a few lawless settlers who risked losing both their capital and their heads. Even if she didn't lose her own head, going to the New World was like going to the next world. She would never see her relatives again: so far as they were concerned, she might as well be dead. And if it was lonely in Lohughat, imagine how isolated they would be in New Zealand! The few settlements were notorious for their grog shops, their dens of debauchery and blasphemy, populated by scoundrels of every sort. There were no cities like Calcutta, no garrisons like Cawnpore or Meerut, no hill stations, no avenues, no servants.

Isabella realized that throughout the evening she had sensed

7

a suppressed excitement in Charles, and in the children too; even Miss Sutherland was in on it. Isabella had been the last to know. She felt as if she was being jogged along like a passenger in the jhampan of her family's destiny, unable to get out and walk.

Why, she asked, need they leave India when they had been happy here for twenty years? Charles's answer was that India was destroying their health. If they wanted to live, they had to leave, but if they retired to England how could they survive? Their class dictated that they could not go into trade, or follow any ungenteel pursuits. The only proper thing permitted by their social station was to buy land, which they could not afford. Instead, they would have to live on slender means in some chilly seaside resort, watching their acquaintances' eyes glaze over as Charles, no longer a man of consequence attended by a swarm of servants but a yellow-faced bore, regaled them with tales of battlefield glory. All the luxuries they were used to would vanish, and Fred would have to become a clerk, a profession for which he was totally unsuited, while the girls would turn into pallid governesses.

Besides, after twenty-six years in India, Charles had come to see 'Home' as wretchedly fog-bound and poverty-stricken, particularly since reading the latest instalments of the new Dickens, *David Copperfield*. To Charles, England was a world of match-sellers, sweatshops, dark satanic mills, Nonconformism, an angry urban proletariat barracked in tenements and slums and the even less fortunate incarcerated in the workhouse. Only just emerging from the Hungry Forties, it did not appeal.

New Zealand, on the other hand (according to Hursthouse), was perfect. The natives had been tamed by missionaries, and the settlers by English law. There was not one single dangerous creature, no man-eaters to terrorize the villagers, no snakes.* It offered an English climate with four seasons, so their health would recover. There was cheap land, and a huge potential to make an income from what grew on it, what lay beneath it, what swam around it, and with that the prospect of putting abundant food on the table, and setting up the children. None of them need be governesses or clerks. Charles would no longer be a humiliated member of the East India Company's Invalid Establishment, of no use to his regiment and a burden on the Company. Instead he would be a landowner, possibly involved in politics, framing laws, guiding the affairs of a young nation. Why not? He would be the squirearchy of the new land.

Charles was fired up by the possibility of buying land for mere shillings per acre, when in five years it would be worth pounds. 'One of the most fatal errors of emigration', Hursthouse wrote, 'is the error of delay. Thousands, sensible of the advantages of emigration, linger on from year to year, sink from bad to worse, and then when they have nothing left to emigrate with, emigrate as a last resource.' For Charles it was now or never. Already emigration to Australia was increasing rapidly, pushing up the price of land, and whatever affected Australia also affected New Zealand.

How, Isabella enquired, would they make their living? The answer was sheep. Hursthouse provided a dazzling array of figures to prove that the markets in Bradford and Leeds, and in France, were begging for fine combing wool. Feeding on New Zealand's lush pastures, the sheep would grow quickly and

---

* Just one timid, rare and mildly poisonous spider, the katipo.

cheaply, allowing Charles to undercut local markets. It was the dawn of international trade; steam shipping and railways were truncating distance and would whisk his wool around the world.

That was a comfort, but Isabella was brought up short when she tried to picture her husband anywhere near a mountain of oily rancid-smelling fleece. The poetically minded Charles as a red-necked farmer? Those tapering fingers sawing down trees, or working a plough? It was grotesque. Charles was already forty-six: too old to transform his character overnight. As for her, elegant and sociable, turning into a ruddy-cheeked farmer's wife up to her elbows in the washtub? No!

What about friends? Family? Society? Charles said they would persuade relatives in England to join them. Charles's brother John had ten children to provide for; his eldest son Bamber was, by all accounts, an excellent young gentleman and the perfect age to share in the Gascoyne adventure.

Charles Hursthouse declared his wide-ranging credentials to be 'A New Zealand Colonist, and former visitor in the United States, the Canadas, the Cape Colony, and Australia'. Compared with these other colonies, New Zealand was, he declared, Heaven on Earth. Isabella doubted the motives behind his hyperbole. His book was pure propaganda, an unashamed attempt to persuade the reader to uproot and settle at the other end of the earth. Why? As a member of the New Zealand Company, a land-buying agency, and an owner of land himself, Hursthouse was writing from self-interest. The more people who bought land, the more his own would rise in value. He admitted as much himself, but argued that just because he was going to make a profit, it did not make his advice any less worthwhile. It was as absurd to reject it as it was to refuse to buy a hat just because the milliner would profit from the sale.

Isabella laid the volumes on the bed. She had married Charles for better or for worse, and she would go with him wherever he desired. However, this proselytizing Hursthouse would have to bear the responsibility for uprooting her family and transforming not only her own destiny but also that of her children, her nephews and all the generations thereafter. Hursthouse's book was dismissed in T. M. Hocken's *Bibliography of New Zealand Literature* (Wellington, 1909) as 'Tiresome and verbose, as are all this writer's pamphlets.' Ultimately Isabella would have cause to condemn it as 'one of the most deceiving and mischievous books ever published of this colony.'

TWO

Up the Country

Like Charles, Isabella came from the fringes of the aristocracy. Also like Charles, she was the younger child of a younger child, so with slender means and even leaner prospects.

Her father, Captain John Campbell, was the seventh son of the Fourteenth Constable – or 'Captain' – of Dunstaffnage. This forbidding castle, built around 1220, is one of the most ancient in Scotland. Its blank walls, pocked only with gun holes and latrine closets, grow sheer out of a hunk of rock on a promontory that guards the entrance to Loch Etive where it meets the Firth of Lorn, guarding access by sea to the Pass of Brander, and from there to the very centre of Scotland. During the Jacobite Rebellion it was home to Flora Macdonald, who, after helping Bonnie Prince Charlie to escape to Skye in 1746, was briefly held prisoner behind its eleven-foot-thick walls.* John Campbell could boast something better: legend had it that during the ninth century his family home had housed behind

---

* By imprisoning Flora Macdonald in Dunstaffnage, from where she was shipped to the Tower of London, the Campbells rather unromantically supported the English. The Campbells had been Protestant since long before many other Scottish clans. They held traditional rights to the Captaincy of Dunstaffnage from the Dukes of Argyll, heads of the Campbell clan.

those massive walls the Stone of Destiny, which was used as a throne for the coronation of Scottish kings.*

John Campbell met Isabella's mother soon after she left school, and they were quickly engaged. Born in 1784, Eliza Monro was equally Scottish, from a cadet family of the Monros of Foulis Castle in Ross-shire. Her father, James Monro, had fought for the British in the American War of Independence[†] and died aged forty-eight in Trinidad, leaving his children orphaned and penniless. His eldest son was awarded a pension by the government 'in consideration of his father's great service during the American War', while his youngest daughter Eliza, still a child, was adopted by her father's friend General Sir George Osborn of the 40th Regiment of Foot, and his wife Lady Heneage Osborn, a daughter of the Earl of

---

* The Stone, on which Jacob laid his head when he dreamt of the ladder of angels that reached from earth to heaven, supposedly remained at Dunstaffnage until, in an attempt to unite his kingdom of Picts and Scots, Kenneth Macalpine moved it to Scone, from where it was stolen by King Edward I and taken south to become part of the Coronation Chair in Westminster Abbey. In 1996, 700 years later, it was returned to Scotland and housed in Edinburgh Castle.

† James Monro and his brother Robert travelled to America where they made a fortune, married American women and settled in North Carolina. But at the outbreak of the American War of Independence Robert took the side of the 'patriots' against the British, while James took the side of the crown. James Monro was authorized by the Governor of North Carolina to erect the King's standard and 'to oppose all rebels and traitors', including his own brother. He returned to Scotland where (at his own expense) he raised a loyalist battalion, chiefly among members of his own clan, to fight for King George III, on the understanding that the British government would incorporate his battalion into the British army and repay his expenses. James Monro accompanied his corps back to America and fought with distinction as its colonel, with a price on his head. But when the war ended the government reneged on its promise, the battalion was disbanded and Eliza's father was ruined.

Winchilsea. Sir George and Lady Heneage had Eliza educated in London to the highest degree in the arts of music, sketching and French.

After completing his medical training in Edinburgh in 1800, John Campbell found work as assistant surgeon to the 14th Native Infantry in Madras. He was twenty-six, but had to wait until he was thirty before Eliza was able to join him. She travelled out under the protection of her favourite brother, Archy Monro, who was taking up a post with the 7th Native Cavalry in Madras. They nearly failed to make it: the journey from Cromarty to London was frighteningly stormy, and then they narrowly escaped being taken prisoner by the French. Nevertheless in March 1805 Eliza and John were married in Calcutta, and John was promoted to surgeon with the 8th Madras Light Cavalry.

After five years of India's heat and sickness, Eliza Campbell's health failed. She said goodbye to her husband and returned home in the *Sovereign*, a splendid East Indiaman of 617 tons, three decks, 132ft long, commanded by her husband's favourite brother, Alexander Campbell. With her was baby Isabella Augusta Eliza. Born on 7 April 1810 in Madras, she was baptized two days later at Fort St George, a ceremony hastily arranged because of the possibility – or probability – of the infant's death. The *Sovereign*'s passenger list also includes four-year-old Archibald Campbell (named after Eliza's brother, who had remained behind in Madras with John); three-year-old Osborn (named after Eliza's adoptive parents); and five-year-old Alexander Aeneas, named after John's brother the captain, and John's great friend Aeneas MacIntosh, a Calcutta merchant.

They joined the ship in Madras with three native servants, and sailed north to Calcutta. At the height of the Napoleonic Wars, even that short journey was fraught with hazards. Just four days out of Madras, on 16 September 1810, Captain Campbell notes, 'AM saw a strange sail, made signal to Honourable Company Ship *Astele* [with whom they were travelling in convoy] and cleared Ship for action, which prevented the performance of Divine Service.' There is no mention of any action so the danger must have passed, but it was a tense and exciting time on board for passengers and crew. The next day the crew were 'employed under boat as usual',* but they also took the precaution of exercising the great guns and small arms, which may or may not have re-assured the passengers.

While in the harbour in Calcutta the *Sovereign* was washed, the rigging overhauled, and a cargo of saltpetre loaded. They sailed for England on 8 January 1811 in fair weather with light winds, but on 15 January the lookout at the masthead sang out that he had spotted a strange sail and again the decks were cleared for action. This alarm was repeated several times. They ran into hard rain with thunder and lightning, terrifying for the children, and the crew pumped ship every two hours. The sea was too unsettled for Captain Campbell to perform divine service. Later that month the quartermaster died, while in February one of the crew was given three dozen lashes for inso-lence to the third officer and boatswain. By March, Captain

---

* This meant that the crew were employed as usual under the boatswain, the officer in charge of the sails and rigging, who summoned the men to work with a whistle.

Campbell was concerned about a leak in the stern due to bad caulking.*

They were travelling in a small convoy, commanded by a naval frigate. When the lookout spotted a strange sail on the horizon, the frigate gave chase, and soon two ships returned to the convoy, both showing English colours. To everyone's excitement the frigate had captured a French ship called *La Manche*, and they escorted their prize to Portsmouth where they landed on 15 May 1811. The journey had taken over eight months.

Eliza Campbell spent the next four years with relatives in and around Cromarty in the far north of Scotland. She also visited Dunstaffnage Castle, which had recently burnt down, leaving it standing like a rotten tooth on its crag while the Campbells built a new house nearby. Eliza yearned for her husband, but there was no question of his abandoning his career and returning to Scotland; there were no prospects for him there. As Walter Scott said mournfully, India had become 'the corn chest for Scotland where we poor gentry must send our younger sons as we send our black cattle to the South.' In 1815 Eliza, unable to bear being parted from John any longer, decided to rejoin him in India.

Isabella, just five years old, was taken from all she had come to know. The family travelled south, and after her brothers were

---

* The log reveals the tips of other dramas. On 18 January Captain Campbell noted that a Mrs Debrinne had died and was committed to the deep with the 'usual ceremony'. A scan of the passenger list reveals that Mrs Debrinne left behind three children aged between two and six. No husband or servant is listed, so the children had to witness the death of their mother, then continue their journey alone. Of the eleven other adult passengers, one must have taken these motherless waifs under their wing, but who met them at the other end? The log does not relate.

left with a tutor in Cheltenham, Isabella was driven by coach to Bath and deposited at a tall thin Georgian house belonging to a tall thin spinster. Miss M— intended to take in five more pupils from genteel families but so far Isabella was the only one. Eliza left her daughter there and in 1816 departed for India. Miss M— was cruel. She forced Isabella to learn music and other matters 'far beyond my powers or inclination'. When Isabella made mistakes in her lessons the spinster pushed her head into a basin of water and held it there until she almost drowned. Unable to understand why she had been left with this evil woman, Isabella would run into the street calling for her mother, but she would be dragged back into the house and punished for insubordination. When no more pupils were forthcoming, perhaps because the servants had whispered around Bath stories of the bullying, Miss M— wrote to Isabella's guardian and then took her up to London and left her at a high-walled boarding school in Cadogan Place.

Before Isabella had a chance to absorb her strange new surroundings, or even take off her coat, a maid hurried her upstairs to a dormitory where she was ordered to change into black clothes that had been laid out on a bed. She was then rushed down a dark corridor and into the room of a severe-looking elderly woman, who coldly informed Isabella that her father was dead.

Isabella was separated from her brothers, her mother had left her, and now her father had died. Imprisoned in an alien establishment, poor, friendless, disorientated and alone: she was still only five years old. Several times she tried to escape, running down the canyon-like pavements of Cadogan Place below the soaring brick facades, and she would call her mother's name.

Then at last something good happened to little Isabella, something for which she would be grateful throughout her life. Her class was out walking in a crocodile in Hyde Park when a stout but kind-faced woman stopped them, and asked the governess the name of the smallest girl, who reminded her of someone. When she heard it was Isabella Campbell, daughter of the late Captain John Campbell, the woman swept Isabella into her arms, covered her face in kisses and begged that for as long as Isabella remained at the school, she should stay with her every Saturday-to-Monday*. Mrs Skinner was the widow of an American general, and a cousin of the Dunstaffnage Campbells. Isabella would remember her as 'kindness itself'.

Sometimes Isabella was collected from school in an old carriage with a lame coachman and a hump-backed footman, both attired in gorgeous livery. Her destination was the grand but sinister house inhabited by Lady Heneage Osborn, her adoptive grandmother. Isabella later recalled being terrified by the drawing room with its sofas, curtains and hangings of faded thick blue satin damask, and its tables and chairs encrusted with grinning monsters on curious twisted legs. Even more intimidating was Lady Heneage's sister, Lady Helen Finch. She sat upright with her hair high and powdered in Queen Anne style, dressed in peaked bodice, lace ruffles and very high-heeled shoes. She was stiff and cold, but Lady Heneage, who dressed more simply, as a widow, was fond of Isabella and kind to the poor child.

---

* Isabella's memoirs predate the word 'weekend'.

She wanted to leave Isabella a legacy; her chilly sister forbade it.

One night at about nine o'clock Isabella lay in the dormitory, when she was roused and dressed and placed in a carriage with a silent footman in a powdered wig. They drove what seemed a long distance, to Kensington. They stopped outside a well-lit house. Isabella was ushered into a room full of company and kissed as people murmured, 'Poor little thing.' Isabella gazed around her in befuddled surprise. She was put to bed by a woman she had never met but who claimed to be her aunt, and must have been Eliza's sister Anne, who had married a Mr Townsend Pasea, wealthy owner of much of Trinidad. The bed was soft, the covers warm.

In the morning Mr Pasea drove her to a hotel in a quiet part of London. They went upstairs to a drawing room that looked dark and dismal. The curtains were partly drawn. At the far end Isabella saw a woman in black lying full length on a sofa. 'In an instant I knew it was my dear mother, whom I had never forgotten and to whom I had often tried to go. She clasped me in her arms, and I would not be parted from her nor leave hold of her hand for a minute all day.'

Isabella's brothers were summoned from Cheltenham, and the family was – briefly – reunited. As a widow Eliza Campbell's circumstances were much reduced, and she had to take the drawing-room floor of a modest house in Lisson Grove, then a pleasant but unfashionable village north of Marylebone. It was arranged that the boys should go to school in Putney, while Isabella was sent to be educated a few doors away by a Miss Payton, who took in pupils.

Despite their straitened circumstances, it was a happy time for Isabella. Inevitably, it was destined not to last.

Eliza Campbell was a broken woman. After an outward journey of nearly six months in a ship commanded by a cousin of John's, yet another Captain Campbell, she had reached Madras. She could not go immediately to her husband as there was no dock or jetty and ships had to moor in the Madras roads, and wait for passengers to be ferried ashore in small native catamarans. As soon as the ship was spotted, the Indians pushed off from the beach and surfed the breakers with letters and other items of news tucked into their conical straw hats; when the first catamaran reached the ship, all the passengers crowded together to hear Captain Campbell read the news. Not noticing Eliza in the crowd, he read out, 'John Campbell Dunstaffnage is dead. He died of cholera after a few hours of illness, caught while attending at the hospital.' Dr Campbell had died at Secunderabad on 23 March 1816.

So here was Eliza Campbell, who had prised herself away from her children, travelled from Scotland to the west of England then on to London, spent her savings to voyage for six months in a frail craft over six thousand miles of ocean: a huge wheel had turned, and for nothing. John had been buried a few days before his wife arrived. She had not seen him for five and a half years. She fainted on the deck.

Throughout her life, Isabella kept her parents' letters, which, she wrote, demonstrated the intensity of their love. During the eleven years of their happy marriage, they had been together for only four. All Eliza had to comfort her was John's Bible. On his deathbed he had placed his Bible in the hands of his trusty bearer, and told him to take it to the Memsahib and place it in her own hands. No longer able to write, he had managed to send his wife a message by turning down a leaf and underlining a verse. It was in effect his last word to her. 'Leave thy fatherless children and I will preserve them alive, and let thy widows trust in me.' That was all she could do: trust in God. Isabella would keep her father's dog-eared Bible for the rest of her life.

In 1818 Eliza's beloved brother Archy Monro, still out in Madras, died too. Eliza never recovered from these shocks and lingered in Lisson Grove for only three years. Despite the attentions of the most eminent doctors, who gave their services for free because Eliza was the widow of a medical officer, in 1820 Isabella saw her mother laid out in her coffin in the darkened drawing room, her face waxy as a death mask. It was a sight she never forgot.

Now orphaned, Isabella was sent to board (miserably) at Miss Payton's school. One afternoon Isabella was shown into the parlour and presented to a whiskered gentleman who sat studying her silently, leaning on a cane with a carved ivory top. He had a friendly face, and instead of shrinking, Isabella dared to gaze back at his whiskers and a large gold chain slung across his waistcoat, and one knobbled finger that was adorned with an enormous ruby ring. His skin was dark, burnt by the sun. He lifted her onto his lap. She smelled his agreeable spicy smell.

'Are you very unhappy, my dear?' he asked gently.

She nodded.

'I believe I shall take you away from here. I have a more superior school in mind, more suitable for a Miss Campbell of Dunstaffnage.'

Aeneas MacIntosh had been her father's greatest friend, and

in his last will and testament John Campbell had bequeathed to him the care of his four children. Mr MacIntosh was a nabob who had retired from the great mercantile house of MacIntosh, Fulton and McClintock in Calcutta with a fortune of £30,000 – today worth £1,400,000.* Now he had retired to a five-storey mansion in smart Montague Square, overlooking a huge communal garden. From that day Isabella spent every holiday with her guardian. As a bachelor he observed propriety by inviting a woman with daughters to chaperone Isabella and keep her company.

For two years Isabella attended Miss Montier's school in Clapham, where she met several other daughters of the Empire who she would later run into in far-flung British outposts, then she was sent to a finishing school called Oxford House. Two elderly sisters, the Misses Priscilla and Susannah Brown, ran this establishment of sixty pupils. Miss Priscilla was stately and dignified and never seen without her head swathed in a turban. She hated men, and dismissed them as 'odious creatures, necessary evils'. When out walking two by two (a governess at every fourth row) the girls were obliged to cover their faces in green veils, and if a gentleman passed by they had to turn their eyes to the wall. It was a very refined school, and they were taught by French masters of drawing and dancing who also attended Princess Victoria.

Mr MacIntosh did not know much about girls, and treated his ward as a small woman. From the age of fifteen until she left school in 1827, Isabella attended all his dinner parties, which were exceedingly grand, and in the drawing room with

---

* Later the collapse of this firm would ruin many rich old Anglo-Indians.

its full-length windows opening onto an elegant little balcony she met, as she put it, 'many of the great men of the day'. She listened to discussions about free trade, Catholic emancipation and the independence of states in South America, Mexico and Greece, and she loved to hear the talk of India, the land of her birth. It was a time of excitement about Abroad – its colour and vivacity – while England stood on the threshold of a colossal boom. It was also a time of agitation and social discontent, of transition between a rural and an industrial society, the age of the Radicals and their demands for parliamentary reform.* Perhaps around the dinner table in Montague Square there was also talk of art and literature, of Scott, Keats, Shelley, Wordsworth and, until his much-lamented death at Missolonghi in 1824, Byron. For those like Isabella literate in French there were Stendhal and Hugo. Up the road in galleries such as the Royal Academy there were exhibitions by Constable, Lawrence, Turner, Rowlandson, and the French artists David and Géricault.

Sometimes Isabella stayed with John Goldsborough Ravenshaw, who lived at 9 Lower Berkeley Street, close to fashionable Piccadilly. Mr Ravenshaw was another old friend of Isabella's father and a director of the East India Company. Through him she may have met his fellow company directors, such as James Mill, who was 'Examiner of Indian Correspondence'. Mill was not only employed in the company's magnificent offices in Leadenhall Street – the very epicentre of the burgeoning empire – but was also a follower of the philosopher Jeremy Bentham, whose

---

* George IV was on the throne and his reign was spanned by Lord Liverpool's Tory ministry, dominated first by Castlereagh and then by Canning and Peel.

search for the greatest good for the greatest number of people informed Mill's hugely influential three-volume *History of British India*, published in 1817. This was the first such history, and the first to make severe criticisms of the conquest and administration of India. It taught that the Indian subcontinent was riddled with vice, ignorance, despotism and the cruel customs of Asian misrule, and suggested that the role of the British in India was not to plunder the subcontinent, but to bring about a total change in the system of government in order to free the poor enslaved Indian from the yoke of ignorance and tyranny, and to dispense liberal democracy and justice along benevolent British lines. James Mill was the father of the radical socialist and Benthamite John Stuart Mill, one of the most influential philosophers of the century, who was also employed in London by the East India Company. Isabella may not have read their works, but their ideas permeated her milieu.

Isabella left school in 1827 and spent the next few years in Scotland, staying in Argyllshire with her uncle and guardian Captain Alexander Campbell, who had retired from the East India Company and bought the lovely Innistore, near Dunstaffnage.* She was surrounded by Campbell cousins, including her uncle Niall Campbell, who was now the fifteenth Captain of Dunstaffnage. From the way the orphaned Isabella was welcomed, it is clear that she was warm-hearted and popular. She was well finished and well connected; she was also a beauty with dark hair that she wore in abundant ringlets, huge doe-

---

* Isabella loved her uncle Alexander Campbell so much that when she found he had stolen a legacy left her by her father, she couldn't begrudge it. He only took it, she declared loyally, because the poor man needed it more than she.

like eyes, a high forehead and wide cheekbones and a slender figure.

By now Mr Ravenshaw had supplied all Isabella's brothers with cadetships for the East India Company. These commissions were not bought – in fact if money was seen to have changed hands, the cadetship was void. Instead the process was more like being proposed as a member of a club. Nominees were recommended by a friend or acquaintance, who passed on their recommendations to a member of the Court of Directors or Board of Control, each of whom had a fixed number of nominations for each season. Thus membership of the East India Company was kept comfortably in 'the family'.

One by one Isabella's brothers departed for Bengal – Alexander in 1821, then Archy and Osborn in 1825. Isabella was left alone, with no home or immediate family. She missed her brothers, particularly Archy, who had always been the most affectionate and in their few years together had always acted as her protector and guardian. His letters took up to six months to reach her, by which time the news was stale, and contained replies to questions which had long since ceased to be relevant. It was heartening to know that Archy was well when he wrote, but by the time his letters arrived she had no idea whether he was even still alive. He longed for Isabella to come out to India and join him, perhaps to keep house for him, and in 1833 wrote that he had been promoted from cornet to lieutenant, and also appointed adjutant to his regiment, the 1st Bengal Light Cavalry. This appointment doubled his pay, making it about £1,000 a year (around £50,000 today), giving him more than ample means to send the £120 (£6,000 today) for her passage.

It seemed a perfect opportunity. Isabella had nothing to keep her in Britain, and at twenty-three she was the right age for such an adventure – young enough to withstand the rigours but old enough to be wise to its dangers. However, in the 1830s very few women travelled to India. The voyage was long and hazardous. Isabella's world was filled with images of shipwrecks, like Géricault's immense painting *The Raft of the Medusa*, which had been exhibited in Piccadilly to great acclaim in 1820, and within six months had been seen by forty thousand people. The collective imagination was fired up by such scenes, along with poems and plays which portrayed the drama and disasters of the high seas. It was no fantasy: *The Raft of the Medusa* was based on contemporary accounts of the dramatic wreck of a ship en route to Senegal.

Despite the warnings, Isabella would happily have started at once, but Aeneas MacIntosh insisted that if she was determined to go, she should not do so alone. She needed a companion. But who? Letters were sent, and the word put out, but it was a year before Isabella found someone suitable. The Honourable Mrs Ramsay was a kindly woman she had met in Edinburgh, who had decided to take her children out to Bengal to join her husband. Mrs Ramsay was admirably connected: her husband was Major General the Hon. John Ramsay, in command at Meerut and the Upper Provinces, where Archy also happened to be stationed; General Ramsay's brother, the 9th Earl of Dalhousie, had until 1832 been Commander-in-Chief of India.* The Ramsays' daughter Anne, a plain but ladylike girl, would make the perfect companion for Isabella.

---

* The Earl of Dalhousie's son, the Ramsays' nephew, became the 1st Marquess, and Governor General of India in 1848.

Mr MacIntosh invited Isabella to stay in Montague Square while she prepared for the voyage.

First she had to book a passage, then buy her outfits, which, Isabella points out as if to emphasize her frugal nature, lasted for many years after her marriage. At the East India Docks she bought what she needed on the voyage, including all the cabin furniture. She was advised to take a sofa with a mattress that would double as a bed for the night and seating for the day. She needed a pillow and a chintz cover for the daytime, and a hanging lamp, a looking glass with a protective sliding cover, a chest of drawers, a foul-clothes bag and an oilcloth or carpet. She was advised to bring a good supply of papillote (curl) papers, a case of cologne water, hair powder, hartshorn (smelling salts) and aperients (laxatives). For her amusement she was encouraged to bring carpet and crochet work, drawing, knitting and netting, with the reminder that silver needles were best since the moisture of the fingers at high temperature would rust an ordinary needle.

Her ship was the *Broxbournebury*, a magnificent old East Indiaman of 709 tons. Though relatively small, the *Broxbournebury* was built with an eye to cargo capacity rather than speed so was broad in the beam (35ft 6in. wide), while the height between the three decks was 6ft, allowing Isabella to stand upright. She and the Ramsays saw her first through the mist on an early April morning at the East India Docks, the great masts festooned with rigging, sails hung up like sheets to dry, the cargo being humped aboard, merchants muffled in cloaks standing around on the quay. They talked a foreign language of bills of lading and saltpetre and indigo.

Isabella recalled that 'among our fellow passengers were

several whose names were afterwards famous in the annals of Indian warfare; they were then cadets and young civilians.' This included eighteen-year-old Henry Ramsay, Anne's brother, later philanthropist and General the Hon. Sir Henry, KCSI, CB, of the 53rd Native Infantry. Isabella added, 'At that time, those who sent their younger sons into the Military and Civil Service were far superior in birth and social position to those who now compose Indian society, especially the Artillery and Engineers Departments.' This rather snobbish remark was one made by every generation of Anglo-Indians about their successors.

The cabins opened onto the central saloon, and here at a long central table the passengers congregated. Eighteen of them sat down to dinner, a convivial party, although an unusual rule aboard the *Broxbournebury* compelled the men and boys, including Anne Ramsay's brothers, to sit at one end of the table, and the women at the other. These prudish *placements* would remain throughout the journey.

They were joined for tea in the cuddy by Captain Alfred Chapman, commander and, until recently, principal managing owner of the *Broxbournebury*. He was a splendid figure, majestic and autocratic, and he greeted his passengers with affable condescension. He explained to the assembled company that he kept a calm but well-organized ship, and insisted on strict segregation. There was to be no dancing. The seven unmarried young women on board were his responsibility and he did not want to be responsible for any ruined reputations. Then he crooked his elbows towards Anne and Isabella. 'Miss Ramsay? Miss Campbell? As I am not a young man, but a happily married father of four, I am entitled to the pleasure of your company. Would you do an old but respectable gentleman the honour of keeping him company while he takes the air on deck?'

After being sickeningly buffeted by the English Channel, it was lovely to watch the gulls flashing overhead, the great sails swelling in the wind. England had disappeared but Isabella felt no sadness of parting: her brothers and her life lay ahead of her. The passengers were cast adrift, the *Broxbournebury* a solitary speck under a full moon that shone down through the masts and rigging with a lustre Isabella had never seen before, cutting a path through the lead-coloured sea. Isabella was impressed by the way under Captain Chapman's calm and measured command the ship seemed to find her way with such certainty over the deep, as if she was marching along an invisible Roman road.

Captain Alfred Chapman turned out to be one of the most delightful men Isabella ever knew, a perfect gentleman who treated both her and Miss Ramsay like his own daughters. He was forty, only slightly younger than Isabella's father would have been, and, for the next six months, he made an excellent surrogate. He had travelled this route countless times, and there was nothing he didn't know about India. Moreover his wife Caroline was the sister of the famous Sir William MacNaghten, who as secretary to India's Governor-General, Lord Auckland, would later propel the British into the First Afghan War, which saw so many of Isabella's friends slaughtered – including Sir William himself.

As they headed south they had some brisk and exciting days. Isabella was intoxicated with the speed and the beauty, and may have dreamed of having someone special to share it with. Early in the voyage she had celebrated her twenty-fourth birthday. Did she feel time running out? Was she a precursor of the Fishing Fleet, those hordes of women who would later flock to India in search of husbands? Pride and propriety would never have allowed her even to hint at such a thing in her memoirs.

At the Cape the wind died and they were becalmed. The officer of the watch paced the afterdeck and gazed hopefully at the sky but it remained relentlessly blue. Every sail was set, but without a breeze the *Broxbournebury* wallowed impotently, canvas sagging. A sense of ennui set in. Each evening, once the blast of the sun had faded, the passengers strolled on deck in small groups with a cigar or a dish of post-prandial tea. As the days wore on they began to lose their bright-eyed look. Their smiles wilted. They sat around, and hauled themselves from meal to meal. They were living cargo, nothing more. Although Captain Chapman required the crew to wash the ship twice a week, the stench from the livestock, quite apart from the humans, grew formidable. Tempers frayed.

Day after day, week after week, they were alone. The *Broxbournebury* was the only real-seeming thing in space. Then one day a white dot was spotted on the horizon. No longer afraid of capture by the French, spirits lifted at the prospect of a chance meeting with other human beings. After months of seeing no one, their eyes and glasses were glued to the skyline. Over the next few hours the dot swelled into a fully rigged ship, and slowly its national flag took shape. Cheers broke out: it was a Union Jack. As the two ships drew closer cheer upon cheer rang out, then grew fainter as they drew apart, and by dusk their unknown friends had shrunk to nothing more than a dot on the horizon again. Everyone felt maudlin: while the others were going home, they were heading across the globe, possibly never to return.

Then the breeze picked up and they felt the ship dipping. After such a long silence the passengers heard the slap of the *Broxbournebury*'s bows hitting the water, the swishing of her wake, and they felt their moods lift. They heard the order – calm but firm – to shorten sail, and the 'Aye aye, Cap'n,' as sailors climbed the shrouds to reef the topsails. Others closed all ports, while still more ushered the passengers down into their cabins. The ship groaned as the sky turned a deeper blue until it was almost black. The masts quivered, the rigging began to sing, the ship began to plunge and rear like a horse being broken, and the officer of the watch roared at the helmsman to fling the wheel hard down. The solid old *Broxbournebury* heeled over, sending books and needlework flying, and tossing Isabella bruisingly across her cabin.

Near Madras the nights became beautiful. The full moon hung brilliantly in the western sky, moving in and out of shapely clouds. Then it was 'Land ho!' and everyone rushed to the larboard side and peered along the moon's path. Isabella thought of her mother's arrival, of her anticipation at seeing her husband again after nearly five years apart, and then the hammer blow of his death. She panicked at the thought of finding that her brothers were dead too.

After they moored in the Madras roads, small native boats began swarming round the ship, piled with strange-looking fruit and other goods for sale. The men paddling them were naked but for a tiny thong, and on their heads they wore comic pointy hats. They shouted out for passengers who wanted to go ashore. Isabella was placed in a chair resembling half a barrel with the side cut out, then lowered in worrying jerks from the deck onto a catamaran. In this frail little surfboat she crested the breakers and was flung onto the beach, where she was gripped by the strong hands of her oarsmen and unceremoniously humped above the tide line.

When her feet met solid ground for the first time in nearly five months, it must have felt less steady than the ship. This was the beginning of her new life, but she had no idea what form it would take, or whether it would continue to feel so unstable.

Isabella was astonished by the sweep of white sand with the blue hills in the distance, the white buildings tucked in green trees, the dark faces and bodies, the flowing robes and white turbans, and among them the sombre and incongruous sight of English gentlemen in black frock coats and pinstripe trousers, sporting top hats as if they were in Piccadilly. Throughout her life she had heard tales of India, seen pictures of exotic-looking natives adorning the walls of Montague Square and Lower Berkeley Street, read her brothers' letters describing the strange customs of the East, but seeing them for herself and smelling the humid hothouse smell must have made an impression that even in a few moments outweighed in intensity a lifetime of imaginings.

The *Broxbournebury* spent a month in Madras. Isabella does not describe the final leg of the journey to Calcutta, but fortunately the letters of a fellow passenger have been preserved. The Hon. Thomas Babington Macaulay, later Lord Macaulay – politician, essayist, historian and poet – was en route to take up a post in Governor-General Lord William Bentinck's newly created Supreme Council.

Up the Country

3rd October 1834
Calcutta

My dear Mrs Cropper,
After breakfast [in Madras] *I made inquiries about the ships which were then lying in the roads bound for Calcutta. The largest and the best was the Broxbournebury, under the command of a Captain Chapman, a brother-in-law of my friend MacNaghten, the Chief Secretary to the Government. MacNaghten begged me to go with his relation, if I could contrive it. I therefore sent for the Captain, and engaged a passage in a very good cabin, which had been vacated by a lady whom he had brought to Madras. The cabin was part of the poop. I furnished it, – not as I furnished my little room in the Asia* [the ship in which he had recently travelled out from England to Madras] – *but in the very simplest manner. One strong table served for dressing and for writing. A large brass basin which I had used on my journey and two jars of the same metal contained water for my ablutions. The couch of my palanquin sufficed for a bed. We were not likely to be many days on the water, and at this season of the year carpeting and curtaining would have been mere annoyance . . .*

On the evening of Tuesday the 16th [of September] *I went on board the Broxbournebury. I was carried through the surf in a native boat. But I think I have already described all that to you. I was honoured with a farewell salute of fifteen guns from Fort St George, and greeted by as many from the Broxbournebury. I found my cabin tolerably comfortable. I had laid in two dozen bottles of soda water, a little sherry, a little sugar, and a few limes; – so that I was able to bid defiance to thirst. Captain Barron sent on board*

33

a large supply of fruit and fresh vegetables from the
Governor's garden.

I amused myself during this short voyage with learning
Portuguese; and made myself as well or almost as well
acquainted with it as I care to be . . .

I did not like Captain Chapman quite so well as Captain
Bathie . . . He is an excellent navigator, and manages to have
the business of his ship done very well, with less noise and
scolding than I ever heard even in much smaller vessels. He
seems to be very humane and conscientious. But he is a
shallow, fanatical fellow, a believer in the tongues, and in all
similar fooleries. He brought out a missionary to Madras
with whom he had long and fierce theological contests. He is
famous for the care which he takes to prevent flirtations
among the young ladies and gentlemen whom he carries out.
They sate separate at table; and I was told at Madras that, in
order to prevent them from giving any signs of partiality
under the table, he had buckets, painted alternately white
and green, into which all his passengers were forced to put
their legs. This was a lie, as you may suppose. It is true,
however, that he would not allow dancing and that psalm-
singing was the only amusement of the poor girls on board.
He is, in short, a good sort of man who understands his
profession, but who is not overburdened with brains.

We had a remarkably fine passage up the Bay of Bengal –
at least for the time of year. The voyage in September is often
more than a fortnight. We performed it in a week. At two in
the morning of Tuesday the 23rd we saw the floating light
which marks the entrance of the Hoogley. At break of day we
procured a pilot. At noon we saw the island of Saugur; and
by dinner time we anchored for the night at Kedgeree.

The following morning we weighed anchor, and

proceeded up the river with wind and tide in our favour. We
had a most unusually good run. The day was fine and not
oppressively hot. The banks of the Hoogley were far prettier
than I had expected. Indeed, I think that justice has never
been done to them. They are low. But they are of the richest
green, well wooded, and sprinkled with pretty little villages.
They are far superior, I am sure, to the banks of the Thames
or the Humber. I was a little surprised to find Bengal more
verdant than Leicestershire in a moist April. But I came at the
end of the rains; and the bright, cheerful, silky green of the
rice-fields was in all its beauty. The least agreeable part of the
scenery was the river itself. It comes down black and turbid
with the mud collected in the course of fifteen hundred miles.
For many leagues out to sea the water of the Ocean is
discoloured by the filth which the innumerable mouths of the
Ganges pour into it. The Hoogley often brings down with it
great masses of jungle, whole trees, and acres of shrubs and
brambles. We passed several of these floating islands. But this
is not the worst. The boiling coffee-coloured river swept
several naked corpses along close to our ship. This ghastly
sight would once have shocked me very much. But now I am
more used to the sight of death as a subject of contemplation.
If we had taken one of the fine houses at Garden Reach
which are close to the river, we should have been forced to
keep a man whose only business would have been to push
away the corpses from our garden into the stream.

The *Broxbournebury* sailed up the Hoogley into the city that
was the very essence of empire. The wharves were lined with
huge three-masters and country craft. To the right rose the heap
of ramparts and barracks that was Fort William, the East India
Company's fortified trading post. It was ringed by the green

space of the maidan, on which stood the palatial Government House, and topped by the spire of the garrison church – for Isabella a comfortingly familiar sight in all this strangeness. To the left lay the leafy expanse of the botanical gardens. Power and religion on the right bank; beauty and nature on the left. Then came the mass of the central city, plastered white. Isabella remembered her schoolbooks and their illustrations of ancient Rome – there were Doric pillars here, Corinthian there, vast colonnades, and stucco mansions set in their own grounds like Roman villas, in a dreamlike evocation of the ancient classical world of which the East India Company Raj was the heir.

Isabella may not have been aware of this at the time, but the *Broxbournebury* was carrying more than Bentinck's second-in-command. She had flowed in on a tide of liberalism that was embodied by Macaulay. More evangelical than before, more utilitarian, he brought a new sense of mission to reform an Indian society considered heathen and degenerate. This new tide flowed strongly against the earlier more tolerant stance of the East India Company, which had appreciated and enjoyed Indian art and literature and customs, and through intermarriage had often become part of it. There had never been any doubt about the superiority of the Christian religion and British character and industry to anything found in India; social equality between them and those they regarded as pagan was out of the question; but whereas in the past there had been a laissez-faire attitude of live and let live, and a desire to prevent any cultural clashes from interfering with Anglo-Indian trade, now there was a benevolent but sometimes misguided urge to *improve*. Macaulay, like all his generation, was steeped in the utilitarian ideas of James Mill's *History of British India*. He and his successors sought the greatest happiness for the greatest number of Indians, and naturally assumed that they should define that happiness.*

In Calcutta, Isabella parted from the Ramsays and was received by the Hon. Mrs Udney, who lived in the Bank of Bengal, on the Strand at Chaundpaul Ghaut. Mrs Udney's son was Treasurer and Secretary of the Bank, and his mother lived 'above the shop' in tremendous grandeur.

The arrival of the Ramsay party caused a stir in Calcutta society. Although the Calcutta season would not begin for another two months, when the city would be besieged by races, theatre, fancy-dress balls, dinner parties and boating parties to the botanical gardens, nevertheless invitations flooded in. Isabella declined them all. She was, she declared, not interested in that sort of life. She had come to one of the most worldly cities on earth, where fortunes were still made and lost at cards, where the nabob still flourished and ladies still smoked the hookah, only to announce that she had spent many hours on board ship listening to conversations in the cuddy between Captain Chapman and Mr Macaulay and the missionary, and had been so impressed by Captain Chapman's disavowal of materialism

---

* The company itself was changing. A year before Isabella's arrival it had lost its commercial monopoly, leaving India open to anyone for trade. In ceasing to be a trading concern, the company was metamorphosing into a kind of sovereign agency that administered the British possessions in India on behalf of the Crown. This was the beginning of change not just in India but throughout the empire. By 1830 all the signatories of the Congress of Vienna (1814–15) had abolished the slave trade, and in 1833, the year before Isabella embarked for India, ownership of slaves was also banned in the British Empire. The Royal Navy, the world's greatest maritime power, was now in the business not of capturing French ships but of patrolling the seas to liberate slaves.

that she only wished to stay indoors and read improving texts.

This was frustrating for Mrs Udney. Having a beautiful young woman to chaperone cast a reflected glow on her, making her the centre of attention since the sole topic of conversation in every drawing room for several days after the arrival of a ship were the age, height, features, dress, manners and background of the marriageable female cargo. In the 1830s men still vastly outnumbered women, so girls of any sort were a welcome addition, particularly pretty ones.* It was generally assumed that each new arrival was in search of a husband and Mrs Udney would have been congratulated had she managed to secure a propitious match for her charge. Instead she was resented for not bringing the girl out and giving Calcutta's ladies a chance to catch up on the latest London fashions.

Studying the Bible and praying, Isabella sat for hours in the drawing room, an immense lofty room on the second floor with many full-height windows. The high ceilings, sparse furniture and exposed rafters gave the room an inspiring church-like feeling. The only fabric in the room was the punkah, swaying back and forth.† With the room dark behind closed Venetian blinds, the lamps on the walls had to be lit, and these were sheltered

---

* This was a very different India from the twentieth-century Raj when the journey by steamer from England was quick and cheap, and came loaded with hordes of Delhi debutantes eager for sundowners and race weeks.

† An Indian invention, this was a huge wooden frame, perhaps twenty feet long, covered with a cloth and suspended from the ceiling; with the help of a system of ropes and pulleys it was swung to and fro by a servant outside the room.

from the punkah behind tin tops. When she wrote, Isabella had to use a paperweight to stop the punkah from whisking her letter away.

After tiffin, Isabella would doze on the sofa, the air thick around her, the house dark and silent. Then a servant would appear with a reviving ice cream, which consisted of ice made in the up-country during frosty nights, or else the more superior ice that an enterprising speculator had shipped over from North America. Isabella lived off almost nothing else. Sometimes when the heat outside was so intense that it could melt metal, Isabella was almost as cool as if she had climbed into one of the pits where the ice was stored. With this combination of prayer and ice cream, time passed.

Isabella eschewed Calcutta's fading decline-of-Empire frivolity not only because she disapproved of it, but because she was beside herself with worry. Her youngest brother Osborn, who she had hoped would meet her in Calcutta, had disappeared. Other members of his regiment, the 43rd Infantry, might have revealed his whereabouts, but she could not find out where the regiment was stationed. Her brothers were all she had; there was no other family.

One day she was informed that a gentleman wished to see her. 'Upon his entering the room I rose to greet him, whereupon he came forward and took my hand and said, "You do not know me, but I would know you as a Dunstaffnage Campbell anywhere. My name is McIntyre."'

Isabella gazed at him questioningly; the name was faintly familiar.

'My parents were cottagers on your father's estate,' he explained. 'My mother was foster-mother to your uncle Captain

Alexander Campbell, who brought me out to India in his ship. All I have I owe to him. I am happy to say that I am now a rich man. Can I serve you in any way?'

Isabella revealed her anxiety about Osborn. A few days later Mr McIntyre called again to tell her that Osborn had been very ill and had been sent up the River Ganges for a change of air. McIntyre had discovered that Osborn's doctor had ordered him on sick leave to Europe, but Osborn had been ashamed to admit that he was unable to leave the country because he was too heavily in debt. 'Mr. McIntyre then added, "I have seen his principal creditors, paid all his debts, booked a passage for him in the next ship that sails for England, and given him money to meet all his expenses. I should be glad to do anything else I can for you." You can well imagine that I was overcome with gratitude. With many expressions of regard, we parted. I never saw him again. But numerous are the instances I could relate of the generous, warm-hearted, noble conduct of old Anglo-Indians, giving assistance most liberally to brother officers in less fortunate circumstances than themselves, and providing for their widows and orphans.' Osborn returned to India with a wife, survived being dangerously wounded in a duel and lived until he was sixty-six to die in his bed in Bayswater. MacIntyre had saved his life.

After six weeks the Ramsay party and Isabella set off up the Ganges to Cawnpore and thence to Meerut to join General Ramsay and Isabella's beloved Archy. Cawnpore lay 633 miles upriver, and would take three months to reach.

They travelled by budgerow, a lumbering flat-bottomed Noah's Ark-like barge, with aft cabins lit by Venetian windows. Oarsmen sat in the bows, the captain at the huge tiller at the stern, and a mast projected from the cabin roof. Progress was hard against the current and they covered about twenty miles a day.* When the wind was favourable they could sail, but most of the time they had to be hauled along the banks by half-naked boatmen, three or four to a boat, their heads down as they strained at ropes over their shoulders. Sometimes the men were forced to wade into the river, and even swim, their backs glistening in the water while the manjee urged them on.

Mrs Ramsay's fleet consisted of one large budgerow for her family and, because she had two growing sons, a smaller one for Isabella to use as a separate sleeping boat. There was also a cooking boat packed with fowls and goats to be slaughtered en route and several others for baggage, and no fewer than thirty servants who slept on deck under the sail. Three years later a young woman named Emily Eden would accompany her brother Lord Auckland, Lord Bentinck's successor as Governor-General, on a journey of several years through Bengal; her letters, which vividly but often acidly described her experiences were later published as *Up the Country*. Emily Eden set off up the Ganges in 1837, at the same time of year as Isabella, and described enviously how the men of the party were able to sleep on deck, while she was incarcerated down below without a punkah, sitting up in bed fanning herself. 'The native servants

---

* At exactly this time, in the autumn of 1834, a steam ship named the *Lord William Bentinck*, which had been built in England and shipped out to Calcutta, was making its first trip up the Ganges as far as Allahabad, a distance it covered in thirty-eight days, less than half the time it took the Ramsays; however, the first regular steamship service would not begin on the Ganges for another nine months. When it came, it was largely thanks to the encouragement of one of the principal assistants to the Chief Examiner of the East India Company, the poet Thomas Love Peacock.

sleep any and everywhere, over our heads, under our feet, or at our doors; and as there are not partitions but green blinds at the sides and gratings above, of course we hear them coughing all night.'

Isabella watched the banks glide by. Thatches of roots that had been exposed by the river forever altering its course supported huge trees. She saw bullock carts rumbling along the foreshore, wheels squeaking, timbers groaning. She saw ghats with steps crumbling down into the river, some where people soaped themselves all over and lowered themselves into the stream (their ablutions intriguingly public), others in front of pyramidical Hindu temples where barbers sat shaving the heads of the faithful, and holy men ground up brilliant-coloured pigments to smear on people's foreheads, and the shaved and anointed men dunked themselves in the holy Ganga while chanting prayers in Sanskrit. At burning ghats she saw men clustering round a corpse, vultures lurking near by. Isabella did not describe suttee – the government was just beginning its well-intentioned campaign to have it outlawed – but most Europeans were appalled by the barbarity of this act of living sacrifice.

Each sunset they drew close to the shore, and a plank was thrown from deck to land. Isabella would gaze at the Indian plain, immense and awe-inspiring. The rice harvest was finished, and the fields were rectangles of brown stubble under a dun-coloured sky. There were no hedges, just a vast emptiness, featureless, flat and dusty. The servants gathered with their wives and families in circles on the shore where they lit small fires. Each was tended by a different caste or family, each with its appointed cook who produced bags of rice and spices and concocted different mixtures in earthenware kedgeree pots. There was a smell of garlic and ghee and spices and burning cowpats. Isabella loved these times, the squatting groups chatting and singing or smoking their hookahs, the fires flickering. She also became very fond of her ayah, who taught her Hindustani.

As they entered the 'up-country' Isabella began to emerge from her virtual convent. At each military station the commander of the garrison delivered messages of welcome to Mrs Ramsay and her delightful entourage, and dinner parties were promptly organized in their honour. Isabella began to feel it was churlish to refuse. The officers were deprived, poor things, of social life, and these dinners certainly broke the tedium of the journey. Captain Chapman's strictures against the frivolity of dancing retreated downstream. When they halted at Cawnpore to find that the officers of the 5th Bengal Light Cavalry, who were garrisoned there, had booked the Assembly Rooms and engaged a band, Isabella forced herself to accept their invitation to the ball.

Torches flickered at the gate as the Ramsay party alighted from a carriage. Two gorgeously turbaned sowars stood to attention each side of the Assembly Rooms' door. Inside was a whirl of blue and gold and silver uniforms, glittering sabretaches, twinkling chandeliers, punkahs freshly washed and trimmed with crimson flounces, walls hung with wreaths and draped with regimental colours. It looked just as glamorous as a ball in London, but Isabella and Anne Ramsay – almost the only single girls in the entire station – received far more attention than they would have back home. As soon as they removed their shawls they were set upon by a throng of officers who each tried to outdo the other in praising the young ladies' charms, and making chivalrous offers to bring drinks, find seats, escort them to supper and book them for every quadrille. The girls basked in the adulation.

When the heat and crush became overwhelming, Isabella extricated herself and sat down. A young man, who had held himself aloof but had been watching her, looked down. Tall, with a mop of black curly hair, he had heavy-lidded eyes, a long nose and sensitive lips, and strong dark eyebrows. It was a handsome intelligent face, yet faintly supercilious. Introducing himself, he explained that he was her brother's most intimate friend. Isabella looked up with her great doe eyes. 'Lieutenant Gascoyne. Yes. He has often mentioned your name.'

Charles Gascoyne told Isabella that he and Archy had met as cadets on their way out to India in 1826, where they both joined the 5th Bengal Light Cavalry. They had done everything together – studied Hindustani with the same munshee, shared a bungalow, shared a tent. When Archy had fallen ill with fever, Charles had nursed him, and when Charles had felt cast down with melancholy, Archy had cheered his spirits. They had been pig-sticking together in the Jumna valley, and shot black buck in the hills. Then Archy had transferred to the 1st Bengal Light Cavalry, and Charles had missed him.

For the rest of the evening Charles monopolized Isabella. At last the wallflowers sagged, the lamps flickered and the carriages were brought to extract the tired guests. The few remaining officers removed their jackets and tucked into the remains of supper, ordered pegs and cheroots and broke into song. Charles left them to it and wandered along the ghats until dawn, looking down at the Ramsays' flotilla and wondering which boat sheltered the sleeping Isabella.

Isabella spent two weeks in Cawnpore, with Charles Gascoyne frequently in attendance until their burgeoning friendship was truncated. The Ramsays were to continue to Meerut by boat, but the impatient Archy had made arrangements to transport his sister overland, which would be quicker.

This was the last leg of the journey that had begun in Scotland nearly two years earlier. By now Isabella was used to discomfort and independence, but even she might have been daunted by what lay ahead. She was to travel without the Ramsays 250 miles north-west across the plain by palanquin dak. Her vehicle was to be an airless coffin in which she was to half-lie, half-sit for the next forty-eight hours. She would be carried on poles by four jogging bearers while others ran alongside, changing places with each other every few miles. When a sheet of water blocked the way the bearers would put the palanquin on their heads and wade or even swim across. She would travel by night and day across bumpy trackless terrain entirely in the hands of a team of unknown Indians, carrying her most precious possessions. Behind every mound or thorn bush might lurk bandits or the infamous Thugs, the hereditary fraternity who roamed the land clutching square knotted cloths with which to strangle their randomly selected victims, and said to be particularly active around Cawnpore.*

More to the point, Isabella was leaving a man who attracted

---

* It was claimed that Thugee disposed of about thirty thousand travellers every year, and although this is an unverifiable and barely believable number, the point is that many travellers were afraid of being throttled.

her, and who she would probably not see again for months, if ever. As she said goodbye to the Ramsays and was about to commit herself to her palanquin, the object of her thoughts materialized dashingly on the back of a grey charger. Charles sprang from his horse with a basket of delicacies that he had brought to sustain her during the journey. He helped her into her seat, and then tucked the sweetmeats and wine around her, and Isabella was touched – and intrigued – by his thoughtfulness. She would never forget the taste of the wine.

Enclosed in her box, Isabella set off at a trot across the roadless plain, listening to the rhythmic grunts of the bearers and the jangling bridles of the two sepoy escorts provided by the Civilian of the district. Then at seven o'clock in the evening she heard a horse galloping up behind the palanquin. Isabella dared to raise her curtain just enough to see that the sepoy guards were now miles ahead. So much for her protection! She was alone with only her unarmed bearers. She forced herself to look at the rider, and was astonished to see Lieutenant Gascoyne. At first she was afraid, but he quickly reassured her that he meant no harm, and had only come to see that she was safe, and make sure she had everything she needed. He accompanied her to her first dak, where she could stretch and take on a new team of bearers. During the hot season she would have spent the day here, slept and eaten, but being January it was cool enough for the bearers to keep going throughout the day as well as the night. Soon Isabella was back on the road and in a cloud of dust Lieutenant Gascoyne disappeared.

Her dearest brother Archy rode out to meet her, and their

reunion was joyful. She was welcomed into his home and into Meerut society. Naturally she had an introduction to General Ramsay.* She was also befriended by the doctor attached to the regiment, an Alexander Davidson who was the son of a gentleman of Cromarty whose family Isabella knew well. He and his wife were 'most kind people' and she was soon quite at home with them and their delightful baby boy.

After a fortnight the Ramsay party arrived, bearing a letter for Archy from Lieutenant Gascoyne. He wrote that he had asked for leave of absence for a month on 'urgent private affairs', and would be in Meerut almost as soon as his letter. His service record shows that he was given leave from 15 February. However hard he rode, he cannot have covered the 250 miles from Cawnpore in less than three days, so would have reached Meerut on or soon after the 18th. Six days later, on 24 February 1835, Charles Gascoyne and Isabella Campbell were married by special licence in St John's church.

Archy performed the painful task of giving away his only sister, while poor plain Anne Ramsay performed the perhaps equally painful task of being her bridesmaid. The witnesses were the Ramsays and the Davidsons. They had their miniatures painted, Isabella a beauty, painted in profile with her dark hair swept up on the back of her head, and falling in three

---

* Emily Eden, who disguises General Ramsay as General N in *Up the Country*, mocks him for his thick Scottish accent. 'He is the Governor of the district, a good-natured old man, but he has quite lost his memory, and says the same thing ten times over, and very often it was a mistake at first. George [Lord Auckland] asked him how many men he had at Meerut; he said, "I cannot just say, my Lord; perhaps sax and twenty thousand" – such a fine army for a small place.'

ringlets at the sides, her neck rising white and serpentine from her fashionably sloping shoulders. As for Charles, even allowing for artistic flattery, he was exceptionally handsome, with black curly hair and chiselled features.

Three weeks later the newly-weds returned to Cawnpore. So, here was a pretty but portionless young woman who apparently intended to live with her brother and take care of him, yet within three weeks of meeting him again after an absence of ten years, had married his best friend, with whom she then disappeared to a garrison 250 miles away. Were there censorious tuttings from the ladies of Meerut at the unseemly haste with which they tied the knot? Probably not, as the speed of their union was quite normal. Fanny Parkes, the most entertaining female eyewitness in India at that time, who crossed paths with Isabella several times, wrote in 1824, 'we have weddings, and rumours of weddings. The precipitate manner in which young people woo and wed is most ridiculous; the whole affair, in many cases, taking less than a month . . . marrying and giving in marriage is, in this country, sharp, short and decisive; and where our habits are necessarily so domestic, it is wonderful how happily the people live together afterwards.'

In a sense Archy had lost them both. Archy was so fond of Charles that he named his son Charles Gascoyne Campbell, and his descendants would continue to name their babies Gascoyne until 1932. Isabella admits that after her marriage Archy was 'so depressed and lonely' that he applied for leave to visit Calcutta in order to find a wife for himself. 'On seeing a young lady in the Cathedral on the first Sunday after his arrival, he made inquiries as to her name, residence and family, wrote to her father, an indigo planter up the country, stating his name, position and so on; and referring to his commanding officer for his credentials, he asked permission to pay his addresses. He always was of an impetuous, enthusiastic temperament, warm hearted and entirely unselfish. The young lady was exceedingly pretty, her age sixteen – a Miss Emily Payter. Her mother was a native lady who, having separated from her husband, lived in her own house in Calcutta, where I afterwards visited her. Emily was an only child. She had been brought up and educated by some of her father's friends in Calcutta. Archy and she married on July 11 1836, and they spent some days with us at Cawnpore on their return journey. My brother was one of the few to whom marriage made no difference to his love for his sister. While he lived he was the most devoted, loving relative I ever had.'

Was there an air of desperation about both Charles's and Archy's marriages? For young bachelors, army life was often stultifyingly boring, at least after they had lost their initial excitement about the novelties of the East and liberation from the strictures of home. Officers often hung listlessly around the mess, leafing through out-of-date copies of *Blackwood's* or the *Edinburgh Review*, all the time oppressed by heat and lust. This was stimulated by the overtly sexual nature of Hindu culture, but they had no way of assuaging their desires. India had few single English women available to marry: in *Up the Country* Emily Eden describes attending a ball in Meerut in 1838, at which there were only *three* young ladies, one of whom was already married, and the other was Anne Ramsay.

However desperate they may have been, marriage was in fact discouraged as it was thought to have a detrimental effect on a Bengal officer's devotion to duty.* If he had to marry, it was hoped he would wait until his first home furlough, which was given after a minimum of ten years of service. Besides, it was usually only once an officer had worked his way up the regimental ladder and was nearing middle age that he became desirable marriage material to most young women – or at least to their parents. As for Indian women, they were increasingly off-limits, unless marriage was in mind, which was tricky owing to a growing awareness of caste, religion and race. (Emily Payter had been brought up by Europeans so in her case this barely featured.) Brothels were an alternative, but they carried the danger of possibly deadly disease. Lonely widows may have been a source of supply, but they often came hampered by a brood of children. As for extra-marital affairs, the few regimental wives who had not returned Home were fiercely guarded by their husbands, and single women were unlikely to destroy their marriage prospects by becoming 'fallen' women.†

Charles's and Archy's haste to marry was not just about loneliness and sexual frustration; there was also the ever-present sense of death, the sense that time was short.

Charles and Isabella's union was not an obviously advanta-

---

* As steam ships truncated the length of the journey from England and brought more marriageable British women, so the officers spent less time with their men, and their consequent loss of contact was thought to be one of the causes of the Mutiny in 1857.

† Not every single woman was snapped up within hours of arriving. The passenger list for the *Maidstone*, returning to London from Calcutta in 1840, includes Miss Ramsay, so despite being the most ladylike-looking person in Meerut, Anne was considered to be returning home in disgrace, satirized by the more malicious members of Bengal society as a 'spin' who had failed to capture a spouse.

geous one; neither married for money or ambition. However, Charles was well connected, which mattered almost as much. His cadetship to the East India Company had been recommended by the 2nd Marquess of Salisbury, who was married to his first cousin. The fortunate Frances, known as the Gascoyne Heiress, had married Lord Salisbury with a dowry of numerous estates that by chance lay on the estuaries of both the Mersey and the Thames, at the time when Liverpool and London were mushrooming. At the moment of Charles's marriage, Lady Salisbury was recording in her diary her grand life at Hatfield House, which was not a house but a vast Elizabethan and Jacobean palace with a great hall, long gallery, libraries, full-length portraits, lake, maze and terraced flower garden. She mentioned as if in passing dinner with Mr Wordsworth, tea with little Princess Victoria and a meeting with her intimate friend the Duke of Wellington (then Foreign Minister), who had given her away at her marriage and was godfather to several of her children.

Charles's application to the East India Company had been witnessed by his wealthy uncle General Isaac Gascoyne, a military hero, friend of dukes, favourite of King William IV, and Tory MP for Liverpool nine times between 1796 and 1831. Isaac Gascoyne was one of the oldest and most familiar figures in the House of Commons, where he championed measures to improve conditions in the army, and like his brother Bamber, Lady Salisbury's father, who had been one of Liverpool's MPs before him, he had vigorously supported the business interests of the city, which meant the healthy continuation of the slave trade, at least until 1807, when it was abolished by Britain. Later, when Charles and Isabella went on furlough to England,

Charles took Isabella to spend the day with Isaac's daughters in the family mansion at 71 South Audley Street in Mayfair, where she was awed by the pillared portico projecting over the pavement into the street, and by the magnificently ornamented marble fireplaces and statuary and family portraits and panelled walls and triple Venetian-style windows and pediments and ornate stucco walls and ceilings. She was deeply impressed by the powdered footmen and a butler who waited on them at table.

This was Charles's background, but being the youngest son of a youngest son, he had been educated not at Eton or Harrow but at humble Swansea Grammar, and although he was both interpreter and quartermaster to his regiment (more than doubling his pay) he was not much richer than Isabella.

Why not permit their union to have been a genuine coup de foudre? Hastiness was not out of character for Charles or Archy, both of whom Isabella described as impetuous and romantic. Charles had met the female version of his best friend; perhaps he felt he already knew her, that Archy was the forerunner. For her part, it is likely that Isabella was attracted to the same sort of people as her favourite brother, and she respected his judgement. Besides, a dashing twenty-nine-year-old cavalry officer was hard to resist, and Isabella had no parents to cramp her style: she was free to marry whoever she chose, and if that person lacked prospects, who cared! There was also the question of expediency. Charles had been given a month's leave on 'PA' – private affairs – after which he had to return to Cawnpore. He had only a month in which to woo and marry Isabella, or he might lose his chance forever.

Isabella adored Charles. 'Now I must tell you that he was

no ordinary character. He was the most perfect gentleman in manner and appearance generally that I ever knew. As a boy he was his mother's favourite, and it was a great grief to her that he chose the military profession. He was a scholar and linguist speaking French fluently and writing it, and afterwards becoming proficient in Persian, Hindi, Urdu, Arabic and Hindustani. He was appointed interpreter to his Regiment. He wrote many pretty pieces of poetry, and from his boyhood had a strongly poetical, chivalrous, imaginative, but unpractical turn of mind. He had peculiar views on many subjects, and was inclined to melancholy and withdrawal from general society. The few friendships he formed were deep and lasting, and he was a sincere Christian. His voice, accent and manner had a strange, rather peculiar charm, and his reading aloud of Shakespeare and indeed of all poetry, was greatly enjoyed by all who heard him. He was naturally graceful in every action, and courtesy itself to womanhood, whether young or old, rich or poor. It was almost impossible for his wife and mother to help worshipping him.'

By his 'peculiar views' Isabella may have meant his failure to share the new well-intentioned belief that the poor suffering heathens ought to be saved by the British – and their religion. As Fanny Parkes remarked in 1830, 'People think of nothing but converting the Hindus.' In a letter to Lord Salisbury in 1841, Charles described how circumstances had conspired against him to prevent him from partaking in active service, and instead he had mixed as much as possible with the Indians. Until his marriage, whenever he had a few weeks' leave of absence, he had travelled throughout Upper India, visiting almost 'every place of note'. This was partly in order to perfect his languages, but it was also to steep himself in the Indians' 'customs, observances and moralities'. He did not criticize those moralities, but simply observed, and enjoyed. Isabella on the other hand – a herald of the new Victorian evangelical attitude – was less willing to immerse herself in Indian culture, more shocked by disease, by a perceived immorality and by the disparity between rich and poor (although like most memsahibs at the time, she was happy to maintain the double standards of employing servants in almost slave-like conditions herself).

This different attitude to life may have lain behind events that would engulf them twenty years later – and some said they lay behind the horrors of the Mutiny that would tear India apart at the same time.

In 1835 there was no hint of future violence, and Charles resumed his duties. The regiments of the Bengal Army were like private companies in that they were given a lump sum which they could spend as they chose on fodder, uniforms, equipment, barracks and food – everything except arms and ammunition. The colonel had to be an accountant and a businessman. As quartermaster and interpreter, Charles was responsible for the distribution of these goods, and for liaising constantly with the native officers and troops, with whom he could converse fluently.*

Cawnpore was a major military station on the Ganges, which here was so broad you couldn't see the other bank. It was stuck in a treeless wasteland with no buildings worth visiting,

---

* A regiment of light cavalry consisted of three squadrons of six troops. Each troop consisted of one subedar, one jamadar, five havildars, four naicks, one trumpeter and seventy troopers. Naicks and troopers were armed with one royal-pattern cavalry sword and a pair of pistols, and fifteen men in each troop carried a carbine each, in addition to the sword and pistols.

but there was a substantial British community to provide amusement. The cantonment was neatly laid out with the cavalry, infantry and artillery lines side by side in rectangles, next to the officers' messes, hospital, commissariat, armoury, powder magazine, treasury, parade ground, latrines and so on. There were also the civil lines with the pillared law courts, the residence, assembly rooms, theatre, treasury and the wide-verandaed mansions of the civil servants, who attended the church and filled its well-stocked graveyard. The native town sprawled across the plain, but in line with standard company practice the cantonment had been built several miles away, separated by the clear expanse of the maidan that not only kept the natives at a distance but, with piquets installed at each corner, also provided the cantonment with a open field of fire without needing to make it into a fortress. Of course, this became a source of vulnerability in 1857 when the attack came not from across the maidan, as expected, but from within.

Charles installed Isabella in married quarters that were slightly more spacious than his bachelor abode, in a row of more or less identical white bungalows built by the government using the same plan, each set in a walled compound. The bungalow was a British invention, a European version of the *bangla*, the long single-storeyed Bengali cottage, with an overhanging thatched roof and an unrailed veranda running round the front. Smaller ones were for subalterns like Charles, larger ones for field officers. Along the compound's back wall stretched the servants' quarters in flat-roofed whitewashed buildings of baked mud, which were crowded and astir long before daybreak.

The new Mrs Gascoyne received visits from all the

regimental ladies, many of whom she had met at the ball when she was still plain Miss Campbell. Now, just a few weeks on, she was one of them. 'The officers and their wives were like one family,' she enthused, 'with Colonel and Mrs Kennedy as parents.' Here at last she found a home, with Colonel Kennedy standing in for Captain Chapman as her father-figure; in fact the 5th Bengal Light Cavalry really was a family affair since the Kennedys' two daughters had married two of the five regimental captains, Alexander and Blair.

The denizens of Cawnpore relied for entertainment on each other. There were few visitors, no news, no regular post. Calcutta was a three-month boat ride away, and there would be no railway for another twenty-four years. Nevertheless, Isabella enjoyed station life. The highlight of her day, after being immured since morning by the heat, was the evening promenade along the Mall. Until the hot season depleted their numbers, the Mall thronged with the residents of the garrison, some in open carriages, others on horseback, some carried in palanquins, others in a palankeen carriage or on a camel. They called to friends, waved graciously at acquaintances, paused at the bandstand where they gossiped – anything but listen to the music – and for a few brief moments before darkness fell and the buggy lamps were lit, took the opportunity to inspect the fashions.

Often there was a musical soirée, or a dinner party, when Charles in his glittering uniform would have seemed especially glamorous, outshining the drab civilians even if their salaries were larger. Isabella or one of the other ladies would be persuaded to play and sing, and the men would stand around in groups discussing the performer's charms. Some of their wives had left for England, which allowed the remaining ladies more than their fair share of attention. Isabella's mother Eliza had been such an excellent performer of Scottish songs that one evening in Madras the men had crowded in so tightly that she fainted. The other guests chatted desultorily, and surreptitiously scratched their mosquito bites. Refreshments were brought, and then it was time to face the barrage of palanquin drivers who physically fought for custom at the door. Sometimes there were amateur theatricals, which occupied a great deal of time in rehearsals, stage design and costumes – although these were increasingly frowned upon for their frivolity.*

Cawnpore had extra entertainment in the shape of Nana Sahib. Born in obscurity and poverty, he grew up in a small village near Bombay where his father was the local priest. Bajirao II, a deposed peshwa who lived in luxurious exile in Bithur, near Cawnpore, was desperate for a son. The priest's boy was taken north and adopted, taking the 'household title' of Nana Sahib, in imitation of the greatest of the Peshwas. When his adoptive father died, Nana Sahib inherited his huge wealth, much of which he enjoyed spending on lavish dinners for the officers and civilians of the Cawnpore garrison and their wives. Guests were seated at a table twenty feet long (formerly the mess table of

---

* After dinner, women such as Honoria Lawrence, wife of the British Resident of the Punjab and hero of the siege of Lucknow Sir Henry Lawrence, were startled to see the hookah being produced, even before the ladies had withdrawn. The stand was set on the floor, like a candlestick with its upper bowl for tobacco and balls of hot charcoal. The lower part was a ball filled with water, and from it emerged a snake-like tube, which curved under the smoker's arm, with the mouthpiece (wrapped in a napkin) placed between his lips. Honoria Lawrence found something faintly obscene about the process, and as more women came to India so the hookah gradually disappeared.

a cavalry regiment) and dined from a bizarre mixture of gold plate and remnants of broken china.*

Nana Sahib intrigued Isabella, but he also frightened her. He was self-assured with charming manners, but when his guests strolled through his Westernized reception rooms, they whispered about secret inner apartments covered in pornographic paintings. That would have alarmed and shocked Isabella, but what she feared was an underlying sense of hostility, perhaps even a secret hatred of the British. Late one evening in Bithur, while beautiful jewelled nautch girls were entertaining the guests, Isabella noticed the native servants going around the reception room shutting the doors and windows. The Black Hole of Calcutta sprang to mind. 'I told my husband and insisted on his taking me outside, where we found the flat roof of the building crowded with spectators, watching some magnificent fireworks which the natives were letting off. My husband laughed at my fears, for I had thought they were going to murder us; I felt sure they would do so sooner or later.'

Isabella had arrived in Cawnpore in March, the start of the hot season when anyone with any sense escaped to the hills. However, as quartermaster and interpreter, Charles was trapped in the plains, where he remained throughout that hot season and the next, until November 1836. His new wife stayed with him. The sky turned into a furnace, and desiccated and

---

* Although he inherited the wealth, Nana Sahib's succession as the titular Peshwa was not recognized by the British government, which therefore refused to pay him the pension that it had paid his father. For this Nana Sahib bore a grudge against the government, and he went to England to argue his case. He failed, but when he returned, his now more Western-style parties became even grander. Everyone hoped to be asked.

baked the earth beneath. If they ventured down to the river, they found it a murky shade of green in which floated half-cremated corpses and the occasional crocodile.

Throughout the hot season Isabella endured the extra boiling torture of being pregnant. Encased in stays, and as many cumbersome layers of flannel, muslin and cotton petticoats as she would have worn in England – with no concessions to the climate – Isabella's baby burned like a hot-water bottle inside her. The barometer in the Gascoynes' drawing room rose remorselessly. Although by May there appeared clouds and occasional light showers, the first harbingers of monsoon, the midday temperature in the shaded drawing room was still 100 degrees (F). Then the clouds would roll away; the wind would rise and stir up dust that came roaring across the plain, black and solid looking as a cliff. Everyone would run for cover, banging doors behind them. Thunder crashed and lightning flickered malevolently through the crepuscular afternoon. When people emerged they sometimes found their verandas deep in sand, and strange creatures – a lizard or a toad – were found sheltering in the drawing room. The sand smothered books and clothes, and even turned the dinner to grit.

The house became a fort against dust and sun. The arches of the veranda were screened by tatties of odoriferous khus-khus grass, which were doused with water; as the water evaporated it cooled the air and brought delicious scents into the rooms. But by June 1835 life was almost unendurable. Isabella's health could stand it no longer, and the baby was at risk, so Charles took her back down the Ganges to Calcutta, where if she did not recover they would take a ship home. This interlude did the trick and they returned to Cawnpore, where in December 1835, just over nine months after her wedding, Isabella gave birth to Isabelle Eliza Forsyth Gascoyne.

Isabella loved her daughter. She gave the baby her own name, but planned to give her the childhood she never had. She may also have been filled with foreboding: every disease lay in wait, not only typhoid, pneumonia and typhus fever, which were common in Britain, and the childhood plagues of whooping cough, scarlet fever, diphtheria, measles and smallpox, but also the exotic diseases of the East. There was leprosy, ague (which we call malaria), dysentery, every sort of worm and above all the scourge of cholera, which had spread with terrifying speed since its first major outbreak in 1816, when it killed Isabella's father. Then there were snakes, venomous spiders and rabies carried by pariah dogs, for which there was no cure other than sucking out the poison, or amputating the stricken limb before the poison spread throughout the rest of the body. In *Up the Country* Emily Eden remarked that almost everyone she had met on her travels in India had died, none of them living beyond the age of fifty.

There was much on offer as both diagnosis and cure, but little that was of any use. Advances in medical science and hygiene had not spread at the same speed as empire; water was untreated, there were no drains, and food was prepared by often unwashed servants, but none of these were linked yet with infant mortality. Cholera, which had broken out of the sub-continent to work its way westwards, reaching Britain by the 1830s, was a disease of vomiting and diarrhoea which could kill its victims within half an hour. It was still thought to be caused by eating fish and meat at the same time, or by a vaporous miasma, and was often treated by applying a red-hot ring to the patient's navel, causing a 'revolution in the intestines'. Fevers were brought down with ice, but ice was rarely available up the country for more than four months a year. Malaria was treated by bleeding, and if no surgeon was available, the vein was simply opened with a pocket knife. It was still believed that claret could cure the other ills of the subcontinent – women were advised to drink at least a bottle a day – but while wine was recommended for medical use on the one hand, it was condemned for causing drunkenness on the other. Drunkenness was, in fact, considered 'a prime cause of disease and mortality in the East Indies Command 1828–1835'. However, cheap arak, often mixed with datura, was more to blame than claret, and neither were appropriate for a sick baby.

Mother and baby survived both the bacterial onslaught and the heat that was more ferocious than ever. In 1836 there was no rainy season at all; a drought had begun that would soon lead to famine. Isabella was pregnant again, and on 29 March 1837 baby Charles Cecil joined the family, named after his father, and after Charles's patron, James Gascoyne-Cecil, the Marquess of Salisbury. Isabella lovingly described her son's flaxen curls, his large blue eyes, his skin like snow.

This time they were not so fortunate.

Another rainy season failed to arrive. Isabella made no complaints, but in *Up the Country* Emily Eden cursed the dust that got into everything. 'We all detest Cawnpore,' she wrote of her Christmas in the garrison in 1837/8. She was appalled to see how the crops failed, the cattle died, and the people were dying too or fleeing. Those living in Cawnpore itself were relatively well off because government funds had been set up to help the less able. Those who lived outside the city travelled vast distances to obtain the government handouts of food in Cawnpore, but many died along the way, and their corpses lay strewn across the plains. Eight hundred thousand people were estimated to have died. 'The women look as if they have been buried,' Emily Eden observed. 'Their *skulls* look so dreadful.'* The famine only served to reinforce the growing sense of mission. The Anglo-Indians felt their presence here was essential; without their (Christian) handouts, many more thousands would have starved.

Baby Charlie was not another famine victim. Isabella says simply that in July 1838, at the age of sixteen months, her first son wasted away in her arms. She had no time to mourn him because the very next day, on 25 July, she gave birth to her second son, Frederick John William. A death and a birth: two babies in her arms within twenty-four hours.

While the heat mounted in Bengal, so did the political temperature. Anglo-India now had a land frontier two thousand miles long that needed defending. Afghanistan, secretive and sinister, inhabited by warring tribes and sandwiched between Russian and British empires, was where the Great Game was on the boil. During the 1830s whispers spread of Russia's growing influence in Kabul. In 1839, defying not only public opinion in Britain but also the East India Company's horrified Court of Directors, Lord Auckland decided to invade Afghanistan. The plan was to

---

* Typically, this did not prevent Emily Eden from enjoying interminable dinners in Cawnpore, a lavish Christmas breakfast concocted by the Governor-General's own itinerant French chef, and a ball for the entire station of two to three hundred people, including Fanny Parkes and Charles and Isabella.

win the Great Game by restoring to power the aged but pro-British Amir of Kabul, Shah Shujah, who had been ousted in 1812 by his rival, the possibly pro-Russian Dost Mohammed Khan. Isabella had a personal interest in events because her eldest brother, Alexander, was fighting as a mercenary officer for Dost Mohammed Khan.*

Lord Auckland formed the Army of the Indus and in March 1839, after farewell balls and fireworks, 9,500 Crown and Company troops set off for Afghanistan. With them was Charles's own 5th Light Cavalry. In July 1839 they stormed Kabul, and in August entered the city. It was all a great success. Shah Shujah was restored as Amir of Kabul, while his rival Dost Mohammed Khan, with Isabella's brother Alexander in tow, was forced into exile in India. Dost Mohammed Khan's eldest son, however, slipped away into the mountains.

Most of the British and Indian armies returned to India, leaving behind some troops and officers including those of the 5th Light Cavalry, who settled in to enjoy themselves. Setting up camp on a plain east of Kabul, they built a race track, skated on frozen ponds, played cricket in the dust, rode in the hills and (naturally) organized amateur dramatics.

Charles remained behind in India because he was ordered to act as detachment staff on court duty with Lord Auckland, and in November 1839 Charles joined him and Emily Eden on their

---

* Alexander Campbell lasted only six years in the Bengal Native Infantry before being pensioned off in 1827, whereupon he entered the service of Shah Shuja in Afghanistan, and commanded two battalions of natives at the defeat of the Shah by Dost Mohammed Khan at Kandahar in 1834, where Alexander was wounded three times. His soldiering so impressed Dost Mohammed that he was taken on at double the salary by his former opponent.

journey to Kurnaul.* Naturally Isabella accompanied Charles on the march, despite being seven months pregnant. The contents of their house were sold and their few treasured possessions packed into tin boxes for the road. Not that 'road' was exactly the word: along the river lay the bund, a causeway up to eight feet high above the plain, just wide enough for the wheels of a buggy which trundled over the heavy sand in parallel ditches cut out by vehicles in front. Isabella was heaved into a horse and doolie with babies Izzy and Fred and their ayah. It was her first experience of camp life, of becoming a piece of baggage herself, a gypsy without a permanent home, moving from boat to bungalow and bungalow to tent, but Isabella made no complaint. She was bound up with the regimental family, in which it was normal to follow your husband to battlefields and – if necessary – beyond.

Each officer was allowed at least ten domestic servants, and each regiment had stretcher-bearers, plus bihishtees, saddlers, blacksmiths, darzees, syces, dhobiwallahs, cooks, stable boys, dancing girls, herdsmen, sweepers, butchers and religious instructors – maulvis for Muslims, pandits for Hindus, granthis for Sikhs – and all their wives, children, parents and prostitutes. This immense peripatetic camp symbolized the boundless self-confidence of Anglo-India at this time. Politically, India was on a roll. The British had assimilated the vast territories acquired the century before, and now most of the subcontinent – an agglomerate mass of districts and states – was under British

---

* Perhaps Charles was chosen as a friend of the family: before her marriage to Lord Salisbury, his cousin Fanny Gascoyne had rejected the attentions of Lord Auckland's younger brother (inspiring some of Emily Eden's more vitriolic remarks).

suzerainty. The East India Company was committed to expansion, and within four years would claim all of the Gangetic Plain as far as the River Sutlej.

In Kurnaul the Gascoynes made their home in a vast tented camp alongside the Governor-General's party. Emily Eden rubbishes Kurnaul as an ugly scattered cantonment, all barracks, dust, guns and soldiers, with not a tree in sight. 'The fashions were even again behind those of Delhi,' she sneers. 'Mrs V appeared in a turban made I think of stamped tin moulded into two fans, from which descended a long pleureuse feather floating over some very full sleeves.' Emily Eden disguises her characters, so Mrs V may be Isabella, but the pleureuse feather does not sound like her style. Emily Eden describes a ball that she gave with Lord Auckland, which Charles and Isabella would have attended. 'There are between sixty and seventy ladies living here – most of them deserted by their husbands, who are gone up to Cabul; and they generally shut themselves up, but last night they agreed to come out. I wish you could see Mrs—. She is past fifty – some say near sixty – wears a light-coloured wig with very long curls floating down her back, and a gold wreath to keep it on, a low gown, and she dances every dance . . . but except that pretty Mrs J. who was at Simla, and who looked like a star amongst the others, the women were all plain.' Perhaps Isabella was that pretty Mrs J, but again this is unlikely because at this time Isabella had plenty to occupy her beside her attire. On New Year's Day 1840, in a tent in Kurnaul, she gave birth to Mary Catherine Helen.

Two months later Charles was given a sick certificate to visit the hills for six months, his first leave for three years. The family travelled into the Himalayas to Mussoorie, up at 6,570 feet.

The hill stations had been invented only recently, once the imperial armies had reached the foothills of the Himalayas, and Simla was still the only other British foundation. They rented a bungalow called the Hermitage, which stood with just one other in a beautiful wooded cud. Here Isabella found not only physical beauty, but also a sense of release: elevated above the Indian masses, she could relax with her babies in a climate more like that of Scotland (although the 'gentleman's houses' tucked into every nook reminded Fanny Parkes of the more prosaic Isle of Wight). Isabella adored it. Although she had enjoyed Cawnpore and Kurnaul, she responded with far greater intensity to the Himalayas. 'I cannot give you any idea of the magnificence of the scenery of the Hills, with the cedar forests, the lovely valleys full of rhododendron, walnut and cherry and many other flowering trees, and all capped by the everlasting Snowy Range, the highest mountains in the world. The air, the sky and the earth are all exquisitely beautiful, and the thunder storms in the rainy season grand and awe-inspiring beyond all description.'

Charles strolled along the Mall and 'ate the air' with other sickly gentlemen, but he did not recover. So once again their possessions were sold, and the Gascoyne family descended the hills in jhampans to Dehra Dun, then continued by palanquin dak to the Ganges and by boats to Calcutta. On 23 December 1840 Charles was granted furlough to England, his first since he had left home fourteen years earlier.

THREE

On Furlough

The earliest thing I can recollect is standing on the banks of the Hoogley River in Calcutta, holding my father's hand and watching an English ship come in. I was four years old. The only white people I had seen besides my parents were officers and their families, so these strong 'sailor men' looked very interesting to me. I was a very timid child and would have been alarmed if I had not had hold of Papa's hand.

Very soon I was lifted into the boat and all our native servants were left behind. It was a great grief to me to part with Sudda, who had looked after me, and used to carry me about, and take me for walks; but everything was so new and strange that I soon forgot my sorrow in the excitement of the moment, and only knew that I must keep near my father. We boarded the great ship, an East Indiaman, amid what seemed to me much confusion. The loud shouts and orders to the men, the bustle and excitement, all combined to overwhelm and frighten me.

The doctor had ordered that I should have a glass of Port wine every forenoon, and when we had been some days at sea, my dear father gave it to me thinking I needed it; but my mother said that he was just spoiling me.

Izzy

We sailed in the *Carnatic*, commanded by a Captain Voss. When we were about half way across the Atlantic, late in the evening, suddenly a cry of 'Fire! Fire!' was heard, and smoke and flames were seen coming from the steward's pantry, which was full of wine and spirits and other inflammable goods. The door was locked, and some little time elapsed before it could be forced open and the buckets ranged from the ship's side and handed from one to another in a line, the women and children shrieking with terror. It was an anxious time for everyone, but the flames were soon brought under control and order was restored, by God's mercy. Isabella

The Gascoynes joined Charles's parents in Clifton, a suburb of substantial Georgian villas and terraces built on hills in the sweet air above the malodorous port of Bristol. Isabella was charmed by Charles's French mother, Charlotte. She was, Isabella recalled, 'an earnest Christian, and a noble lady, and I loved her dearly. Her daughters Mary and Sophie,' she added drily, 'did not resemble her in any way.' Isabella also took against Charles's father, a retired naval captain. He had suffered from yellow fever and still played the invalid, demanding constant attention from his dutiful wife and, despite their meagre income, special luxurious foods. Every day Charlotte brought him breakfast in bed and lunch in the drawing room. 'In short,' Isabella pronounced sternly, 'he was a thoroughly selfish man, Mrs Gascoyne the very opposite. It is to be hoped that her qualities may predominate in the succeeding generations.'

9 Frederick Place was part of a steep flat-fronted Georgian terrace of Bath stone.* The children were aghast to find themselves imprisoned upstairs in two nurseries, one for day and one

---

* Frederick Place is still standing. No. 9 was later owned by the actor-archaeologist Tony Robinson.

for night, a far cry from the Hermitage in Mussoorie. Instead of running freely round the veranda or into the garden, they were taken out for daily walks or drives under the strict charge of two nurses. The upper nurse was sour and ugly, very different from their beloved ayah, Sudda, and their other Indian servants who were so anxious to please. On returning from their boring walks they had to toil up flights of stairs to the nursery, and the children asked each other in Hindustani why English people had a 'hall' or 'stairs'. The nurseries were above the drawing room, and poor querulous Captain Gascoyne found his peace destroyed by his grandchildren's feet pattering overhead. Although the children had been told that it was the height of impertinence to criticize a grown-up, they disliked their grandfather. He was greedy and tiresome, and insisted that the children should be seen and not heard; in India they made as much noise as they wanted, and people only smiled at them.

Their grandfather became so irritable that after whispered consultations with Charles, Isabella sent Fred and Mary to stay with her cousins at the Manse near Dunstaffnage. 'Here I knew my children would be more than welcome and would thrive on Highland air and Highland fare. Though,' she added sadly, 'I felt very much the hardship of being parted from my little ones. Izzy, my eldest, was a very quiet, shy, reserved child, and gave no trouble to anyone. She remained in Clifton and went to a day school first, and then had a young lady teacher for two hours every day.'

Charles was worried about his future, and wrote to Lord Salisbury. Even though the Gascoyne Heiress had died of dropsy in 1839, Lord Salisbury received many such letters from his late wife's relations, and often responded generously.

Perhaps he felt guilty about having inherited most of the Gascoynes' family money; he had also taken their arms, and changed his name by royal licence to Gascoyne-Cecil. However much the Gascoynes disliked humbling themselves to grovel fervent thanks for condescending patronage and kindness, Lord Salisbury expected it, and the Gascoynes depended on it.

June 1841
9 Frederick Place
Clifton

My Lord Marquis,
It is with hesitation that I lay before your Lordship the present circumstances of my life – but having formerly presented me with a commission in the EIC Services I have presumed to account your Lordship my patron, and trust that, situated as I am, this feeling may excuse my intrusion.

After fifteen years service in India the medical board have sent me home on furlough, certifying 'that my constitution is utterly broken', and advising me, by no means, to return to the East.

In the event of my retiring from the service at this time – I should probably obtain from the EI Govt a pension of about £100 a year. [£4,428 today.] Having a wife and family to provide for, it would, therefore, be necessary at the expiration of my furlough, to return to India and rejoin my regiment, unless some opportunity for employment should present itself in this country.

In the hope that your Lordship's great influence may render this object attainable, I have ventured to intrude this account of my affairs.

I can only add that should I be successful in obtaining

*employment – whatever its nature – I would by great
perseverance, endeavour to fulfil its duties and do justice to
your Lordship's recommendation.*

*I am – my Lord Marquis – with gratitude for former
kindness – your Lordship's very faithful servant
Charles Manners Gascoyne.*

Lord Salisbury replied unpromisingly,

*My dear Sir,
I have made every inquiry in my power in pursuance of the
object expressed in your letter and exceedingly regret that I
see no prospect of success. Even if circumstances should
enable me to apply to the government for any offers in your
favour, there appear to be no situations to which gentlemen
are eligible after a certain age, and any other employment
than that of government is not to be depended upon as
permanent.*

*I do not know the rules of the Indian Service but I shall
have great pleasure in making every application to the
Director in your favour which you can suggest – and with
sincere regret for the state of your health, I remain
Yours faithfully
Gascoyne Salisbury*

The northern climate agreed so well with Charles that he felt
fit enough to contemplate returning to India after all. He hastened to point out to Lord Salisbury that he loved his profession
and preferred an Indian life to an English one, something he
owed to his Lordship. He was too well-mannered to add that
he was tired of waiting for someone to die before he could get
promotion. He was toiling his way up the regimental hierarchy,

and progress was painfully slow. He needed a job. When Lord Salisbury's friend Lord Ellenborough replaced Lord Auckland as Governor-General of India, Lord Salisbury applied to him on Charles's behalf. Lord Ellenborough replied promisingly that 'where the merits of men are equal, there is no person I should be so willing to oblige as a relation of yours.' Charles was effusive in his thanks.

After twelve months in Clifton, Charles granted Isabella's request (indeed, a promise made before their marriage) that they should visit Isabella's friends in Scotland. They took a furnished house in Elgin for the autumn and winter of 1841–2. Here Isabella gave birth to Emily Charlotte Ann Justina, known as Amy, and employed a Miss Amelia Sutherland as governess. Amelia Sutherland was not the usual pale spinster in straightened circumstances, the bullied Charlotte Brontë type, nor an ugly rod-wielding arm-pinching tyrant of the schoolroom. She was tall, slender and good-looking with a pile of auburn hair, and the children immediately adored her.

In April 1842, when Amy was one month old, they returned to Clifton with Miss Sutherland in tow. Charles was longing to see his brother John, who was Secretary to the Royal Yacht Club in Plymouth, so he lent John the money to move his entire family to Clifton.

In his day John Gascoyne had been charming, good-natured and with 'a very fine presence'. At the age of nineteen he had thrown up his job in the War Office to marry an elderly but rich widow and become an idle man-about-town, driving about the most fashionable London streets in his wife's carriage and four, and urging her to sit well back because her wrinkled face would spoil the turnout. When she died it was found – alas! – that he would get only half her property, the rest going to her children by her first husband. Her £20,000 – the equivalent of nearly £1,000,000 today – was, however, still enough to get by on.

John then married Julia Cumberland, as young and beautiful as his first wife had been old and ugly. They had met at balls in Plymouth, where Julia's father was the admiral in command. Her loveliness shone so brightly that she was known as the Star of Devon, but Isabella disapproved of her dress, which she found too flamboyant and unladylike. John, on the other hand, she described as having 'a remarkably handsome figure and a very aristocratic manner and walk (as had my husband also).' His personality had a few faults, however. 'Shortly before we returned to India, we were disappointed of some remittances. Knowing that Uncle John had just cleared £1000 by some business transaction, my husband frankly asked him if he could return the money he had sent him on the former occasion [to move his family to Clifton]. His reply was characteristic of the man, "My dear fellow, how readily would I do so were the money a real gain, but the fact is, I can hardly call it so, having lost so much in years gone by." He should have said not 'lost' but 'squandered'. So much for Uncle John's character. He loved money more than all else.'

Uncle John, Aunt Julia and their children rented 5 Frederick Place, and the Gascoyne cousins became friends. The girls went to dancing classes together, 'and became rivals in that art', while Fred played with John's boys Bamber and Henry. The children were blonde and angelic.

Much to his disappointment, Charles failed his medical examination at India House and was forced to remain in England for another season. Then he received news so devastating

that Izzy believed it nearly broke her father's heart. He was promoted to the rank of third captain, which he had long wanted
– but it came only because so many above him in the regimental hierarchy had been slaughtered. The invasion of Afghanistan
had turned out to be the greatest military disaster in the history
of the British in India.

In November 1841, while Charles and Isabella were in
Elgin, an uprising had taken place in Kabul. The British Residency was attacked and several officers killed. The British
garrison was besieged, and Dost Mohammed's son, the fearsome Akbar Khan, arrived from exile in Turkestan with a force
of Uzbeks. Akbar Khan summoned the British Envoy, Sir
William MacNaghten, dear Captain Chapman's brother-in-law,
and murdered him. His head was paraded through Kabul, and
his body swung from a meat hook in the bazaar. British morale,
already low, disintegrated. The army agreed to withdraw from
Afghanistan, but the Afghans found they could dictate the
terms of their retreat: the entire British garrison was to depart
at once trailing their thousands of camp followers, wives and
children, and abandon to the Afghans all their treasure and
most of their guns. In return, the Afghans promised them a
trustworthy escort. The British, now frightened, cold and starving, rightly suspected treachery. There was nothing they could
do.

In January 1842, in the depths of winter, the army began its
retreat, the most terrible in the history of British arms. There
now remained 700 Europeans, 3,800 Indian soldiers, and
12,000 camp followers and their families. Almost before they
left camp they were attacked by sword-wielding Ghazis. Footsore, weary and afraid, they entered the desolate snow-buried

country of the Afghan passes. Frostbite set in and, lacking fuel, shelter, food or ammunition, the paths were soon a nightmare chaos of the dead and dying. Eleven English women and their children, including Lady MacNaghten, widow of the ill-fated envoy, were extracted from the convoy and imprisoned, but the rest entered Hell. For the next seven days, the remnants of the army were harried constantly by Afghan marksmen and their knife-wielding children, their assaults becoming ever more brazen, the carnage and terror more brutal. The track was thick with mutilated corpses. The few survivors struggled on through terrible passes and ravines, the stragglers picked off. By day nine, Dr William Brydon, traditionally described as the sole survivor but in fact the first of several, dragged himself into Jallalabad with the news. More than sixteen thousand people had died.

Over the years, Charles's fellow officers and their wives, posted from one military outpost to another, had been drawn intimately together. Reliant on each other for entertainment, their evenings had been spent in the mess or in each other's bungalows. Now most of them were dead. Of the sixteen officers and four cornets in the 5th Bengal Light Cavalry, half had been killed, along with twenty-six troopers. Those 5th Light Cavalry officers who were not killed had survived simply because they were not there. The survivors, including Charles, erected a memorial tablet in St Peter's Church in Fort William, Calcutta. 'The lamented braves whose deaths it records, though greatly outnumbered by a most treacherous foe in snowy wastes and rugged defiles, for several days and nights together, without shelter or even a tent, and suffering from the extremes of cold, hunger and thirst, in the depth of an Afghan winter, sold their lives dearly as became British soldiers.'*

Captain Blair, who was killed in the Jagdalak Pass on 12 January, was one of the worst losses. Three years older than Charles, Edward Blair had been in the regiment since Charles joined in 1827. They had been together at the Cawnpore ball where Charles first saw Isabella. Edward Blair was married to Susannah, Colonel Kennedy's daughter. Susannah Blair refused to accept Captain Blair's death, insisting he must be a prisoner in Afghanistan and would soon make his way back to her over the passes, so instead of returning to England she stayed in Cawnpore with her two daughters. She awaited her husband for fifteen years, almost as long as Penelope waited for Odysseus.

The invasion of Afghanistan was morally indefensible, and the retreat a devastating blow to British morale – the worst until the surrender of Singapore exactly one hundred years later. On hearing the news, Lord Auckland collapsed with a stroke, screaming and raving. He was left partly paralysed, and never recovered. Still, he

---

* Between 6 and 13 January 1842, Lieutenant-Colonel Chambers, Captain Blair, Captain Bott, Captain Hamilton, Brevet-Captain Collyer, Surgeon Harpur, Lieutenant Bazett, Lieutenant Hardiman, Veterinary Surgeon Willis, Riding Master Quantrill: all these men of the 5th Light Cavalry fell with almost the entire roll of the 5th, 3rd, 4th, and 6th regiments, in gallant but hopeless conflict in the retreat from Kabul. Charles also mourned his troopers, known in the cavalry as sowars. Closeness between officers and their Indian troops was fostered by the long marches and sieges and the ever-present threat of death. Before 1857 the Indian armies were generally more humane and relaxed than the British army. Flogging was abandoned in the Indian armies in 1835, while it was inflicted so frequently in the British army that the Queen's troops were nicknamed 'Bloody-backs', until the death of a soldier from flogging in 1846 in London caused such a furore that it quickly disappeared.

did manage to send forth an Army of Retribution (which included Isabella's brother Archy) to wreak an equally genocidal revenge.*

Charles passed his next medical examination – perhaps standards had lowered now that officers were so desperately needed to replace the dead – and the family decamped to London to prepare for their return to the remnants of the regiment. They took lodgings in Manchester Square and visited Madame Tussaud's and the new zoological gardens in Regent's Park, and paid farewell visits to relatives and friends. A great deal of shopping was done, mainly for school books which were chosen by Miss Sutherland, and which would have to last the family for the next ten years at least.

Charles and Isabella had decided to ignore the advice of friends and not follow what Isabella called 'the usual plan' of leaving the children at school in England, despite warnings that if they returned to India they would never grow up properly, or would even die.† Although they had already lost a child, Charles and Isabella were willing to take that risk. Isabella's childhood experiences prevented her from even considering abandoning her children to relatives or boarding school.

---

* Shah Shuja was murdered and Dost Mohammed retrieved the throne. This time Isabella's brother did not accompany him; instead he became Deputy Superintendent of Police in Calcutta, where, having survived war in Afghanistan, he was felled by cholera in 1850.

† Isabella's contemporary Honoria Lawrence had nothing but contempt for the way British children were brought up in a heathen land. She complained that they were spoilt by their parents who, enervated by the climate, whipped one minute and indulged the next. She criticized parents for leaving their children mostly to their ayahs and other native servants who allowed them to do exactly what they wanted, bringing them up babbling exclusively in Hindustani. There was also the question of health. Fanny Parkes remarked that European children in India had a sickly hue, even when they were in the best of health, very different from the 'chubby brats' of England.

Meanwhile Miss Sutherland was either so desperate, or so adventurous, or so charmed, that she left home to travel with the Gascoynes to India, aware that she might be gone forever. As for Charles, he would never see his parents or siblings again.

FOUR

Charles Sees War and is Horrified

The *Seringapatam*, a 1,152-ton frigate with thirty-eight guns, arrived in Calcutta in September 1843 with one more infant Gascoyne than when the family embarked.

Giving birth at sea was not so bad – there was a surgeon on board, and fresh water and supplies had been loaded at Madras. Although they were at least a week away from a hospital, the distance was not much greater than it would have been for many women who gave birth in remote outposts of India, and there were three other married women passengers to act as midwives, along with Amelia Sutherland. However, the lack of privacy was frightful; the cabin walls had gaps between their planks, and sound travelled easily. Everyone was tense, awaiting the sound of a newborn's mew, and when it came there were relief, joy, congratulations, children curious to see their new sister and tots of rum for the crew.

Isabella thought of her new baby more as an intelligent angel spirit than an ordinary infant; she never cried or showed any temper, and there was something about her – the way she was born nowhere, with a faraway look in her eyes – that made people say she did not seem to belong in this world.

Keen to rejoin his regiment in Muttra, Charles and the expanding family departed as soon as possible up the Ganges.

> It was a delightful way of travelling; every evening the boat was moored to the shore and we were allowed to go for walks – such walks! So full of interest and pleasure, with our father to point out and explain everything. He was an excellent linguist, and could easily speak to the Natives who always responded readily to his courteous remarks and inquiries, with a politeness equal to his own. Sometimes we were taken to a celebrated temple or mosque, or to some deserted old palace. A rare treat was to be taken to a bazaar to see all the shops. Always before we entered, the head man of the bazaar was ordered to see that all objectionable sights were removed while we passed through; and this order was strictly obeyed. Such was the esteem in which the East India Company Raj was held, and all its officers too.
>
> Izzy

Soon another tragedy unfolded. At five months old the baby girl wasted away. Isabella grieved terribly. Of course she was prepared for such a death, just one of hundreds noted each month in the Bengal ecclesiastical records, but she never recovered from her loss. Perhaps a baby's death was worse the second time round; perhaps Isabella suffered more because this time she had no new baby to replace her with. Despite her grief, years later Isabella would say she was thankful that the little girl was safe with her brother Charles in heaven, and taken from the evils still to come.

Then Isabella took a chance on grief and in 1845 another baby, another Charles, was born.

The Gascoynes remained in Muttra for two years, now in

more superior captain's quarters. While the British Army of Retribution equalled and even outdid the Afghans' brutality, Charles's regiment licked its wounds and rebuilt itself. In Calcutta, Charles had presented his letter of recommendation to Governor-General Lord Ellenborough: 'He is a relation of mine by marriage,' Lord Salisbury had written, 'and I shall feel really very obliged to you if you can meet his wishes, which I believe only intend to some staff appointment, of which there are many in North India.' Lord Ellenborough was happy to help, and Charles was appointed to a committee that examined horses at the company's central stud at Ghazipore, their beautiful Arab, English and Persian predecessors having been slaughtered in the Afghan debacle along with their riders. Charles's task was to view a selection of over a thousand carefully reared horses, then take charge of the colts passed for the 5th Cavalry and escort them back to Muttra.

Only one power now remained to rival the company: the Sikh empire, which loomed in the Punjab. Lord Ellenborough, a warlike civilian who irritated the Company Directors, was replaced as Governor-General in 1844 by Sir Henry (later Lord) Hardinge, a peace-loving warrior. A distinguished veteran of the Peninsular War who had lost an arm at Quatre-Bras in 1815, Hardinge was revered as a hero. His job was officially to keep the peace in the Punjab, although Sikh accounts accuse the British of a threatening build-up of arms along their frontier. Hardinge prepared to make a tour of inspection of the Upper Provinces, and Charles was ordered to attend with his rebuilt troop of cavalry.

Isabella made preparations to accompany him. She had to sell most of the family's possessions, and pack up the remainder

– yet again. She also had to rent a house in Manooli and send Amelia Sutherland and the children to the safety of the hills, keeping baby Charlie with her. Isabella had rarely been parted from her children; although they had servants to take care of their daily needs, this was an exceptionally close family.*

After the trauma of packing up and saying farewell, Isabella had nothing but enthusiasm for the march. Hardinge's camp was a huge affair, a city in motion. The 5th Light Cavalry, like other East India Company regiments, owned no permanent transport other than chargers, so hired what beasts of burden they could find – camels, elephants, donkeys, mules, ponies, bullocks, hitched to carts and wagons of every description – to form a colourful noisy cavalcade that stretched along many miles of road. Isabella felt proud to be part of this dusty convoy, and to see her husband on his charger at the head of his troop, resplendent in his uniform of French grey jacket decorated with silver lace, the heavy gold ends of his festoons streaming from his shoulder, swans' feathers floating from his shako. His uniform was impractically stiff and hot, and his shako provided no protection from the sun, but he looked marvellous.

Sometimes Isabella travelled in her palanquin, but more often she sent Charlie and the ayah in that while she took the more airy option with the better view in a buggy driven by Dr Spencer, the regimental doctor. It was delightful marching

---

* Honoria Lawrence complained that most women in India talked of nothing but their children, but only as so many additional misfortunes. Isabella genuinely loved hers, which made what was to happen in New Zealand so poignant.

weather, with warm sunny days and clear nights, perfect for camping.

The camp stirred long before dawn. Charles, woken by his bearer, would wash and shave in water heated on a campfire, then snatch a quick breakfast by lamplight while the servants dismantled the tents and loaded them onto camels and bullocks. By 5 a.m. the first columns were played out of the camp by a regimental band, the officers following on horseback, and they marched through the darkness for one and a half hours, led by burning torches. There was a short halt an hour after sunrise for breakfast for the men (cold chapattis which they carried in their packs), then a long steady march, with an advance party going ahead to mark out that day's camp ground and organize supplies. At midday the first column marched into the camp, played in by the regimental band. Campfires were lit, rice boiled up in vats for a lunch of curried vegetables, dal and rice, then the mess tent was erected and each officer's camp furniture and kit set out.

In this way they crossed the Punjab. In the 1840s the Punjab was very different from now. Today it is a mosaic of fields irrigated by the canal system installed by the British soon after this march; then it was mostly untouched jungle criss-crossed by rivers and their tributaries, all of which had to be traversed. Boats tied together bridged some rivers, others had to be forded, and others had ferries. All of these options must have been daunting to this vast army.

The River Sutlej was the dividing line: on one bank lay the empire of the British, and on the other the formidable empire of the Sikhs, built up over several decades by their charismatic one-eyed illiterate general, Ranjit Singh, the Lion of the

Punjab.* When the Napoleonic Wars had ended, Ranjit Singh's army was supplemented by newly unemployed mercenaries who had no love of the British – mostly French but also Italian and American. They had trained up Ranjit's soldiers and dressed and organized them on French lines. By the time Ranjit Singh died (of a stroke brought on by excessive drinking) in 1839, his army had amassed a formidable arsenal of four hundred cannon, thousands of horses and sabres and a fearsome phalanx of foot soldiers. Without Ranjit Singh at its head, his army swelled out of control and the East India Company watched and waited with growing apprehension as the Punjab descended into anarchy. With the British itching for control, a bloody confrontation was inevitable. It was only a question of when.

For the moment everything looked peaceful, so Isabella sent a message summoning the children from the hills. Amelia Sutherland arranged for the house to be packed up, dismissed most of the servants, hired baggage coolies and set off with the children towards the plains. The children had loved their time in Manooli, with freedom to play outdoors in their beautiful garden under the gentle but watchful eye of Miss Sutherland, but they were excited to be on their travels again.

Charles on his charger, Isabella in the doctor's buggy, and the rest of the entourage were heading for the brigade headquarters at Ferozepore, one day's march ahead. They were about a mile from that night's camp when a young officer galloped towards Isabella, shouting, 'Have you heard the news?

---

* The Sutlej flows into the Indus, which has its mouth at Karachi, and is now mostly in Pakistan.

Thirty thousand Sikhs have crossed the Sutlej! An engagement is expected. Every lady is ordered out of the camp today, before noon.' Isabella felt paralysed. Where was she to go? What was she to do? She had a baby with her. On reaching her tent, she saw an elephant with a howdah and trappings waiting, swinging its trunk and puffing through it. Charles was there, reining in his overexcited charger. He explained that Sir Henry Hardinge had sent the elephant to take her back to Kurnaul. She was to leave now. He didn't know when they would meet again.

Each of the officers' wives had been provided with an elephant. After all the dusty miles they had covered, they were forced to set off back the way they had come, but this time without their husbands. Several of them, like Isabella, had babes in arms. It was, Isabella recalled, 'a sad cavalcade'. 'Half way back to Kurnaul, after about 30 miles, we met an officer on horseback with dispatches, and as he had ridden in haste to reach the camp as soon as possible, he requested us ladies to give up one of our elephants to him, his horse being spent, and two of us to ride together. I gave him mine. That night he reached camp just as the battle of Moodkee was fought, and he was killed. I had only thought to do him a favour, poor fellow.'

Charles had been ordered on escort duties only, so was not expecting to fight. Stationed three miles from the camp with orders to keep a lookout for the enemy, he had just taken off his sword and was preparing to have a comfortable hour's rest when his subedar galloped up shouting that there was a cloud of dust visible not far away, which he feared might be a body of cavalry charging towards them. Charles looked through his telescope, which he always carried slung over his shoulder, and saw that the subedar was right. Giving orders to his men, he galloped back to camp and raised the alarm. Almost before they had time to form the regiment into line of battle, the Sikhs had opened fire, and the Battle of Moodkee had begun; Charles later admitted to Isabella that the attack had been so unexpected that no precautions had been taken, or defences made.

> Very many brave officers, my husband told me later, mounted their chargers, joking and saying what capital fun to have a brush with the Sikhs, little realising the strength and trained skill of the enemy, who had French officers among their leaders, and who fought with determination. Many of our fine men were left dead or wounded on the field all night. Three of the ladies who accompanied me on that march back to Kurnaul were made widows, their husbands dying on the field of Moodkee.
> Isabella

That day –18 December – the battle raged until late. Almost all the Governor-General's staff officers were killed, but thanks to the cavalry, who forced the Sikhs twenty miles back to Ferozeshah, the British won the day. Charles and some other officers and a few of their men pursued the retreating Khalsa Dal into the darkness, to find that they were separated from their regiments, and stranded beside a clump of trees. It was close to midnight and bitterly cold. A Major Gough, nephew of the gallant Irish Commander-in-Chief Sir Hugh Gough, proposed that they should try to find their way back to the camp, but they all admitted that they had no idea where they were. For all they knew, they could be in the middle of enemy territory, with hostile Sikhs all around. But Charles had an extraordinary sixth sense of locality, an ability to retrace his steps and find his way when all others were lost (something his son Fred would later, during a different war in a different place, prove to have inherited). Charles offered to lead them, but they hesitated; Major Gough was the senior officer and so by rights should have taken charge, but he had no more idea where they were than the rest of them. Eventually they agreed that they had no alternative but to trust in Charles. He piloted them through the dark to the mess tents of the cavalry where they were welcomed as if from the dead. All hope had been abandoned of their being alive.

> I received letters daily from my husband until the Sikhs cut off communication by Dacok, but he kept a daily journal and forwarded it from time to time. It was a dreadful period of anxiety for the wives and families left behind in Kurnaul. We could, by putting our heads close to the ground, hear the thud, thud, of the artillery guns, and the reverberation along the foot of the hills, although we were sixty miles away. Many an affecting incident occurred. Some rumour would reach us that such or such an officer was wounded or killed, and I remember sitting up with one poor lady whose husband, Colonel Mair, was among the list of those killed. She, poor thing, was in violent hysterics all night and quite delirious. However, Colonel Mair recovered from his wounds.
> Isabella

The families were not safe either. Isabella had sent an urgent message up to Manooli warning Miss Sutherland and the children to stay put, but they had already left and were heading towards the thick of battle. Only when they reached Kurnaul after weeks of travelling did the children discover that their father was at war. The family found refuge with a Mrs Benson, whose husband, Captain Benson, was with Charles at the front.

Mrs Benson accepted us all with the utmost hospitality, my parents of course insisting on sharing equally with the household expenses. There came days of fearful anxiety and waiting, and constant rumours of danger. Now and then a mounted messenger would bring letters from officers to their wives, and you can imagine how eagerly they were read and treasured. The natives were in a state of great excitement and unrest and hoped the English would be beaten.

Izzy

One night an Indian rode into the station with news that the English had lost the day: he had passed a detachment of four hundred Sikhs on their way to destroy the cantonment of Kurnaul. They would arrive in a few hours hungry to loot, murder, pillage and burn. There was time to escape only if they left at once.

All lights were extinguished and the cantonment filled with fright, hurry and bustle. The closest place of safety was Saharanpur, a small station not far from the Himalayan foothills, but everyone needed a carriage and good horses to get there, which Isabella lacked. She woke the children, hastily dressed them, and covered their clothes in blue quilted labodas to keep them warm. There was a question of how to carry money, jewels and other valuables: Isabella decided that she and Miss Sutherland should each be laden with a bag of rupees, while Izzy, Fred and Mary were entrusted with packets of the family miniatures, which were carefully tied on their backs. The soldiers' wives and others with no access to transport were ordered for their safety behind a barricade, while those officers' wives who had carriages prepared to set off in the dark. Fortunately kind Mrs Benson invited Isabella and Miss Sutherland and the babies to squeeze in with her, and the rest of the children were put into a palque gharri, a kind of small omnibus.

It was a false alarm. The British had – just – won the day, and the four hundred Sikhs turned out to be religious devotees off to bury a great leader at a holy spot beyond Kurnaul. The next day, however, several of the ladies decided it was safer to decamp to Saharanpur anyway. Lady Gilbert, whose husband General Sir Walter Raleigh Gilbert was in command with the army, offered to take Izzy and Fred in her landau; the rest went in palanquins.

A few miles from Ambala they tried to cross a bridge, but the enemy, having taken possession of it, refused to let them pass, in spite of their pleading that they were in great haste and must cross. One of the Sikhs on guard drew his sword and threatened to cut them to bits, so they drove further down the river to the next bridge, where they succeeded in getting over.

It was a weary time with much frustration caused by hindrances in getting fresh horses and food. But when we arrived at our destination we were none the worse for our adventure. We had left the bungalow in Kurnaul with all its furniture and contents to the care of the servants, thinking we would never see it again. However, after two months, we returned to find everything was the same and intact.
Izzy

Meanwhile Charles fought an even bloodier battle, at Ferozeshah on 21 and 22 December 1845. Far away in Saharanpur,

Isabella and the children could feel the ground shake with the concussions of the artillery. They and the other women of the regiment waited in terror for news from the battlefield, knowing that their men were hugely outnumbered. At last the British guns were silenced, their ammunition exhausted. The only hope for the European women and children lay in escaping from the cantonment before the Sikh cavalry reached them, bent on bloodshed and rape.

Isabella decided to flee back to Kurnaul, and asked the officer commanding the station for native carts to transport her servants and baggage. 'He replied that he would do his best, but that the natives were in such a state of insubordination that he had little authority over them.' He did manage to get one cart, and Isabella's servants loaded it with goods and chattels. Suddenly an armed man rode up, drew his sword and commanded them to unload immediately. Isabella, lurking behind the tent door, understood his Hindustani, and stepped forward. 'Who are you who dare to order my servants? The cart was sent by the sahib in command.' He replied by twirling his sword around her head, and shouting abuse. Isabella quickly retreated inside the tent, but seven-year-old Fred seized his uncle Archy's sword, which Isabella always carried in her palanquin, unsheathed it and holding it like a bayonet at the charge rushed at the man, slashing viciously at his legs until Isabella pulled him inside. The bandit bolted back to the compound gate, still yelling threats and insults. It was a moment of triumph that Fred never forgot; it fired him with the desire to be a soldier. Isabella recalled this incident differently, as evidence that British prestige had suffered fatally during this war, and that hostility towards the British, which would culminate in the Mutiny, had already begun to emerge.

At the eleventh hour, the British won their battle. Before leaving the field, Hardinge called his generals together once more to thank God for deliverance and victory. The slaughter was appalling; it was, Charles said, like the defeat of the Assyrians in the Bible.*

A troop of British cavalry arrived in Kurnaul to rescue the women and children and take charge of the cantonment.

When the Sikhs again raided across the Sutlej, another battle took place on 28 January 1846 near the village of Aliwal, where Charles led his troop once more into the fray. On the eve of the battle, faced with the possibility – even likelihood – of death, Charles sat in his tent reading his Bible, praying and writing what might have been his last love letter to his wife.

Death raged over the Indian plains, but again the British won. After reinforcements arrived, the Commander-in-Chief, Sir Hugh Gough, attacked the Sikhs at Sobraon. Gough would call this battle the Waterloo of India.

As soon as light dawned across the plain during the early hours of 10 February 1846, the British guns opened their heavy

---

* A Major White of the 31st Regiment painted the scene. Officers on horseback raise their swords to drive on the infantry under their command, the infantry in their short red jackets, white bands strapped across their chests, white peaked caps and red-striped black trousers. A pall of smoke hangs over the blazing tents of the Sikh camp, and turbaned Sikhs flee on horseback; riderless horses run wild in terror; camels look stupidly about; corpses of both races are strewn over the blood-red earth, their bodies draped over captured cannons; wounded horses roll on the ground in agony. In the foreground an Englishman bayonets a Sikh, who bravely reaches forward to grab the bayonet blade in his hand.

fire. The Khalsa Dal immediately returned fire with a barrage of shot and shell. The artillery duel raged for three hours. The Sikhs outnumbered the British by more than two to one, and the odds looked grim, but Gough knew this could be the battle to end the war: he had to win. He resorted to a series of frontal assaults. First three cavalry regiments galloped to within three hundred yards of the Sikh guns, which covered the advance of the main brigade of infantry. They advanced steadily, as if on parade, bayonets at the ready, straight into enemy gunfire. As they crossed no-man's-land towards the Sikhs, it appeared that the earlier artillery duel had barely broken a cavity in the teeth of the Sikhs' defensive position, and the British forces were strafed mercilessly by a barrage of well-directed musket and swivel spittle. Most of the division was driven back, or fell at every step, but the few who continued to advance did so in disconcerting silence. Suddenly they let out a shout, which was described by one of the surviving Sikhs as being 'such as only angry demons could send forth'. The British leapt into the trench, then swarmed up the opposite side on the shoulders of their comrades and made a dash for the Sikh guns, which were still heavily defended. 'But who could withstand such fierce demons, with those awful bayonets, which they preferred to their guns – and not a shot did they fire the whole time.'

The British managed to get behind the Sikhs to cut away their bridge-of-boats across the Sutlej, and thus trap them between the river and the advancing British army. Victory was completed by a cavalry charge down the Sikh lines, and as Charles's superior officer Colonel Alexander had been wounded, it was Charles who not only led his own troop, but triumphantly commanded his regiment.* The Sikhs, with the river behind them, had nowhere to go, and the carnage was terrible. The Khalsa Dal was destroyed, losing 3,125 men and every one of its sixty-seven big guns during the final battle alone. But the Sikhs had fought ferociously. Gough wrote, 'I declare were it not from a deep conviction that my country's good required the sacrifice, I could have wept to have witnessed the fearful slaughter of so devoted a body of men.' British losses were also massive, the wounded and dying filling the dressing stations, their agony only barely relieved by the newly discovered chloroform.

Charles, Isabella was told, had been the coolest and bravest officer in the regiment. A brother officer named Captain Wrench told her that while they stood beside their horses waiting for the order to charge Charles seemed as calm, and spoke as quietly, as if he had been in his tent. Captain Wrench remarked on this to Charles, who replied that he actually did feel perfectly calm, and added jokingly, 'But there, I do not present such a target for the bullets as you do.' Charles was tall and slim, and Captain Wrench a very stout man.

Although Charles led his regiment fearlessly and was not wounded, something in him was killed. He wrote to Isabella, 'I have seen war and am horrified; and I hope that no son of mine may follow his father's profession.' He had shared the battlefield with some of the most famous names in the annals of Raj history – William Hodson of Hodson's Horse, John Nicholson, Henry Lawrence, Herbert Edwardes, and Joe

---

* Colonel Alexander survived, only to lose an arm during the Second Sikh War and die soon after in 1851 aged fifty-five.

Lumsden of the Guides, many of whom were to fight and fall during the Indian Mutiny – but Charles had no intention of waiting around for that. This war had turned him off the whole bloody business.

Decorated with the Sutlej Medal with three bars, Charles promptly took eight months' leave on sick certificate in Simla.

What a wonderful interlude for the whole family seeking post-war rest and rehabilitation. Isabella described Simla as the most delightful place in all of India. The climate resembled that of Nelson in summer and Dunedin in winter,

> the scenery lovely beyond all description, the hills covered with the most luxurious vegetation – rhododendron, cherry, walnut, horse chestnut, deodar and other pines, and many flowering shrubs. The cuds and valleys are covered with wild hyacinth and many of our wild English flowers, wild strawberries and raspberries, and the Cape gooseberry in profusion; and beyond all, the Snowy Range which is the highest mountain range in all the world, and the same white, cold, clear horizon all the year round.

Yet here Isabella and Charles received news that wounded them more than war. In 1845 Archy Campbell had suffered an attack of liver complaint and been ordered on a sea voyage. He packed himself and his family into a ship bound for England. They paused at the Cape, where Archy was so ill that the chief doctor at the Cape Colony insisted it would be madness to think of continuing the voyage until he was better, but Archy replied that he had no choice since he had paid the passage money and could not afford to lose it. Another sick passenger begged him and his family to remain, as he himself intended doing, adding,

'Here is a cheque, my dear friend, for 1000 rupees; and draw upon me for as much as you need.' Within a month they lay side by side in Cape Town cemetery.

Isabella's sister-in-law, with three infant children, was stranded without friends or means – or so she thought – but, echoing her father's deathbed message to her mother, Isabella wrote that, 'the Almighty Friend of the widow and the fatherless was faithful to his promise, "Leave thy fatherless children and I will preserve them alive, and let thy widows trust in me." ' A Colonel Rutherford, hearing of the sad circumstances of Mrs Campbell, whom he had never met, wrote to ask whether she would prefer to take the next ship to England, or return to Calcutta. She chose the latter, and he paid for everything. 'Such were our kind and generous officers in the old East India Company Service.'*

The Gascoynes were ordered to Meerut. Emily Eden dismissed this garrison as 'a quantity of barracks and white bungalows spread over four miles of plain. There is nothing to see or draw'. Isabella on the other hand found it 'a most delightful station', enhanced by romantic memories of her courtship and wedding. Thanks to Charles's progress up the regimental hierarchy, they now had a 'large and commodious bungalow' and Charles made Isabella a present of 'a charming landau and pair'. Of an evening she could now process down the Mall in style, her pretty daughters and baby Charlie beside her, her handsome Fred on his pony, and her splendid husband, a war hero, distinguished on his charger. The Gascoynes remained in

* Emily Campbell later married a son of Lord Egremont, but he spent all her money and was killed falling from a balloon into a lake in Bengal.

Meerut for three years, and in 1846 Charlotte was born, named after Charles's mother. The children and Miss Sutherland resumed their life of six months on the plains and six months in the hills, but Charles remained on duty in the plains all year round, with Isabella at his side.

The combination of sun and the after-effects of the war had left Charles dangerously weak. On 1 December 1848 he joined the Invalid Establishment and took extended sick leave. Isabella's furniture, carriage and horses were sold for less than a quarter of their value and, in 1849, Charles moved the family to the peace and quiet of Lohughat in the Himalayas. Here he took a small estate with three stone bungalows; they occupied the best, and let the other two. Isabella noted flatly that Captain Lockett and Dr Pierson, who was in medical charge of the district, were their only visitors.

Lohughat lies fifteen miles from Nepal in the easternmost part of the western Himalayan tract. Tucked into a chaos of foothills leading north to the great ravines and crags of the Snowy Ranges, on the map the terrain looks as intricately contoured as a pattern of cobwebs. It had once been garrisoned by Gurkhas commanding the fertile valley to the south, but because of the difficulty of getting supplies up to this remote outpost the garrison had long since been withdrawn, and by the time the Gascoynes arrived nothing remained but a few houses and a small bazaar.*

Their compound – houses and garden, stables and servants'

---

* The surrounding soil was made of blue and often red ferruginous clay, which was thought by locals to be the blood of giants. During the rainy season the Lohu or 'Blood' River turned red.

quarters – was unusually large. Izzy loved the garden with its plantains, bananas, pomegranates, date and coconut palms and forest of mangoes; when the apricots ripened the ground was covered in a golden blanket three or four inches deep. For Fred the very word Lohughat would always conjure up the joy of being given his first gun and being taken under the wing of Captain Lockett, the great shikari, with whom he shot a bear. Together they roamed through forests where scarlet rhododendron flowers glowed against the dark green of the oaks. They crushed wild violets underfoot, and gorged on yellow raspberries.

A photograph caught them. Not a fleeting brightly coloured snapshot, but an image captured with the stillness and dignity of sepia. A heavy-roofed, low-browed house. Basket chairs scattered along the veranda. Charles, hand in pocket, elegant and long-limbed in waistcoat and breeches and solar topee. His syce holds his saddled horse, as if Charles has just dismounted, or is about to leave. Isabella stands tall and stately in full-length muslin. Only one child is present – it must be Charlotte, aged about five. She is seated in frilled lace beside a table behind which lurks an ayah and a turbaned servant about to pour tea. The other children are missing and in their place there are eleven servants, as if they formed the family; one little girl with her head draped in a shawl squats below Charlotte, and one tattered boy stands off stage left, as if ready to run out of the picture. The sepia and the static poses, and Charles and Isabella's height and white clothing, give them a statuesque quality hinting at the superior status of the East India Company Raj, but a closer look reveals that the garden is unkempt, the house and garden ramshackle, Charles's horse a skinny nag.

There is little formality and the servants seem at ease around their master, who has either recently taken this house and not yet got round to improving it, or else doesn't have the money or inclination to bother.*

It was a happy time, and the family drew closer. When Fred was twelve, Charles decided that he should at last go to school. They set out from Lohughat to visit a recommended establishment. The principal led Charles into his office to discuss his son, while Fred loitered in the grounds, where he got chatting to some of the pupils. When Charles reappeared they set off back

---

* The photograph is undated, but it must have been taken between 1849 and 1852 when the Gascoynes were in Lohughat. This makes it among the first photographs taken in India, since at the start of the 1850s cameras were not scarce: they were unique. Photography came to India in the 1840s but failed to take off because it faced so many difficulties – damp, rot, heat, bad chemicals, inadequate water supplies. P&O refused to transport the necessary chemical collodion because the active ingredient was also the explosive ingredient of smokeless gunpowder. There was no photographic society in Bengal until 1855, after the Gascoynes had left for New Zealand. In other words, this photograph is exceptionally rare. Who took the picture? Only two photographers are known to have been in Almorah and the surrounding district in the early 1850s. One was John Murray, principal of the medical school in Agra, who went to Almorah, and had paper negatives developed and printed there in 1853. The other was John McCosh, who went with his regiment to Almorah in 1844. He took the first photograph attributed to any individual photographer in India, possibly having taken up photography during his time in Almorah. He travelled into the Himalayas and took beautiful views of mountain ranges and peasant houses. To capture the scene Murray or McCosh had toiled up from Almorah with an army of bearers to carry their hefty equipment. They needed a pyramidal tent, a stock of glass plates, boxes of chemicals plus their replacements in case they fell down a mountain or into a river, heavy glass baths, a camera top, bottles for solutions, spirits and distilled water – about twenty loads, to be carried along with baggage, tents, bedding, cooking equipment and stores, camp furniture, and books, the whole requiring the aid of forty-two coolies at the very least.

along the track in silence. There was no sound but the clop of horses' hooves. Then a firm voice said, 'Father?'

'Yes, son?'

'Father, do you know they flog boys in that school?'

Charles nodded gravely. 'Yes.'

The hooves rang out on the hard ground.

'Father?'

'Yes?'

'I think that if anyone laid his hands on me, I would knife him.'

'Yes, son, I think you would.'

Silence fell again.

'We won't go to that school,' said Charles.

There were dramas. One evening in 1850, the family was sitting in the drawing room listening to Charles reading Walter Scott. Suddenly the roof slabs began to rattle. They were huge stone blocks about three foot square, and under their weight the solid cedar roof beams began ominously to creak and groan. Everyone fled outside and watched the creaking and swaying for another minute. The house withstood the strain, but the servants ran shrieking that one of the officers' bungalows had collapsed. A visiting officer, a Captain Aubert who had recently lost a leg to a tiger, was reclining on his charpoy, his wooden leg propped in the far corner. His bearer had gone to deliver a message. When the earthquake began his fellow officers abandoned him, leaving Captain Aubert shouting, 'Here! Someone give me my leg, for mercy's sake.' He escaped just as the bungalow fell. It was the most severe earthquake to have struck India since the British arrived.

One morning the family woke to find themselves snowed in,

something the children had never seen before. Charles and Isabella stood on the veranda admiring the pristine whiteness, when Charles noticed something that marred it. He demanded of a servant, 'What is that huge log of wood doing on the pathway? Move it off.' When the servant approached it, to everyone's astonishment it undulated away across a gully and disappeared. It was a boa constrictor, partly paralysed by cold.

For Fred the most memorable event was when two kitmagars quarrelled. One seized a tulwar that hung on the wall and struck the other, Panchkauri, who threw up his arms in self-defence. Fred heard a scream and ran into the servants' quarters to find both Panchkauri's forearms had been sliced clean from wrist to elbow. Ten inches of flesh dangled from each elbow. Fortunately Dr Pierson happened to be visiting, and he patched up Panchkauri so successfully that within three months he could wash plates again and help the cook.

Then everything changed. Caroline was born, Isabella fell ill, Charles read *Hursthouse's New Zealand* and abruptly the Indian adventure was over. Charles and Isabella prepared to take leave of the people and places they had known and loved for twenty years, and set off with their seven children for a new life.

FIVE

Goodbye, Lohughat

When it came to possessions, it was hard to decide what to take and what to leave. Hursthouse reminded prospective emigrants that very little was available in New Zealand. What there was had been shipped all the way from England and so was hugely expensive. He recommended taking plate, the best cutlery, glass, earthenware, cooking utensils, table linen, a table, a set of chairs, beds, a mirror and a selection of their favourite books and ornaments. The Gascoynes had an awkward thousand miles to cross before they reached Calcutta, let alone New Zealand, and even with an army of bearers they could hardly travel down the Himalayan foothills, across the jungles of the Terai, then down the Ganges with a piano, dressers, chiffoniers and sideboards, so the largest pieces of furniture were auctioned at Petoragarh. Despite going through this process so many times before, Isabella still felt bereft by the loss of her treasured things, bought so expensively yet sold so cheap.

The chattels not needed until New Zealand were packed in specially made wooden cases lined with tin to protect the contents during their hazardous voyage, the fabrics layered with dry tobacco leaves to keep out moth.

Fred was as reluctant to leave as his mother. During the journey he was offered a commission in the cavalry, but Charles persuaded him to refuse it because he had set his heart on farming in New Zealand, for which he depended on Fred's help. Besides, Charles was determined that no son of his should ever experience what he had seen on the battlefield. But since the age of seven, when he had brandished Uncle Archy's sabre in the face of the bandit during the Battle of Ferozeshah, Fred had been determined to become a cavalry officer. The first sentence of his memoirs, *Soldiering in New Zealand*, is a wistful description of Charles's uniform – light blue and silver braid with scarlet cuffs and scarlet and white feathers – to which Fred added bitterly, 'It took all the charm of a new country and new hopes to reconcile me to the change of career.' He wasn't really reconciled, and his relationship with Charles began to sour.

They left the hills in a huge cavalcade of bearers. The older children rode their shaggy hill ponies, while Isabella, Miss Sutherland and the babies went in dhandies – hammocks suspended from poles in which they sat sideways while two dhandie-wallahs took their weight at each end. Charles rode ahead, and behind came the phalanx of baggage coolies, one with Caroline's crib on his head, while bangy-wallahs carried baskets of clothes.

At the foot of the hills they met the Commissioner of Almorah district, who was lending the Gascoynes his elephants to carry them through the Terai. The great beasts with their sagacious little eyes were tame and amenable; they knelt, as if at prayer, while the family and Miss Sutherland climbed ladders onto the howdahs padded with embroidered red cushions. The mahouts leaped up the trunks and onto the elephants' heads. At first the children felt sick because the elephants, unlike horses, walked with a swaying motion, moving both legs on one side and then both legs on the other (the 'ship of the jungle'), but they got used to it.

In those days the Terai spread the whole way from the Himalayan foothills to the Ganges: dense, untrodden jungle with patches of open grassland prowled by tigers, bears and rhinoceros. Line-cutters led the way, opening a single-file track for the train of servants, with the family on the elephants – above danger, with wonderful views, and able to flee if necessary – bringing up the rear. They were always on watch for the gentle waving of jungle grass that Captain Lockett had taught them meant tiger, and they all felt the excitement and fear. Fred and Charles would release their safety catches, but it usually turned out to be deer. Quail and other wildfowl would squawk up in front of them and many were shot for the pot, while antelopes – too beautiful to kill – scudded away in all directions. Each night, the Gascoynes lay in their tents listening to croaking frogs and cicadas, to the sinister howling of jackals, and to their servants banging drums to keep off the tigers.

Soon the country grew more cultivated and peopled, then at last they reached the Ganges at Allahabad, where they sent the elephants back to Almorah, and climbed into budgerows. The river descended to the Sundarbans, which wound for miles and miles in a myriad of low-lying waterways and tiger- and malaria-infested islands towards Calcutta. Here, four months after leaving, the Gascoynes arrived in February 1853.

Doctor's orders were that Isabella was too ill to go directly to New Zealand, and she should instead go to England to stay with her mother-in-law until her health improved. She also wanted to bid farewell to her relatives and friends for what she suspected (rightly) would be the last time. Lonely at the prospect of many months, possibly years, away from her family, she decided to take Charlie as a companion. Charlotte and Caroline were too young to appreciate it, and Charlie, who had not yet been to England, would probably never have another chance. The others were left, again, in the care of the governess. Amelia Sutherland had lived with the Gascoynes for twelve years, and now decided to throw in her lot with them for ever. She had no marriage prospects back in Britain. Job prospects were equally lean, since (thanks mainly to colonization and war) women now outnumbered men, so Amelia would have been one of thousands of spinsters who, with no husband to support them, were forced to compete for the few badly paid jobs.

Isabella's passage was booked on board the *Hindoostan*, one of the largest East Indiamen ever built (2,018 tons with accommodation for 102 passengers) and Isabella's first experience of a steamer.* She was to travel via Madras, Galle and Bombay and – another first – to Suez. Since the Suez Canal would not be built until 1870, she would travel overland by mule-drawn carriage from Suez to Cosseir, then by special shallow-draft vessel to Cairo, then down the Nile to Alexandria – an eighty-eight hour journey in all – then on by ship to Southampton. This made the journey only six weeks long, at least half that of all the others she had made between India and England.

One evening in February 1853 the whole family came to settle

---

* A P&O ship, the *Hindoostan* was built in Liverpool in 1842 with two funnels, two masts rigged for sail and side paddle-wheels, and could reach speeds of ten knots. This magnificent craft was ultimately wrecked in Calcutta during a great cyclone in 1864.

Isabella and Charlie into their cabin and say goodbye. Everyone returned to shore except Charles, who did not leave Isabella until ten o'clock that night. Isabella felt bereft. She had no idea when she would see her husband again. It would be at least a year, but that was only if they all survived the hazards that she knew lay ahead. She knew too that she would never again see India, the land of her birth, and where the graves of two of her children lay.

> Mine was the stern cabin, and feeling very disconsolate and lonely, and not at all inclined to sleep, I climbed up on the bulkhead before the windows and looked about me. It was a lovely moonlit night, everything still and silent after all the previous bustle, except for the regular tread of the officer on watch on the deck overhead. Suddenly the tramp overhead ceased, and I heard a plunge, as of someone or something overboard, and presently a most extraordinary sound of gurgling and choking, and splashing. Straining my body forward, I caught sight of a white thing floating alongside, and the same horrible noise was repeated. I then saw it was a man wearing a heavy cloak and a white solar topee. I threw over some rope that was beside me and shouted with all my might to awake some natives asleep in a small dinghy. Happily I succeeded and one native was overboard in an instant, dragging the drowning European into the dinghy. At once all the cabin doors burst open. Every lady passenger, in a state of great alarm, appeared, believing it was her husband who, after having wished her goodnight and gone to enjoy a little extra conviviality with the officers, had stumbled overboard. 'Oh, I'm sure it is my husband,' was the cry from twenty cabin doors. Only upon our learning that the individual was a bachelor was peace restored.
>
> Isabella

The drowning man was an officer in the Bengal service with the improbable name of Captain Bemply Baugh. He gratefully acknowledged that he owed his life to Isabella, and for the rest of the voyage behaved like her son, attending to her every need. When they landed in Southampton he escorted her and Charlie to Clifton.*

---

* Another passenger was the earthquake survivor, legless Captain Aubert.

SIX

Weeping Water

Charles, Miss Sutherland and the rest of the children took a passage on the *Marlborough*, a huge sailing ship of 1,600 tons bound for Melbourne. For fourteen-year-old Fred the most memorable event on board was his first duel. In his autobiography Fred does not reveal who was the challenger or what was the cause; all he states is that his opponent was a midshipman named Quirll, and their weapons two of the captain's swords, which they had 'borrowed' when they had been taken forward to be cleaned. They agreed that the first man wounded would be declared vanquished. Fred had been given lessons in swordsmanship by his father's troops, so he was easily able to lock Quirll's blade and slightly wound his sword-hand. As only the sailmaker and two other midshipmen witnessed the duel, Fred was able to hush the affair up, and Charles never knew.

The *Marlborough* reached Melbourne at the height of gold fever. Fred, bitter at being deprived of his military career in India, lit up at the sight of streets thronging with prospectors. Most had come from England and America with the single aim of making their fortune; those who had already done so were spending it as quickly as possible in the brothels and bars. Fred would never forget the atmosphere of hunger and excitement, a hunger that would gnaw at him until he was able to assuage it nearly a decade later. Had he been a few years older, he might have stayed to try his luck. Charles, on the other hand, rejoiced in meeting the only man beside himself more interested in land than gold. John Tinline was a shrewd-looking Scot whose flowing biblical beard had earned him the nickname of Old Fizzlebilly. He had lived in New Zealand for over a decade.* In three weeks' time he was due to sail on the *Belle Creole* to Nelson, on the northern shore of the South Island, and he urged Charles to book a passage on the same ship.

Tinline filled the gaps in Charles's knowledge of his new country. Charles learnt that although a coherent programme of settlement in New Zealand had begun only in 1840, there had been a few settlers there since the turn of the century, but because of the perceived blood-thirst of the natives, the country had been considered too dangerous even for convicts. Instead the islands had been braved by hard-boiled whalers and sealers who were followed by a fluctuating population of sailors, traders, escaped convicts and renegades of every sort. Hot on their heels and frantically trying to rein in their excesses

---

* Ever since Nelson was founded in 1842, Tinline had worked there as a merchant and run a store. More importantly, as his biography coyly records, he had 'had a Maori companion in his home'. As a result he spoke Maori and in 1844 had been appointed Clerk to the Court and Native Interpreter, through which post he became closely involved with land-claim disputes between Maori chiefs and the New Zealand Company. As Sheriff, and Deputy Registrar of the Nelson District, he knew all there was to know about land purchasing, about Maori unrest over land issues, and about the New Zealand way of life. Tinline would go on to become a wool baron, a member of the Nelson Provincial Council, chairman of his county council, and a benefactor of Nelson College and the University of New Zealand. If success was contagious, the Gascoynes' connection with him surely boded well for their future.

TOP LEFT: Eliza Monro, Isabella's mother. TOP RIGHT: Isabella Campbell, aged five, in 1815, holding a miniature of her father, Captain John Campbell. BOTTOM LEFT: Charles Gascoyne, 1830s. BOTTOM RIGHT: Isabella Gascoyne, 1842.

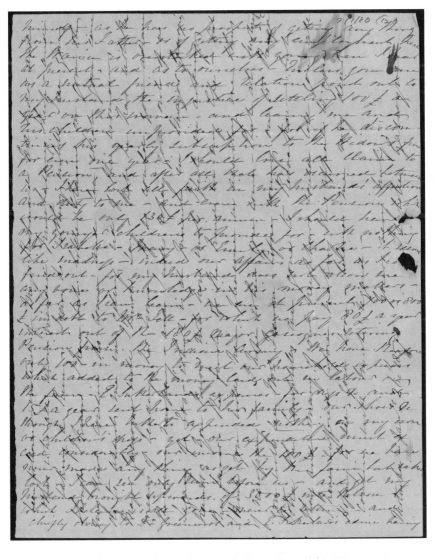

ABOVE: Cross-written letter from Isabella to Donald McLean, 1857.

OPPOSITE TOP: The Bungalow, Lohughat, c.1852.
OPPOSITE BOTTOM: Fred and Marion Gascoyne with their neice
Caroline Gascoyne, Hastings, 1890s.

Maori pa, 1860s.

TOP: The impenetrable Urewera Country. ABOVE LEFT: 'Strangerland'
– a letter from Isabella to McLean. ABOVE RIGHT: Pangatotara:
the Motueka River, with cabbage trees and flax, 1875.

TOP LEFT: Major Charles Gascoyne, early 1870s. TOP RIGHT: Isabella Gascoyne. BOTTOM LEFT: John Greenwood, 1848, by his mother Sarah. BOTTOM RIGHT: Dr John Danforth Greenwood, 1852, by his wife Sarah.

TOP: The Motueka River at Pangatotara today, with the Arthur Range.
LEFT: Isabelle Greenwood, née Gascoyne.
RIGHT: Isabella's grave in the Baptist cemetery, Nelson.

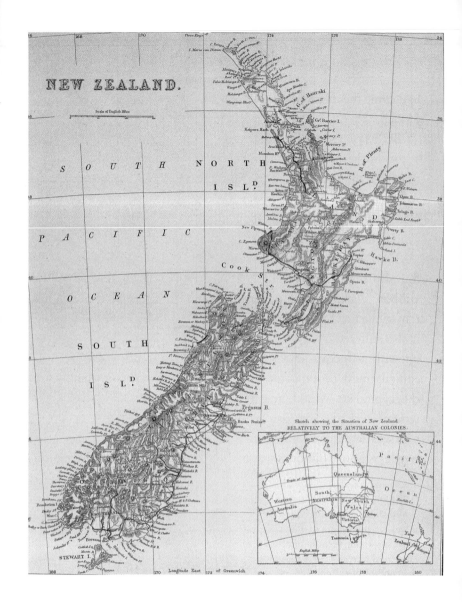

New Zealand in 1880.

had come the missionaries, who clustered in the far north from 1814.*

By 1839 there were still only 2,000 permanent settlers, 1,400 in the north island, and 600 in the south, mostly clustered on the coasts, and all British apart from around fifty Americans and twenty French. But in 1840 the New Zealand Company sent out its first shipments of pioneers, who included Tinline himself.

The New Zealand Company was a land-buying agency founded by a remarkable Whig reformer named Edward Gibbon Wakefield. Like many people, Wakefield recognized that while newly industrialized Britain had a surplus of capital, it also suffered from a surplus of labour.[†] Unlike others he came up with an active solution: if a balance of both labour and capital could be exported voluntarily to some suitable place, the capitalists would invest in the land, and the labourers would work it. This could create a completely new kind of overseas settlement: not a settlement for convicts with oppressive legislation, but one where land was bought cheaply by the

---

* The missionaries found the Maori willing converts, quickly lured away from cannibalism. Human flesh had never been a regular part of Maori diet; eating it was a symbolic act of violation and humiliation performed on enemies, usually after killing them in battle. The ritual eating of Christ's flesh and drinking His blood were of course its opposite, a celebration rather than a violation, but the concept of eating a man was at least a familiar one.

† Until now, the solution had been to export that surplus to the colonies, whether as convict transportations to Australia, or 'free' shiploads to North America. As someone who had himself been imprisoned for the felony of abducting a rich schoolgirl and persuading her to marry him in Gretna Green (he needed her money to get into Parliament), Wakefield was a vehement opponent of transportation: not only did it corrupt the morals of the convicts, but it also ruined the colony for any respectable person wishing to emigrate there.

Company, and sold expensively to the capitalists, raising money for further expansion. The self-financing and self-perpetuating system would be maintained by selling land at a price high enough to prevent labourers from buying it and therefore ceasing to work on it, at least for the first few years. Profits would be used to buy more land and so more work for labourers would be generated. This was to be not mere land speculation; the 'capitalists' would be concerned with politics and civil rights, Christian religion and education, and would participate in a coherent policy of settlement with a utopian ideal behind it: to create a new society in a new world that would take the best from the old, and improve on it.

New Zealand was an excellent place to try this experiment. The land was perfect for farming, with abundant rainfall and lush pastures. The natives (it was reported) were eager to exchange their land for muskets, boats, nails and other useful goods. They were also reportedly intelligent, sophisticated, brave and honest, and instead of killing sheep as the Aboriginals did in New South Wales, they were keen to look after them and even to own some themselves. Through the influence of missionaries, and of civilized settlers and British law and government, they would undoubtedly succumb (in Wakefield's words) to 'wonderful peaceful conquest'.

Wakefield hoped to model the New Zealand Company on the East India Company: a private monopoly backed by the government. Unfortunately the Colonial Office doubted the altruism of some of the members, many of whom were shippers, land speculators or politicians, and refused to support it, so Wakefield abandoned his search for official recognition and decided instead to buy land not for the British government but for the Company, dealing directly with the Maori chiefs.

The Colonial Office warned the Company that if New Zealand ever became part of the British Empire, the government might not recognize its title to the land. Ignoring the warning, in May 1839 the Company sent out Wakefield's brother as agent to buy as much land as possible. Deeds of purchase were signed on a total of no less than 20 million acres, comprising the lower half of the North Island and the upper half of the South.*

At this stage the British government was reluctantly imperialist. The American colonies had been lost, and while some in the Colonial Office were keen on expansion, many said good riddance to an expensive overseas folly. Overseas trade was welcomed, but why go to the expense and trouble of governing these far-flung dots on the globe? Nevertheless under pressure from missionaries and evangelical metropolitan groups in England, particularly the Aboriginal Protection Society, who claimed that lawless settlers needed to be controlled by British law and that land was being forcibly or duplicitously taken by

---

*According to Edward Gibbon Wakefield's son, Edward Jerningham Wakefield, payment for the entire area consisted of 6 single-barrelled guns, 5 double-barrelled guns, 100 red blankets, 5¼ hundredweight of tobacco, 20 muskets, 50 iron pots, 2 cases of soap, 20 kegs of gunpowder, 1 keg of lead slabs, 50 cartouche boxes, 100 tomahawks, 20 pipe tomahawks, 20 gross of pipes, 24 spades, 50 steel axes, 1,000 fish hooks, 72 shirts, 200 yards check (cotton), 120 handkerchiefs, 24 slates, 200 pencils, 60 looking glasses, 120 pocket knives, 60 pairs of scissors, 60 combs, 1 cask of ball cartridges, 500 flints, 6 quires of cartridge paper, 60 jackets and trousers, 12 Flushing coats, 12 adzes, 2lb of beads, and 12 shaving boxes and razors. Payment did not end there: Wakefield headed east and signed a further confirmatory deed and handed over 10 single-barrelled and 3 double-barrelled guns, 60 muskets, 100 red blankets, gunpowder, axes, pipes and beads.

the New Zealand Company from the Maori without their full understanding or consent, the Colonial Office ordered the Governor of New South Wales to extend his colony's boundaries to incorporate New Zealand.

Captain Hobson, the new Lieutenant Governor, quickly issued proclamations that gave the Queen of England complete government over the land, recognized Maori title to their own land and forbade the sale of that land to anyone except the Crown. With a full guarantee of Maori rights and citizenship Hobson proclaimed British sovereignty over New Zealand.*

The Treaty of Waitangi was 'signed' by over five hundred Maori chiefs on 5 February 1840. The setting was near a beautiful cascade named Waitangi, which meant Weeping Water.

A chief of the Ngapuhi tribe described the event to an early settler named Frederick Maning, who later became a distinguished judge. His words demonstrate the utter confusion on both sides.

> Then came a chief of the pakeha who we heard was called a Governor. We were very glad of his arrival, because we heard he was a great chief, and we thought, he being a great chief, would have more blankets and tobacco and muskets than any of the other pakeha people, and that he would often give us plenty of these things for nothing. The reason we thought so was because all the other pakeha often made us presents of things of great value, besides what we got from them by trading. Who would not have thought as we did?

---

* The Treaty was drawn up in two versions, Maori and English; the poor translation of the English into Maori meant that there were differences between the texts, which still have ramifications today.

The Governor, he heard, had a piece of paper he wanted the chiefs to make a mark on.

Some of us thought the Governor wanted to bewitch all the chiefs, but our pakeha friends laughed at this, and told us that the people of Europe did not know how to bewitch people . . . Some said the Governor only wanted our consent to remain, to be chief over the pakeha people; others said he wanted to be chief over both pakeha and Maori. We did not know what to think, but were all anxious he might come to us soon; for we were afraid that all his blankets, and tobacco, and other things would be gone before he came to our part of the country, and that he would have nothing left to pay us for making our marks on his paper.

Well, it was not long before the Governor came, and with him came the other pakeha chiefs, and also people who could speak Maori; so we all gathered together, chiefs and slaves, women and children, and went to meet him; and when we met the Governor, the speaker of Maori told us that if we put our names, or even made any sort of a mark on that paper, the Governor would then protect us, and prevent us from being robbed of our cultivated land, and our timber land, and everything else which belonged to us.

Some of the people were very much alarmed when they heard this, for they thought that perhaps a great war expedition was coming against us from some distant country, to destroy us all; others said he was only trying to frighten us. The speaker of Maori then went on to tell us certain things, but the meaning of what he said was so closely concealed we never have found it out. One thing we understood well, however; for he told us plainly that if we wrote on the Governor's paper, one of the consequences would be that great numbers of

pakeha would come to this country to trade with us, that we
should have abundance of valuable goods, and that before long
there would be great towns in every harbour in the whole
island. We were very glad to hear this; for we never could up
to this time get half muskets or gunpowder enough, or blankets, or tobacco, or axes, or anything. We also believed what
the speaker of Maori told us, because we saw that our old
pakeha friends who came with us to see the Governor believed
it . . . We all began to write as fast as we could, for we were
all very hungry with listening and talking so long, and we
wanted to go to get something to eat, and we were also in a
hurry to see what the Governor was going to give us; and all
the slaves wanted to write their names, so that the Governor
might think they were chiefs, and pay them. But the chiefs
would not let them, for they wanted all the payment for themselves. I and all my family made our marks, and we then went
to get something to eat; but we found our food not half done,
for the women and slaves who should have looked after the
cooking, were all mad about the Governor, so when I saw that
the food was not sufficiently done, I was aware that something
bad would come of this business.

Later a Maori chief would observe to the Governor, Sir
George Bowen, that the name Waitangi – Weeping Water – was
prophetic of the blood and tears which would soon be shed on
account of the Treaty, throughout all the murderous conflicts
which would rip the North Island apart over the next thirty
years.

Having established their first settlement in 1840 at Port Nicholson (the port for what would become the city of Wellington),
the Company planned a second on the northern tip of the South
Island. The site was not perfect since it had only a very modest
natural harbour, but it did form the gateway to some 46 million acres of fertile soil and superb grazing lands to the south
and east.

Late in 1841, the first settlement party under the leadership
of another Wakefield brother, Captain Arthur Wakefield RN,
landed in Nelson with engineers, surveyors, labourers and
apprentices, and a cargo of surveying equipment, forges, pre-
fabricated barracks, wagons, tents, saws and other tools and
deal boats.* The process began of surveying land, carving it up
into streets and sections to make a town, and into plots of farmland, and allocating them to settlers. Huts built of dried mud
and grass known as cob grew up in tiny clusters along the
shores. But Nelson worked better on paper than in reality. Too
many absentee landlords and speculators had no intention of
spending capital on felling trees, clearing, planting grass, or
building fences; instead they were waiting for prices to rise so
that they could sell on and make a profit, which meant that
there was not enough employment. There was also a shortage
of decent farmland – the settlement was hemmed in by mountains to the south and sea to the north, and some of the land
offered for sale was covered by the sea at high tide, or by the
overflow of rivers and streams. Many people who had bought
land in advance, before they had even left England, arrived to

---

* A deal is a plank of fir or pine, nine inches wide, not more than three inches
thick and at least six foot long.

the news that there was nothing suitable available. The Company's utopian ideal turned to dust.

The Land Claims Court began its investigations into the validity of the Company's purchases. First it had to define the New Zealand laws of property ownership, and lay down for the Maori what constituted their legal right to sell out of many rights to ownership. The Maori had no law governing ownership of land; it was regulated by custom.* Having established the legal framework, the court could turn its attention to 'sales' already agreed, and most of the New Zealand Company's purchases were ruled unlawful. Settlements at Wellington, Nelson, New Plymouth and Wanganui: all were built on disputed land. Much of it was demanded back – and some duly returned.[†]

Pressure to find more farmland inspired pioneering expeditions inland, but when in 1842 British surveyors were ordered by a Maori chief off land he claimed along the Wairau River, a massacre followed. Four Maoris and twenty-two settlers, including Captain Arthur Wakefield, were killed. The Wairau

---

* Many tracts of forest and shore had been won by one tribe from another through war, or marriage, or through one of its chiefs being cooked and eaten on the ground; each claimed the land, but one wanted to sell while the other did not. It was all tribally held; no individual had any rights of ownership, or therefore any right to sell. Each tribe, or iwi, held land communally, but it was subdivided amongst the hapu, or clans. A single chief inherited each hapu, but the tribal territory remained as a whole and its defence was the highest duty of each member. A tribal chief may have wanted to sell, but the hapu leaders did not. If they did agree to sell, how was the money to be distributed? What should be the fair payment?

[†] John Tinline himself was investigated for his purchase of Maori land in Golden Bay in 1839.

Massacre dealt a serious blow to the settlers' morale, and relations between the whites and the Maori were soured.

Without land, Nelson's settlers found life exceptionally grim. Workers and their families had been recklessly dumped on the shore with little attention paid to their future. By 1845, many were reduced to near starvation, and would not have survived had the Maori not shown them which ferns were edible, and how to follow the birds' lead: what berries the birds ate, they could eat too. People stayed only because they had no means of leaving. Meanwhile a war had broken out in the North Island between the settlers and the Maori, and this discouraged others from immigrating. It looked as if the whole New Zealand experiment might collapse. After sending out over fifty-five ships and 18,900 settlers, the Company was wrecked, and in 1850 it was wound up.

Later in 1845, Captain Robert Fitzroy was replaced as New Zealand's Governor by the charismatic George Grey, and the situation began to improve.* Grey was clever, and more unscrupulous than Fitzroy in his dealings with the Maori. With only a thousand imperial troops at his disposal – comparable to a small tribe – he was forced to use subtler means than brute force to win them over, and instead adopted what the historian James Belich has identified as the four means of persuasion: God, money, law and better-organized and more legitimate land sales. The Maori responded eagerly. By 1847 the wars in the

---

* This was the same Robert Fitzroy who had commanded HMS *Beagle*. He was appointed Governor and Commander-in-Chief of New Zealand in 1843, but his obvious sympathy for the Maori made him unpopular with the settlers, and the Admiralty recalled him.

north had ended, and peace was maintained more or less for the next thirteen years.

The 'golden age' of land buying began. Men like John Tinline set off on horseback and mule to follow Maori trails over mountain ranges and river gorges, through phalanxes of spear grass and manuka scrub, over swamps and rocks, to explore the South Island. They found vast tracts of apparently empty pasture, and on these they acquired rights to run sheep. The first wool from the Wairau district was exported from Nelson in 1851, and good wool it was too.*

In 1852 Governor Grey claimed that peace had been fully restored and the Maori largely civilized. In communications with the Colonial Office, Grey boasted that now both races formed 'one harmonious community, connected together by commercial and agricultural pursuits'. The British government felt able to reward New Zealand by granting the colony self-government. It was split into six provinces, each of which was in effect a separate colony, one being Nelson. Each had a Superintendent, who governed the district, and a Provincial Council, while central government structures were set up by 1854. As Edward Gibbon Wakefield had originally envisaged, the settlers now controlled most of their own affairs. The first ever meeting of the General Assembly was convened a month after Charles arrived, and the following September a ball was held

---

* By that year, New Zealand's European population had grown to 26,000, while there were 223,000 sheep; by 1858 there were 59,000 colonists and 1,523,000 sheep; and by 1861, 99,000 colonists and 2,761,000 sheep. Sheep outnumbered the Europeans, and they themselves hugely outnumbered the Maori.

in Nelson to celebrate the first elections under the new constitution.

Tinline told Charles that he was exactly the sort of person Nelson needed: they wanted not only labourers, but also those able to defend the settlement – in other words, military or naval officers. The inducement was a money certificate of £200 (£9,800 today), which was offered not to absentee landlords, but to those who would live for two years on the land they bought. The same year Sir George Grey halved and halved again the price of rural land from £1 to 10/- to 5/- per acre.

Tinline introduced Charles to Alfred Fell, a pioneer who had arrived in Nelson in 1842 and opened a shop and auction house selling imported tools and equipment of all sorts. Fell had his finger in every sale, from maiden ewes to milch cows, butter in kegs, treacle, Java sugar, ironmongery, candles, cutlery, even horses shipped from Sydney. Fell had also become a shipping agent and went into partnership with Henry Seymour, marrying Seymour's daughter. Fell & Seymour's warehouse in Bridge Street had a glass-panelled office known as 'the Glass Case', and here they met Nelson's other dynamic personalities to drink and talk politics and gossip, discussing the price of food, delays of ships, Maori trouble, the New Zealand Company's misdeeds and Nelson's lack of drains.

This powerful group, some of whom would later form Isabella's circle, included one of Charles's old acquaintances from India, Francis Horniblow Blundell. There was also the run-holder and provincial council member, Edward Fearon; the surveyor, Nathaniel Edwards; Dr John Danforth Greenwood, a medical doctor, newspaper editor, and founder of Nelson College; Thomas Tudor, a peripatetic Maori-speaking curate; and

Nelson's Superintendent, Resident Magistrate and Land Commissioner, Major Mathew Richmond. Between them, albeit overseen by the new legislature and thence by the distant imperial authorities personified by the Governor, they ran the province.

Each of Charles's new friends offered him conflicting advice about how to invest his capital. Major Richmond advised him to buy a run – a huge area of land on which to pasture enormous flocks of sheep, in the Australian style. In 1853, a run of a thousand acres could cost as little as £250 (£12,250 today), and land would never again be so cheap. Mr Tudor, who knew the country well, backed this view: with a bit of luck, and willingness to endure a life of tedium and hardship, Charles could expect rapid profits. Mr Tinline suggested that since Charles had no experience it would be easier for him to buy not land but sheep and 'put them out to terms' – in other words, place them in someone else's run that was not yet fully stocked (possibly Tinline's own). In return he would receive an annual sum in lieu of wool. Others proposed that Charles should buy land, lay down English grass and make a permanent estate of it, though they admitted that this required much experience and money, both of which Charles lacked. Eventually Dr Greenwood persuaded him to farm as *he* did, in a more traditional mixed English way with sheep, cattle, wheat and other crops.

This appealed to Charles. He could become a gentleman farmer, build a charming house overlooking his land and live in a gracious style that he could never have afforded back in England. But the town of Nelson was not the place. All of the land had already been taken, and penetrating further inland into the mountains was still virtually impossible: there were no roads, just a few Maori trails. The only viable means of communication was still the sea, so John Tinline urged Charles to continue his journey westwards along the coast to the infant settlement of Motueka. However, by the time Charles arrived, most of Motueka's coastal plain was already spoken for, so despite the lack of access, he was forced to look inland. He bought eight hundred acres of bush that had recently been surveyed on the east bank of the Motueka River, six miles upstream, at a place named Pangatotara. In June 1854, Charles formally cut his losses and retired from the East India Company. He was rewarded with promotion to the rank of major, with a consequent rise in pension, and committed himself to New Zealand.

SEVEN

A Boisterous Passage

Fourteen thousand miles away, Isabella was happily ensconced with Charles's mother in Clifton. Captain Gascoyne had died in 1845 so there were no complaints about six-year-old Charlie's noisy footsteps. They were joined by Charles's brother John.

Idle fashionable John, who loved money above all else, was bankrupt. He had invested the fortune he had acquired from both his wives in the York and North Midlands Railway Company, and lost the lot. Suffering 'great pecuniary distress', he wrote in desperation to Lord Salisbury, asking him to use his influence to help him 'obtain a situation' as an official 'assignee to bankrupts' – this being one of the few professions of which John had experience. Lord Salisbury was unable to help. Over the next few years John wrote again and again, charting his downward progress as he moved from one drab lodging to another, fleeing landladies from Clifton to Liverpool to the Isle of Man, flogging his furniture en route to buy food for his children, and each year the number of them grew: by 1852 he had seven sons and three daughters. John described himself to Lord Salisbury as not only ruined, but perfectly bewildered, and with no idea what to do to earn a crust – he would do *anything*. Some of his bankrupt friends had been made inspectors of post offices, or heads of police, and John fancied something like this himself. Perhaps he could be an agent to a nobleman or gentleman's estate? Lord Salisbury replied that, painful though it was, he was now in opposition to the government so it was improper for him even to apply for any such position on John's behalf.

Isabella felt that John had become mean and overcareful. Perhaps she didn't realize quite how desperate he was; his swarm of children, having expected to be gentlemen and ladies of leisure, had nothing with which to set themselves up. One son had spent four years at sea in HMS *Phaeton*, but without a salary. He had another two years to go before he could become a mate and support himself.

The solution, Isabella was convinced, was for the boys to emigrate to the New World. In part this was self-interest: she dreaded leaving this family which had been such a source of friendship, especially as it was certain that she would never see them again, so the prospect of having Gascoyne boys with her in New Zealand made her own future less bleak. Charles wrote from New Zealand promising to help them find 'situations', to take care of them and give them a home.

Isabella's last ever winter Christmas was dramatically cold. Snowfalls drifted three feet high outside houses, trapping their inhabitants inside, covering railways and disrupting the mail. Everyone was amazed that the fifteen-acre glass roof of the Crystal Palace (now moved from Hyde Park to the hill at Sydenham) managed to withstand tons of snow.

Without the support of a husband, Isabella made her way through this Siberian winter from Clifton to London, and found herself a ship to New Zealand. The *Balnaguith* was described

in Lloyd's Register of Shipping as a fine barque,* classified AI,
sheathed in 'yellow metal', an alloy of copper and zinc hot-
rolled into thin plates.† She was the fourth ship of the line
owned by Young and Co., 61 Cornhill, London (loading in the
East India Docks). Being of modest means, Isabella secured and
furnished not the top-class stern cabin – this with its large windows provided more space than she and Charlie needed – but
a small first-class poop cabin, about 7ft square, with a window
on the port side from where the prevailing winds blew, scour-
ing the cabin clean.

Isabella also ventured to Brown's seabed and furniture warehouse in Leadenhall Street, where she could buy almost
everything she needed for the voyage, and Brown's provided the
ship-joiners to fit up the cabin for her. The journey would last
twice as long as any journey to India, so on Hursthouse's advice
Isabella bought an easy chair with cushions for deck use,
blankets, sheets, mattress, pillows, clothes, a straw hat (indispensable in the tropics), sewing kit, books, towels, a metal
footbath and marine soap – a variety that was meant to lather
in salt water, but usually failed. For Charlie there were titbits
such as jam, biscuits, a plum cake, dried fruits and some toys.

---

* As a barque, the *Balnaguith* had three masts, but these were square-rigged
on the fore and masts only, as opposed to a 'ship', which had square-rigged
sails on all its masts.

† For around fifty years, between the 1780s and 1830s, it became increasingly
common for ship builders to sheathe their larger vessels in copper. However,
the copper was both hugely expensive and short-lived. In 1832 an Englishman
named George F. Muntz patented his 'yellow metal' or 'Muntz metal', an alloy
which did not corrode so quickly as copper, and because of the high zinc content cost much less, but which was flexible enough to adapt itself to a wooden
hull. By the 1840s this was widely used.

The East India Dock teemed with noise and bustle, shouting sailors and hammering carpenters still busy in the cabins, sheets and halyards twanging in the December wind, sails being mended hanging up to dry and gangs of 'lumpers' hoisting on board packing cases and boxes and stowing them in the hold. Passengers watched anxiously as all their worldly goods were tipped into the gaping hatchway.

Tearful farewells were made on the dock. Every passenger was aware that once they had travelled fourteen thousand miles to the Southern Oceans (supposing they survived the Roaring Forties) they would rarely be able to afford the journey home, or be willing to risk it. They would probably never see their friends and families again.

In the midst of a blizzard – not an auspicious start – Isabella and Charlie embarked for New Zealand on 27 December 1853.

The first week was a vortex of anxiety and anticipation. Isabella was travelling to an unknown land where she knew no one other than her immediate family. In that respect, India had seemed like an outpost of Home: the instant community of the East India Company with its rules and regulations had provided a structure for almost every day of the Gascoynes' lives; New Zealand was uncharted, and unstructured. Isabella had no script to follow. The British had been in India for two hundred and fifty years, but in New Zealand for only thirteen. The New Zealand colony was as old as Isabella's daughter Mary.

So far, Isabella's only experience of New Zealand had been during the family's furlough in 1842 when they had visited the Polytechnic in Regent Street and, among the strange and wonderful artefacts from around the world, had seen a human head, cured and preserved by Maori warriors. It was remarkably lifelike, far more so than the waxworks at Madame Tussaud's. Fred had loved it, and Izzy called it a pretty thing, but Isabella had been revolted by the bruise-coloured tattoos, and its barbaric provenance. The British government had recently prohibited further importations after evidence reached the Colonial Office that the Maori frequently murdered people to obtain their heads for barter.

Isabella faced this uncertain future alone, yet she also faced months of intimacy with sixty-four fellow passengers. They were a mixed bunch, not the familiar East India Company employees, but strangers leaving all they knew and loved forever, as well as all they loathed – poverty, hunger, industrial squalor and oppression.*

The *Balnaguith*, as the *Wellington Independent* reported with tactful understatement, 'had on the whole a very boisterous passage', especially in the Bay of Biscay. Isabella knew only too well the hazards of such a journey, when the sea turned mountainous, and sent the ship lurching up to the peak of a

---

* The *Balnaguith* heralded a colossal exodus. Between 1853 and 1876, over four million emigrants left Great Britain, which then included Ireland, and of this astonishing number 804,366 went to Australia and New Zealand. Many more went unrecorded. It was like a human explosion out of Europe. However, it was not until the 1870s that mass government-assisted migration to New Zealand really took off; in 1853 immigration was still sporadic, partly because of the problems the settlers had faced, and partly because passenger ships to New Zealand were still under sail. A small barque like the *Balnaguith* could never have carried enough coal to create the steam to drive her fourteen thousand miles, the longest commercial sea voyage on the globe. No regular steam ships would come from England for another five years. While the average journey still took 110 days, the *Balnaguith* took 132 days. This must have seemed interminable when at the same time expectations of speed had risen: Isabella's last trip from India to England via Suez had taken only six weeks.

wave, then plunging down into a watery abyss, flinging the passengers across their cabins. However tightly the hatches were
fastened, water always penetrated; during the nineteenth century, at least thirty ships sailing to Australia and New Zealand
were sunk, with horrendous fatalities.*

Then there was the danger from within. On the *Balnaguith*
there was not a single fatality, but this was unusual. Epidemics
could spread like fire through the cabins, especially in the foetid
air of the hold. The surgeon's journal of a New Zealand Company ship called the *Perkin*, which reached Nelson in 1850,
describes mustering the emigrants on deck before departure for
a compulsory inspection by a government agent. Anyone found
ailing was dumped ashore – at least in theory. The risk was min-
imized by taking precautions that now seem obvious but which
were not yet commonplace. Surgeon Müller describes the assid-
uous airing of bedding on deck every few days, except during
the first fortnight when everyone was too seasick to move, or
during storms. At his insistence the berths were thoroughly
cleaned out, and chloride of zinc sprinkled about and poured
down the water closets, which were checked daily. Between
decks was regularly swept and 'holy-stoned', meaning they
were scoured with soft sandstone, then sprinkled with chloride
of lime. When the air grew humid in the tropics, Müller insisted
on portable airing stoves being kept lit all day, which may have

---

* Just as the *Balnaguith* left London, the *Tayleur* left Liverpool for Australia,
but got no further than the Irish coast where she sank amidst scenes of what
the *Wellington Independent* described as 'the most frightful horror'. In 1854,
only a year after Isabella set sail, the *Guiding Star* vanished en route from Liverpool to the New World, taking all 546 passengers and crew. It was supposed
that she had hit an iceberg but there was not one survivor to tell the tale.

made the cabins unbearably hot, but emitted cleansing smoke and kept out the damp. He recorded a few accidents (a child falling down the main hatchway; a crew member slipping on deck and getting a big splinter in the eye; someone tripping over the anchor and injuring his leg) but mostly it was cases of sea-sickness, which he tried to allay with rice water and lime juice, while the children were served plain boiled rice. Then there was the odd case of diarrhoea, griping, fever and a touch of syphilis amongst the crew. There was only one burial at sea and that, tragically, was of Müller's own wife.

Contemporary diaries show that most people accepted the dangers and discomforts without fuss, and even enjoyed their months at sea. Charles's cousin, nineteen-year-old Cecil Gascoigne, travelled to New Zealand in 1896.* In letters home he described the cabin passengers aboard the steamship *Rimutaka* setting up an amusement committee which corralled any musical talent to perform. Despite the growing heat, the younger passengers played cricket on deck, held competitions of athletic sports (which Cecil won) and organized a fancy-dress ball (where Cecil's Maori chief costume won him the 'best-dressed' prize). Sometimes wonderful things happened. Cecil marvelled when the sea was a mass of phosphorescence, and when it filled with hundreds upon hundreds of icebergs, varying in shapes and sizes from a foot square to a great beast four miles long; the *Rimutaka*'s captain managed to avoid the fate of the *Guiding Star* and weaved around them, and Cecil described the

---

* Cecil Gascoigne knew nothing about the existence of Charles and Isabella, but like many young men was being sent out to New Zealand to labour on a farm in the hope of making a man of him after he had done badly at school.

moon turning their crevices a 'simply lovely blue'. By the end of the voyage, most young men – including Cecil – had lost their hearts to pretty girls on board. This was normal. The *Adelaide*, the largest ship to set out from England in the New Zealand Company's first wave of settlement in 1840, caused some concern when she failed to arrive. When she finally docked, it transpired that she had been delayed by jealousies amongst the ladies so fierce that the captain had had to put in at the Cape to allow for no fewer than four duels, one of the principals being the captain himself.

Hursthouse suggested that if hands must often be idle on board ship, there was plenty of work for the head. 'The emigrant,' he wrote, 'may profitably devote a few hours a day to a course of useful reading, master some popular work on agriculture and dairy farming, on the sheep, ox, and horse, on the growth and preparation of flax, and various raw materials which might constitute additional exports; procure Archdeacon Williams' Maori Grammar (Stanford's, 6 Charing Cross), so as to land with a useful smattering of the native language; and practice sketching in watercolours, so as to send Mamma or Lucy a picture of the new home he has reared in Zealandia.'

For all the fun and profitable study, there was often a sense of listless tedium. The watch bell rang every half-hour, measuring out the days, and at the end of eight bells the watch changed. The long day was punctuated by meals. At nine o'clock, Isabella and Charlie took their seats at the saloon table where they breakfasted communally on tea or coffee (with sugar and preserved milk), hot rolls, toast, butter and marmalade, a dish of mutton or pork chops and a slice of cold meat. Lunch, at twelve o'clock, comprised slices of ham, tongue, beef and pickles, followed by bread, butter and cheese. Dinner was at four o'clock. It began with mock turtle or pea soup, with preserved salmon three days a week, followed by fowls or ducks, then puddings, pies and tarts, cheese and finally dessert of biscuits, figs, nuts and raisins. Only three hours later passengers were summoned to a tea of hot cakes and toast, and sliced ham, tongue or German sausage, and finally at ten o'clock a buffet was set out with cold meats and bottled stout. Most people would have got disgustingly fat, but the reality was that after a few weeks the quantities reduced, the live sheep, pigs and fowls were all slaughtered, and the monotony of dried meat and ship's biscuit detracted from the excitement of meals. Anything fresh disappeared from the table, and the water was brackish.

'Below decks' was another world. On the *Balnaguith* twenty-seven steerage passengers lived for 132 days without light or fresh air in what was a converted cargo space, and which in many ships (though not the *Balnaguith*) would be converted back for the return run with a load of wool. During storms, steerage passengers were battened down below for days on end. According to the surgeon of the barque *Birman*, bound for New Zealand, the stench was enough to make you faint. There were no private cabins, simply rows of rough-hewn (and easily dismantled) bunks that opened onto the main eating and living area; privacy was no more than a curtain. Married couples were provided with bunks six and a half feet long and three and a half feet wide, and this had to accommodate not only themselves but also all the possessions needed during the voyage.

Steerage passengers were permitted, at certain times, to crowd onto the main deck to take the air, but the larger poop deck was considered by cabin passengers to be their exclusive recreational preserve for which they had paid, and any steerage passenger found there was chastised for trespassing.

Steerage passengers were also deprived when it came to meals, as they were allocated a smaller allowance of food each week, which they had to cook themselves in work parties, and while chief cabin passengers received twenty-eight quarts of drinking water each week, second cabin and steerage passengers received only twenty-one quarts. What the steerage passengers were fed was still considered a supplement to the provisions they carried on board themselves. Although from 1842 the British government insisted that the minimum weekly allowance for each passenger should be seven pounds of bread, biscuit, oatmeal, rice or potatoes, this and other rules proved impossible to regulate and were usually ignored. Several cabin passengers expressed shock at the treatment of steerage passengers (lifeboats, for example, were reserved for cabin only) but few attempted to do anything about it.*

Throughout their subsequent careers in New Zealand, these early settlers were defined by how they got there. A 'cabin' or 'poop passenger' meant someone with capital and education who arrived with the means to set themselves up in some line of business or to buy decent pasturage; their children were 'poop children'. 'Steerage' meant poverty, lower class, filth and being looked down upon by the cabin class as a servant or

---

* Samuel Butler, who was on his way to make his fortune in New Zealand aboard the *Roman Emperor* in 1859, did succeed in setting up a steerage choir, and wrote to his father that he enjoyed getting to know the poorer passengers. He was unusual.

a labourer who would have to pull himself up by his own hard work and luck. Nevertheless many of the diaries describing those early journeys show that the nearer they came to New Zealand, the more the distinctions between these classes blurred.

Although some ships called at Madeira, Cape Verde and the Cape Colony to load fresh water and supplies, the *Balnaguith* did not stop anywhere before the long haul south and east, down to the Southern Ocean below 40 degrees latitude, beneath Australia and Van Diemen's Land. Captains were often prosecuted for skimping on the rations and profiting thereby, but this was not Isabella's experience. Quite the reverse: when provisions ran out, Captain Smith distributed his own personal supplies amongst his grateful passengers. Forced by a lack of fresh water to make an unscheduled landfall at Lyttelton, the passengers wrote appreciatively to the captain, and asked the editor of the *Lyttelton Times* to publish their letter in his paper. They thanked him for the handsome manner in which he had behaved, and invited him and his chief officer, Mr Pearson, to a delicious dinner of fresh food and drink, at their convenience.

EIGHT

New World

Aotearoa, Land of the Long White Cloud: in letters home, settlers often described the relief after months at sea of their first sight of it. They described the way the forested mountains plunged straight down to the shore, and the way everything was exaggerated: the mountains higher, the waves rougher, the fjords and inlets more majestic, the land more volatile, the rain heavier, the light clearer and the sea bluer than any they had seen before.

On 7 May 1854 the *Balnaguith* glided into Port Nicholson, Wellington's port, and furled her sails. Isabella probably felt a mixture of pleasure and pain: pleasure at the beauty of the enclosed bay with its crescent of mountains rising behind, dubbed the Naples of the South, but pain at the disappointing lack of civilization. She had left an England that was thrilling to the expansion of railways, to bridges of technological brilliance, to the conquest of nature, and was still triumphant from the Great Exhibition with its celebration of art, science and industry, of steam and iron.* By setting foot in New Zealand

---

* Isabella was particularly aware of this having spent so many months in Bristol – home of Brunel, his Great Western Railway and his huge steamer the *Great Western*.

she was part of that propulsion of Progress, yet it must have seemed as if she had shifted into reverse gear and plunged back in time. Wellington was one of the largest settlements in New Zealand – so where were the mansions, the theatres, the warehouses bustling with commerce? All she saw was a scattering of modest weatherboard cottages, barracks and a little cabin-like church, divided up by a few dirt tracks. As for the hinterland, this was so mountainous and wooded that clearing it for sheep looked not only prohibitively expensive but physically impossible.

At least Isabella had the advantage over her fellow passengers of being accustomed to native peoples, so she would have been less alarmed than them by the Maori who clustered on shore. Charlotte Godley, who arrived in 1850 and went on to become virtual queen of Christchurch, dismissed them as 'picturesque but frightful, their faces horribly tattooed even on their lips'. She noted how they squatted about the place wrapped in red blankets, their brown faces crowned with a mop of shiny oiled hair, pipes in their mouths, and how 'if anything obliges them to move, they slide along more like monkeys than anything human'. In her patronizing way, typical of women settlers, she was amused by the way the men and women, young and old, barrelled down the main track through Wellington laughing and chatting while playing with old-fashioned whipping tops, like English children with hoops.

Jostling alongside the Maori on the wharf were the settlers. Some waved shyly or tearfully at long-lost relatives; others were on tenterhooks waiting for goods. The average journey from England took 110 days, but owing to her 'boisterous passage', the *Balnaguith* had taken three weeks more. Over a month before her arrival, Wellington's merchants had been advertising her cargo for sale, and the longer she was delayed, the more concern there was at the possible loss of her drapery, millinery, boots and shoes, beer, Geneva, stout, pickled herrings, and furniture consisting of 'Brussels, Velvet Pile, Axminster, Patent Felt Carpets and Druggets, and Cane-seated chairs French polished'. English goods like these reached Wellington only about four times a year.

All the waiting settlers were also desperate for letters and craved news about the world. Most were happy if they got an answer from home within a year; there would be no international telegraph for another twenty-five years, so every word came by ship. If a ship went down, the news was lost. The Governor knew no more than the governed, since there was no other way for him to get information either.* In three months, the *Balnaguith* was the only British ship into Wellington. Most of the news she carried concerned the build-up to the Crimean War, and the isolated colonists did not discover until the end of July, when the next news came in, that Great Britain had in fact *already* made a declaration of war the previous March, while the *Balnaguith* was at sea. For all they knew, their loved ones

---

* One month before Isabella arrived, Captain Hayes of the *Waterlilly* from Sydney brought news from Europe which had left England on 10 January, eighty-one days before that, and the *Nelson Examiner* gloried in the fact that this was 'the shortest time in which news has ever been transmitted from England and published in New Zealand'. Once the telegraph was invented, whereby electrical signals were sent along copper cables, Britain was able to link up with all major colonies, and messages could travel in hours rather than weeks. By 1854 telegraphic cables were laid across India, but the first to link New Zealand with the outside world via Nelson, Botany Bay, Indonesia, Singapore, Madras, Bombay and Suez was not laid until 1878.

could have been at the front for three months, and could have been killed, and this was the first they had heard about it.

Charles had not managed to make the journey from Motueka to Wellington to greet Isabella and Charlie, but amongst the dockside crowd, waiting to receive them 'most kindly', was Robert Strang, Registrar of the Supreme Court and one of the grandees of Wellington. He had arrived in Port Nicholson in 1840 in the first shipment organized by the New Zealand Company. In 1851 his daughter Susan had married a distant Dunstaffnage Campbell cousin of Isabella's named Donald McLean. Susan had died tragically in childbirth, leaving baby Robert Donald Douglas McLean, who was being brought up in Wellington by his widowed grandfather.

Isabella became deeply attached to Mr Strang and 'dear little Dougie'. They became part of her world, nothing to do with Charles. Dougie was shy at first but by the time they parted the two were such great friends that she wished he could live with her own 'little people' as a playfellow, since he had no siblings or mother of his own. This was a serious suggestion and, over the next few years, as events in her own family unfolded, she yearned to have him near her.

After ten days, Isabella and Charlie took a passage across the notoriously bumpy Cook Strait to Nelson. Then they paid 2s 6d to sail on to Motueka, which lay the other side of Blind Bay (so named by Captain Cook because he was unable to see the end of it). Perhaps Isabella felt blind as she sailed into her own unknown future.*

The boat crossed the bay with the current, then approached

---

* Blind Bay is now known as Tasman Bay.

Doctor's Creek. There was no jetty or dock; the boat beached on shingle and a sailor stood thigh-deep in the sea, hefted Isabella onto his back and dumped her ashore with as much dignity as a sack of coal.

Isabella's disquiet at the informality of her landing was compounded by the primitive state of Motueka. If Wellington was a seaside village, Motueka was a collection of forlorn shanties. A bullock cart lumbered her and Charlie through the 'town'. The High Street was nothing more than a thin surveyor's line marked out in the bush; the trees had been felled and rolled to one side, but it would be another two years before their fire-tarred stumps were cut down to the ground and the soil levelled to give it the appearance of a road. What remained of the forest was now deprived of shelter, and dying. The dead trees rose like skeletons from a sea of mud. A few weeping willows and peach trees had been planted to replace the native forest but their winter branches were bare.

In the 'town centre' the houses lined just one side of the track, opposite fern and swamp. Raised on piles out of the mire, they were built to a colonial template with wooden-floored verandas jutting out in front. Nailed on top of the few shops were crude signs with roughly painted graphics; one announced itself as Wilkie's Store, with windows displaying nothing but metal tinderboxes. At regular intervals tracks crossed the High Street at right angles, although like the High Street they were not yet roads but hopeful lines marking them out for the future. A white-painted wooden church with a modest tower stood at one junction, while another 'road' led to the Maori pa, the small fortified settlement. Another petered out in manuka scrub and an inlet the Maori used as their port, filled with cartloads of carved figureheads and remains of huge canoes, and there were well-built but empty Maori whares – empty because someone had died in them, rendering them tapu.

Like Nelson, Motueka was a strip of flat land about seven miles long and four miles wide sandwiched between sea and mountains. East towards Moutere the houses became more and more widely dispersed in bleak hedgeless plots, some of up to seven acres. The bullock dray bumped Isabella past them, across the roadless plain.

Charles had rented a farmhouse called Hurstmanceaux from rich young Teddy (later Sir Edwin) Dashwood, who had fought heroically alongside Charles at the Battle of Sobraon then left the army to become an explorer and farmer in New Zealand. Lonely in this remote outpost, Lieutenant Dashwood had taken to drink and to living with another man's wife, but he had seen the error of his ways and returned to England to raise more money to invest in New Zealand, and to find a wife of his own.

As the bullock dray approached Hurstmanceaux, Isabella's anticipation mounted. She had endured a separation of sixteen months, and she envisaged their reunion as a mirror of her return to Lohughat after recuperating in Almorah: the ebullience, the enthusiasm. Throughout her journey this picture had sustained her, even during the darkest days of storms and loneliness. Soon after they parted in Calcutta, Charles had written, 'Years – long years – seem to have elapsed since I parted from you, my dear wife, on board the "Hindoostan", and months must yet pass before I hear of your safe arrival in England.' She shared his longing.

She may have been anxious too. Sixteen months was an eternity in a child's life. Would the younger ones even remember her? She was approaching the full stop at the end of her voyage, but it would also mark the beginning of the next sentence. Her new life. What would be expected of her? How would she cope? At least she could reassure herself that she would have Charles to support her.

The family was gathered on the veranda. There was Charles, as handsome and distinguished as ever. But his welcome was not warm, it was off-hand. Isabella was taken aback, and confused. She was wrong-footed, and did not know how to respond.

Miss Sutherland held a child in her arms. It must have been Caroline, not the tiny baby Isabella had left, but an unfamiliar girl of two. The other children clustered round their governess, and for an instant Isabella saw them as the perfect family unit, forgetting she was missing from the scene. The children did not greet her with love – no tiny arms clasping her legs, no embraces from the older ones; instead the little ones clung to Miss Sutherland and the older children seemed awkward, embarrassed even. Everyone was subtly altered, not just by time or their unsightly freckles, or by their forearms scorched brown in the Antipodean sun, or Fred by the hardening stubble on his chin. No, it was a sort of independence that was unfamiliar.

Here at Hurstmanceaux, Isabella spent the winter, attempting to adjust to her new life. She felt isolated, not just from society – there was no society – but within her own home. Charles maintained his air of aloofness. It was almost as if he resented her intrusion. As for the children, there was a bond between them and their governess that Isabella felt excluded her. The family had shared many trials – travelling across the world, finding a place to live, adjusting to the new world – and their relationships seemed to have cemented without her. Now when the infants had tears that needed drying they ran not to their mother for comfort but to Miss Sutherland; to Isabella they were cold and unloving. Charles did not encourage them to love their mother. He and Miss Sutherland had always shared a rapport based on their mutual interest in literature, but here in Motueka they presented a united front on domestic matters too. It was as if the mother, wife and mistress of the home had become superfluous. She was paying the price of absence.

Her sense of alienation was not helped by the fact that she had left England during an exceptionally cold winter and arrived in New Zealand during an exceptionally wet one, which followed a year of drought. Everyone had praised the climate; Hursthouse had described it as being as lovely as Madeira's – warm but not too warm, bracing but not too bracing, perfect for English constitutions – and of all New Zealand, the climate was at its most serene and dry in Nelson. Hursthouse forgot to mention that rain could plummet from leaden skies and turn the land into a quagmire. The climate was not simply a matter of spoiled boot leather: it was considered to be the prime cause of good health or disease. Isabella's health did not improve.

The *Nelson Examiner* provides an insight into other problems faced by this nascent settlement. On 8 April 1854, a month before Isabella arrived, it was announced that people should no longer drive their carts or ride wherever was most convenient but were to stick to the roads. Tenders were invited for building these roads. However, owing to the labour shortage, all landowners were asked to deal with their own stretches of track themselves. By July (mid-winter) such roads as did exist had become impassable, and the bridges entered the last stages of decay. There was also a desperate need for public works such as drainage: Nelson was a mess of dung heaps, open drains, cesspools, pigsties and slaughterhouses, all of which fouled the well water and made it undrinkable. This was particularly dangerous as the population was increasing and disease spreading, but there was no one to do the work.*

Labour was not all that the settlers lacked. In March 1854, a shortage of paper meant that the *Nelson Examiner* had to appear on bright yellow paper, while on 31 May 1854, an editorial apologized for printing on 'miserable tea paper', explaining that there was no alternative available until the arrival of the *Spray* from Sydney, which was not expected for another ten days. When the *Spray* did eventually dock on 30 May, a week late, the paper was found to be buried so deep in her hold that it was impossible to reach, so printing had to be postponed anyway.

Daily life revolved around the fundamentals. Offered for sale from the ship *Maori* were hand grabbers, bullock chains, plough traces, plastering and pointing trowels, tree-felling axes, steeled harrow tines, shepherd's crooks and cleavers. Another

---

* The 1853–54 electoral roll for the Province of Nelson, which then covered most of the South Island, an area of 46 million acres, bigger than England and Wales combined, recorded thirty-six farmers, seventeen sawyers, twelve labourers, four carpenters, three storekeepers, three carters, four shoemakers, two bricklayers, one innkeeper, one engineer, one tailor, one baker, one surgeon, two gardeners, one stock-keeper, one clergyman, one boatman, one miller, one builder, one solicitor, one boat-builder, one butcher, one publican, one schoolmaster, one clerk and seven 'gentlemen', one of whom was Charles.

tradesman offered from the same ship ('by late arrivals') ink-stands, sealing wax, quill pens ('very superior'), slop pails, iron boilers, shower baths and iron bedsteads. In September 1854, it was announced that a fine stag had been brought out from England on the *Eagle*, and turned loose near the Waimea River; now two hinds were expected any day, and people were asked not to disturb them so that red deer could be established on the island. When Teddy Dashwood returned the same month, he brought not only a bride but also trout sperm frozen in blocks of ice, purebred French merino sheep and a few brace of pheasants, which he released in Motueka where they multiplied.

People leaving the old country trapped British birds in cages and carried them fourteen thousand miles, and by 1864, when the first so-called 'Acclimatisation Societies' had been set up, New Zealand could boast eight partridges, twenty-six blackbirds, five thrushes, seventeen starlings, seven grey linnets, ten goldfinches, one robin, five greenfinches, three yellowhammers, one sparrow, twenty-three chaffinches, twenty larks, two redpoles, six Australian sparrows and seven black swans. The Societies not only extended New Zealand's range of wildlife but also were intended to make settlers feel at home, and therefore keen to stay.*

---

* They also destroyed many native species; by 1870 the Maori would voice concern over the disappearance of many small native birds, which they blamed on the introduction of bees. The small birds gathered food by dipping long tongues into blossoms of native trees, but the same blossoms were sought by bees for honey, and the Maori believed that while concealed in the flowers the bees stung the birds' tongues and killed them. The Maori would compare the fate of these birds with their own, saying that while unconscious of the dangers introduced by civilization they fell into them, and became their victim – and just like the birds, they were disappearing. By destroying the forests themselves, the settlers finished off several more native species.

New World

From this story of a burgeoning new world emerged the occasional tip of a human drama. In July 1854, a Mrs Wheeldon respectfully offered her services of needlework to the ladies of Nelson. She was residing presently at 'immigration depot no. 15' (the barracks), having been left destitute after the *Mahomed Shah* on which she was travelling from England to New Zealand had in May 1853 caught fire off Mauritius, destroying every possession and piece of cargo on board. 'Orders for dresses, drawn bonnets, baby linen &., will be thankfully received, and punctually executed.'

Although only a few Maori lived in the South Island, most congregated in Motueka. Many were frighteningly tattooed, and pioneer mothers feared that their children might be cooked up in a 'koppa Maori'. Instead the Maori were friendly. Curious rather than hostile, they crouched on settlers' verandas, smoking, and inspecting the possessions, and when anyone played the piano they clustered round the windows, turning the rooms dark. One settler built a house near the pa, where lived a Maori of an 'inquiring turn of mind'. He was considered a great nuisance because he would come in and sit on the floor, whereupon the women would get the broom and try to dislodge him. He would shift from place to place, but eventually would retreat outside, 'finding the women too painfully clean for his liking'.

Most Europeans laughed at the Maori desire for the pakehas' cast-off garments, often wearing them back-to-front and looking, crowed another Motueka resident, 'the most ludicrous figures and so unconscious of it too.' To some, they seemed barely human. In describing the beauty of the Maori burial ground at Motueka the same woman remarked that, 'Even those savages must have had reverence for something to have chosen such a spot.' But there was a feeling of fondness too, and keen interest in this extraordinarily different race. Some of the Motueka ladies enjoyed getting involved in Maori affairs, particularly when the fine-looking chief Enaki fell in love with a beautiful young Maori woman; as she already had a lover, the pakeha women hid her on board a boat and spirited her away to Nelson where her lover, who had come overland, joined her.

Such affairs of the heart could not detract from the overriding concerns that were the price of land, and the price of wool, with attendant interest in scab and dipping. Even more important were the details of the new constitution and legislation – dull in themselves, but extraordinary in the way ordinary settlers with no experience were framing laws for their new country.

In her loneliness, Isabella turned to the one potential ally she had in the whole southern hemisphere. This was Mr Strang's son-in-law Donald McLean, who was based in Auckland. His grandmother had been the last Campbell born in the Castle of Dunstaffnage before it burnt down in 1810, so he was a distant relative. Although she had not yet met him, Isabella felt particularly warm towards him because he was a cousin of dear Mrs Skinner, the woman who had rescued her from misery when she was a tiny child at boarding school in Cadogan Place. Mrs Skinner, who Isabella described as 'kindness itself', was born a McLean.

Donald McLean sent Isabella a welcoming note and she replied at once, anxious to forward letters and gifts from his family. Having heard so much about him from cousins and mutual friends in Argyll she could not consider him a stranger.

'I shall indeed be glad to be as *relations* in this far off and strange land.'

McLean was able to help Isabella immediately. Her arrival had been marred by the loss of three of her cases off the ship, presumably overboard. She had brought only essentials with her, and to replace them would be almost impossible in New Zealand where everything cost about double the English price, sometimes more. However, thanks to McLean's efforts on her behalf, one of Isabella's boxes was found. It had been broken in two at the Customs House and the contents strewn over the bottom of a boat, but a kind neighbour delivered them to her and only one pair of boots was lost. The two other cases were never found: perhaps their loss foretold of others still to come.

Born in 1820 on the Hebridean Isle of Tiree, off the coast of Argyll, Donald McLean landed in New Zealand in 1840 and became a 'Sub-Protector of Aborigines' in the remote North Island province of Taranaki. He acted as a mediator between Maori and settler, and a sort of British Ambassador taking British law into Maori territory. In 1853 he was appointed the government's master-buyer of Maori land for settlement, and by the time Isabella arrived he was already becoming one of the greatest architects of the New Zealand colony, the most commanding personality of the day. He was tall and burly, with wide shoulders and a deep chest. Photographs suggest a thoughtful and upright man, both patriarchal and vigorous, with Churchillian doggedness.

McLean liked the Maori, was fluent in their language, and being a Scottish clansman understood the clannish nature of their society – the strong tribal identity based on kinship, the hereditary chieftains with their limited powers, the endemic inter-tribal warfare and long-remembered slights, and the effect these had on land ownership. McLean understood the problems caused by buying land whose ownership was disputed: the outcome could be a disaster like the Wairau Massacre. He was also more sensitive than any other government agent in arbitrating between the Maori and some of the more aggressive settlers. This made him astonishingly successful in persuading the Maori to part with their land. Between 1846 and 1853 he managed to buy 32.6 million acres, just under half the entire country. Although he was sometimes unscrupulous – there are descriptions of him using alcohol to clinch a sale – most Maori knew what they were doing, and (at this stage) wanted to sell.

McLean was on the move for months on end, riding thirty miles a day through barely penetrable bush, rushing down rapids in Maori canoes, hunkering around the fire in a Maori kainga or making a speech at a korero of many hundreds of Maori. In January 1854, while Isabella was on board the *Balnaguith*, he arrived in Nelson, an event eagerly anticipated because until he concluded his final arrangements with the Maori to extinguish their title to land in Nelson Province, no surveying could be undertaken. Valuable blocks of land were in effect 'locked up from settlement'. To the Nelson settlers' regret, however, McLean was needed on more urgent business in Taranaki where more serious problems were brewing between restless land-hungry settlers and the natives.*

He resolved the disputes, and in April the *Taranaki Herald* reported McLean being entertained at a public dinner to thank

* Taranaki Province was known as the province of New Plymouth until 1859.

him for the 'benefits he has conferred on the Province'. Over sixty guests, including several native chiefs, drank McLean's health, and the chiefs spoke of the good feeling now prevailing between themselves and the settlers, 'and the desire which they entertained of preserving it'. Hopeful words.

Being so peripatetic made McLean difficult to correspond with. Letters often missed him, and were not forwarded. Their correspondence was spasmodic, sometimes pouring forth passionately from Isabella's pen every other week, then nothing for years. Nevertheless, McLean became Isabella's greatest confidant.

NINE

The Succubus

Even though their house at Pangatotara was still only half-
built, when Teddy Dashwood returned in the *Ashmore* in
September 1854 with trout sperm, pheasants and the new
Mrs Dashwood, the Gascoynes had to move. Moving house
did not mean filling a pantechnicon with furniture, since
there was still not even the vestige of a track through the bush
to Pangatotara. Instead the river functioned as a road: travel
by boat, not boot. This was why it was on the banks of this
watery highway that the first inland blocks had been surveyed
and sold. So far the only people to use the Motueka River
other than surveyors were small parties of Maori on fishing
or hunting expeditions; there was no other reason to go upstream. It was also dangerous: the Motueka was twice as
deep and half as wide as it is today, and at times it boiled and
roared.

Unlike a journey up the Ganges, there was no system of
experienced boatmen or well-tried boats. Instead the family
would have packed themselves and their belongings into Maori
dugouts of rimu or white pine coated with tar, just wide
enough for one person. Canoes perilously overloaded with
tools, beds, chairs, tables, blankets, an iron stove and seed

potatoes, they set off. Maori boatmen paddled against the current. Where there were beaches, the Maori waded ashore and hauled the boats upstream, and sometimes they flung ropes around tree trunks and hauled the canoes up on the ropes. They crossed the river time and again, from beach to beach, sometimes fighting through overhanging forest. Fred may have helped, and perhaps Charles too. The going was tough, the river seething with the spring rains, and boulders unstable and slippery underfoot.

The land reared up on each bank, the bluffs stinking and painted white with the guano of a cliff-top shaggery. Then the riverbanks opened out at last into the wider valley of Pangatotara. The flatlands huddled beneath the sharp ridges of the Arthur Range, which were thickly coated in native bush as if clad in fur. This was the Gascoynes' home.

Although sensitive to the beauties of landscape, Isabella never described the majesty of the black beeches with their black trunks and yellow-green leaves, their lovely mix of textures, shapes and colours, their rounded crowns pierced by the sharper rimu. She never mentioned the deafening choirs of bellbirds and tuis at sunrise. Perhaps she was too exhausted by the journey, and crushed by the weight of the tasks that lay ahead.

The half-finished house sat above the swampy banks, supposedly out of reach of floods, surrounded by a graveyard of tree stumps and mud. Though still no more than a wooden cabin, it did become relatively substantial with a pillared veranda and two storeys, making it bigger than most New

Zealand houses even today. Despite its two storeys, Charles named it 'the Bungalow', in memory of India.*

Three adults and seven children squeezed into three rooms while more were added on. The rooms were sparsely furnished, with bare wooden walls like a shed; later they were hung with unbleached calico, and the women made curtains and soft furnishings with muslin that they dyed with onionskins and beetroot. One of the four carpenters in Nelson Province would knock up much of the furniture. Once they had more space, the essential pianoforte would follow them upstream, balanced across a canoe.

Charles, an impractical man in his late forties, drained by the Indian climate and with no experience of physical labour, now had to face the prospect of creating farmland out of forest. Throughout his life Charles had been pampered. In India, his day had begun with a servant's discreet knock to wake him for his morning ride, after which he had changed into loose Turkish trousers, drunk iced soda water, smoked a cheroot and rested or read until he and Isabella had breakfasted together

---

* It was built from a pre-fabricated kit. Britain led the world in manufacturing pre-fabricated houses, which ranged from wooden or iron huts to elaborate cast-iron villas, hotels and even churches. Some houses were sent overseas complete with all their parts, including doors and casement sashes fitted in wooden frames. There were often boxes of glass, nails and spikes, and corrugated-iron roofing stuff or shingles, elegant columns to support the veranda, French windows and matching shutters. These kits were expensive compared with a house built of raupo thatch or cob, and could cost around £200 so were only for the richer colonists. There was nothing odd or laughable about building a house from a kit; even Government House in Auckland was a kit house. They were available in England and Australia, and even in India, so Charles might have shipped his house with him, but it happened that they were also manufactured in Richmond, just outside Nelson, so Charles may have bought the kit locally.

before he went to the barracks. Even during the Sikh War he had servants to attend to his every need. There was always a syce for the horse, a sirdar-bearer to look after his wardrobe, a bihishti to carry water, and any number of valets, messengers and coachmen. This was Major Gascoyne, Isaac Gascoyne's nephew, Lady Salisbury's cousin, hero of Sobraon. Now that meant nothing. All that mattered was to get up at dawn, roll up his sleeves alongside his two equally inexperienced sons – Charlie aged only eight – and chop down the forest, clear the ground, drain the swamps.

The tree ferns that lined the river created sourness in the land that nobody could explain, but which made it infertile, and so these had to be destroyed. One dry day with a gentle breeze, the fern was set alight and the thick matted dead leaves and stringy bark burnt off, leaving the tall trunks and long cane-like leaf stalks to be hacked off while still soft from the fire. The straggling shrub known as tutu that grew beneath the fern was poisonous, sometimes fatally, to cattle and sheep, so this was chopped down with a billhook. All the detritus was left for a few days to wither and dry out before being raked up and burnt. Even the fires had to be carefully managed: if the weather was too dry and breezy Charles risked setting light to his own house; if it rained, the fire fizzled out.

Then they had to break up the soil by ploughing it to about ten inches deep. Somehow they managed to transport bullocks and a strong iron plough overland through the bush from Motueka. After ploughing, they dried out the fern roots for a week or two then raked them for burning, dug up the tutu stumps and burned them, raked the ground to create an even surface (repeated as often as necessary) and finally left the ground at least four months before sowing it with English grass and clover. The Gascoynes could never have managed this feat alone. Despite the labour shortage (what labour they could find cost at least 100 per cent more than in England, and many more times than that in India) they must have found help, possibly employing Maori labour.

Having cleared the tutu and fern, they had to broach the forest itself. This also required outside help; there was no way Charles, Fred and little Charlie could have hacked down the vast rimu and totara, then sawn up or planked the timber. Sawyers cost Charles between £5 and £10 an acre – today around £500. The dismembered trees were left to wither and dry throughout the summer, and were burnt the following autumn. The stumps would remain sticking up like diseased molars for another three years until they could be heaved out by a couple of bullocks.

Charles now had to fence his newly cleared land. This was crucial; newspapers carried endless complaints about livestock escaping into neighbouring plots. No iron fencing or wire had yet been imported, so Charles used his own timber to make posts and rails, reinforced by the fast-growing prickly furze that he planted inside. Only then could he think about buying his first sheep and cattle.

The women toiled in the house. Isabella wrote to McLean that they had no room for a servant, 'but my children with the assistance of a person I brought out from Scotland some years ago do all the work of the family and I look after the little ones myself.' In India, Isabella's day had mostly consisted of reclining in a basket chair on the veranda while her ayah brushed her hair and gossiped about the station, and servants brought tea and iced drinks. After tiffin Isabella had usually slept through the afternoon under her mosquito net, before promenading down the mall. Having never lifted a finger for herself, let alone for her children, she was now forced in cramped and primitive conditions to put her soft white hands to work. Izzy was nineteen and, assisted by Mary and Amy, well able to help Miss Sutherland, but none of them were accustomed to drudgery, and they were all ignorant of the techniques or short cuts a servant would have picked up over the years. The only way was to muddle through.

They fought dirt. By clearing the land the men churned it up, and saturated by rain it turned into a bog. They laid boards as makeshift paths, but the women's full-length skirts were permanently hemmed with mud. In India, Isabella had abandoned the layers of petticoats, starched muslin, corded calico and rolls of plaited horsehair in favour of the newly fashionable crinoline, since this provided the same big-skirted look but without the bulk. Slender as a lily stem rising from its pot, stately as a ship under sail, the rich fabric rustling suggestively around her feet: this was the image of Victorian womanhood. In her voluminous dresses Isabella was an object of respect, even awe. But this crinoline, which continued to sway down the pavements of Paris and London for another thirteen years, was impossible to wield in the bush and had to be discarded, as did the tight-laced bodice, which was too rigid to allow the women to do anything but sit about feeling headachy. Although Isabella had never been flamboyant in her dress, it must have been humiliating for her to forsake these symbols of fashion and femininity.

There were no new clothes to buy. In India, Isabella had had a more-or-less resident darzee camped on her veranda; now the nearest dressmakers were in Nelson, and to reach them required a perilous journey by river and sea, plus the ferry fare, not to mention the prohibitive price of the fabric required for a skirt that usually measured at least ten yards round, in addition to all the ruches and flounces that adorned it. Isabella and the girls had to make do with the clothes they had arrived in. These ripped in the bush and rotted in the sub-tropical humidity, and then were darned and mended until they were nothing more than patchwork, and handed down from one sister to the next. After their long day's work, every evening they had to sit down and sew.

Mud chained them to the washtub. In India, Isabella had had a resident dhobi wallah attached to her at all times, whether in the cantonment, up in the hills or on the march. Now, at least in these early days before a well was sunk, the women had to drag water across the flats from the river and boil it in a big copper on a fire behind the house. The mangled linen was unfurled on bushes to dry, but washing was often disrupted by the weather when the valley drowned in mist.

Mending and washing were just two of the innumerable household tasks. There was also the lighting. Ideally they used clean-burning candles made from spermaceti wax found in the head cavities of sperm whales, but these were hugely expensive and not easy to find. Mostly the house was lit by fish oil in lamps called colza lamps, or by tallow candles imported from Sydney (fish oil was preferred as it smelled less offensive). At times they had to resort to slush lamps – pieces of rag wound round a stick and stuck in a bowl of fat from the frying pan. There were no kerosene lamps or night-lights. Tallow candles had to be watched constantly or they guttered and the stinking tallow ran over the table. They gave off evil-smelling smoke but very little light. Maybugs as big as thumbs zoomed towards the light and singed themselves on the flames, extinguishing the candle. Mosquitoes were attracted too, and could be kept out only by burning damp cow dung and filling the room with smoke.

If one of the younger children woke in the night, or was sick and needed tending, there were no matches to strike a quick light. Instead Isabella or Miss Sutherland had to scrabble for the tinderbox and strike it with a flint and steel until they could get a spark, then wait while it lit a slip of sulphur-coated wood which could light the candle.

While the house was being finished, cooking took place on a camp oven, a huge metal pot with three legs that stood on the embers and was the iron goddess of the pioneer kitchen, to be propitiated at all times – which was hard when fuel in the bush was often damp. Alternatives were on offer. The *Nelson Examiner* of 17 June 1854 carried the following advert: 'On sale a GAS and COOKING apparatus, by which gas may be made from any kind of fat or grease, the refuse of the kitchen &c., producing a brilliant white light which will enable the Cooking Apparatus to roast, boil, and bake.' Whether or not the Gascoynes bought one of these, Isabella does not relate; it is probable that once they were settled in they installed the more common Colonial Oven, a wood-fired range.

What did they eat? In India, Isabella's khansaman had shopped for her in the bazaar; now supplies could reach them only by boat and, once there was a track, by wearisome journeys from Motueka, so although they could store flour, most fresh food they had to supply themselves. They grew imported

British vegetables and fruit, supplemented with whatever the men could fish from the river, or shoot and trap in the bush. There were wild pigs and blue duck, plump dove-grey birds with brown speckled necks and breasts, which were so fearless that anyone could knock them over with a stick. There were teal and cranes, kiwis that tasted like young turkey, and the pukeko or swamp hen, a big beautiful blue-backed bird with a scarlet-topped head like a blob of sealing wax. This slow flyer was easy to shoot and made good eating. Eventually they would have their own sheep, but even then it would be a while before any were ready to butcher. Then every part would be made use of.

None of the household had ever cooked before. In India the khansaman had prepared curries and mulligatawny soup and cutlets, and the khitmagar and other servants had waited on them at table; now they had to begin from scratch on their own.

Isabella suffered not only privations but also a lack of privacy, yet at the same time she was effectively stranded on an island, separated from her neighbours by a sea of bush. Other than by river, there was no way of communicating with the outside world. When Mary Hobhouse arrived in 1859 as wife of the first Bishop of Nelson she described beleaguered little Motueka, and noted that, 'Behind are the hills shutting in some cultivable valleys wherein people of the upper middle-class have perched their houses. Of course the poor womenkind seldom leave them.' Isabella felt buried alive.

It transpired that Isabella had no domestic servant, apart from Amelia Sutherland, not only because of a lack of space and money, but also – as she informed McLean – because Charles had developed a peculiar prejudice against having regular servants in the house. This was odd, given that he was accustomed to a household full of servants in India. Whatever the reason, slavery was the price Isabella and the rest of the family had to pay to indulge him.

Isabella was flattened by the weight of her burden. She was not weak: although she was used to being waited on hand and foot, she had had to manage those servants. Meanwhile she had endured India's punishing climate, given birth nine times (making a total of six years and forty-eight weeks of pregnancy), and made countless journeys in every possible form of transport over mountains, deserts and oceans. She had lived through famine and war, and during sea voyages she had given birth, survived a fire, and rescued an officer from drowning. All this was by the age of forty-three. But New Zealand was harder than anything she had experienced. She admitted to McLean that she was not coping.

Charles was mostly absent outdoors, but he seemed to be absent emotionally too. He remained aloof, and Isabella felt bemused and wounded by the change in him. Far from supporting her in her efforts about the house, he made it clear that he believed her to be totally unfitted for the management of a family in the colony. When Miss Sutherland and Isabella disagreed on some domestic matter, Charles always supported Miss Sutherland. Thus he undermined Isabella.

On 26 December 1854, a year less a day after leaving England, Isabella wrote to McLean and expressed anxiety that she had received no letters from Scotland, for which she longed in 'this far off Strangerland'. She also wrote of her happiness at the prospect of 'dear little Douglas' being brought to visit her, a treat promised by McLean. Although she still yearned for

Dougie to live with her family, she realized this was unlikely until he was older as, she admitted, 'I know from painful experience how much children are neglected even by well meaning and kind people, and your little darling is in need of more tenderness and judicious management than at any future period.'

Isabella added a PS. 'Pray accept the compliments of the season – though I can hardly fancy a Happy Christmas in New Zealand!' Apart from the isolation, and the exhausting toil involved just in getting through each day, everything seemed topsy-turvy. Christmas was at the height of summer when it was hot and humid, and mosquitoes and sand flies a plague. There was no holly or ivy to decorate the house, and what evergreens there were didn't last. Perhaps Charles carved a kiwi, or one of Teddy Dashwood's pheasants; perhaps they all made an effort for the sake of the children to pretend they were happy.

Even in their narrow community Isabella was made to feel unwelcome. The most important family in the district were the Greenwoods, who Charles had met in the Glass Case. Dr AB, as Mary Hobhouse disguised John Danforth Greenwood, was a paragon of settlerhood. She described him as 'a medical man and a person of great practical sense as well as of considerable talent and cultivation. His wife is a clever active well-educated woman, who has never known illness and if she sits up all night is just as fresh next morning! I need not say that they are just the people to colonise. They were amongst the original settlers here, came and lived in the fern in a tent with a heap of little childn & thought it very pleasant!' Using their bare hands they built a large house called Woodlands out of squared logs they cut in the bush, lined with sawn white pine boards and panelled with rimu. It had a slate roof, and small diamond-pane windows that they brought from England. Here Sarah Greenwood gave birth to four daughters, bringing the tally of Greenwood children to thirteen. She embraced pioneer life. Not only did she bring up the thirteen children and run her household on a shoe-string, she also found time to become an artist of note, painting mainly watercolour landscapes and portraits, and her parlour became a place of worship and a social centre where she organized musical evenings. Mary Hobhouse admitted that the Greenwoods were poor 'by the surest test here, viz. that they have no sheep, which is both proof and cause of poverty. But still they live in comparative comfort. Their house is of a good size & solid structure & they have an abundance of all the necessaries of life. If not quite come up to one's own views of comfort to sleep on a straw mattrass that makes one's bones ache, nor to smell the yellow soap on the wash stand as one lies in bed, nor to use coarse unmangled towels, all of which are concomitants of a visit to their house, but the general air of cleanliness, management and prosperity out-weighs these things.'

Bemoaning her limited social circle, Mary Hobhouse cited the Greenwoods as 'a resource in a way that no other family is'. Dr Greenwood had studied medicine at St Bartholomew's Hospital in London, and emigrated to New Zealand in 1843. In return for a free passage he had acted as surgeon on board the ship, and as there were no deaths and several births, including that of his son Alfred, he arrived with his success in Nelson and Motueka assured. He owned little capital but was energetic, a devout Christian and general do-gooder, and gave the land on which the schoolhouse was built in Motueka. He would go on to become a government inspector of schools, editor of the

Nelson Examiner, founder and headmaster of Nelson College (the most important public school in the region), then Sergeant at Arms to the House of Representatives in Wellington.

The Greenwoods began a farm about two miles from Woodlands, which was managed and worked by their son Fred with intermittent help from his brothers. Their daughter Ellen Greenwood was governess to the children of Governor Gore-Browne, the premier family in the land, while John and Graham Greenwood were sent to Auckland to be educated in St John's College, one of the finest schools in the country, which was founded by the eminent Bishop of New Zealand, Bishop Selwyn, who was renowned for championing the rights of the Maori.

Sarah Greenwood needed friends. Writing to her mother in Tooting, she admitted to longing for 'the unspeakable happiness of a chat', but she refused to give in to such thoughts as they would only awaken regrets which, she added stalwartly, 'it is our duty and interest to subdue.' Isabella should have been the perfect person to chat to. Sarah Greenwood came from a more humble background than herself – she was born in Lambeth to a wax chandler – but in a place so short of people such subtle class distinctions mattered less than what they had in common. Apart from the practical burdens that they could have helped each other surmount, Sarah and Isabella were the same age, shared an education in the accomplishments, and before coming to New Zealand the Greenwoods had lived in France, so like Charles they had a strong French connection. Their children were also the same age. Isabella yearned for Sarah Greenwood's approval and friendship.

Instead the Greenwoods received Isabella with inexplicable

coldness. Before her arrival, they had befriended Amelia Sutherland; now they made Isabella feel like an intruder. She was mystified by their rejection, and hurt. When she had joined the 5th Light Cavalry in Cawnpore she was a success, welcomed with open arms into the regimental family; this time she was a failure. Perhaps Sarah despised her for not fitting the mould of uncomplaining pioneer. Isabella could never be the salt-of-the-earth type, plunging her forearms into the brawn. She could never be the much-loved pakeha dispensing invaluable herbal remedies to passing Maori, with never a day's illness and always a cheerful word. Isabella was gentle, nervous; it was the tall handsome Amelia Sutherland who was the capable settler in the Gascoyne household.

The first difficult year over, 1855 began tumultuously with the most severe earthquake yet recorded, the country's worst calamity since it became a colony. The Bungalow escaped unscathed, but every brick building in Wellington was destroyed and the ground level raised by over two feet. Although Isabella was used to earthquakes, and although Mr Strang and little Dougie escaped unharmed, she was distressed by the destruction of a settlement in its infancy, and by the blow to all the settlers' confidence. It was an upheaval that in retrospect Isabella may have seen as a portent.

As the year progressed, to the outside world the signs became more promising. February saw a plentiful harvest in Nelson, and more labourers and other artisans arrived to relieve the labour shortage. There was a drought but rain fell in time to save the potato crop. Donald McLean landed in Nelson to negotiate the final land sales with the Ngati Toa, which meant that more land was available for settlement. The Salisbury brothers (no connection of the marquess) bought land eleven miles further up the Motueka River and, together with six Maori, battled through the bush to build a track up the valley. The track was so rough and steep that any trap driver had to get out and hold the reins with one hand and hang on to the trap with the other as he staggered along on the upper edge of the siding, while his passenger waded through the mud behind. Nevertheless, the settlers could now bring horses and bullocks up to their farms. Prospects for the valley looked good.

Not for Charles, however. After all the toil and sweat and huge outlay of capital, he was forced to admit that the land he had bought – in his ignorance – was too poor and swampy to make good farmland. His great project had failed. As if in grim reminder of his thwarted ideals, a street that runs towards his land was named Hursthouse Street.* In March 1855 Charles wrote to Donald McLean to seek help in obtaining a grant to buy land in Auckland, and put the Bungalow and its eight hundred acres up for sale.

Nothing happened. A year passed and only then, when McLean was again in Nelson tying up the details of the land claims of the Ngati Toa, did he visit Pangatotara at last.

March 31st 1856
Panga Totara

My dear good Cousin,
I hope you are long over this, safe at Auckland and resting a little, after all your fatiguing duties with the Nelson land

---

* In memory of Richmond Hursthouse MP (1848–1902), the first Mayor of Motueka and nephew of Charles Hursthouse. He married Edward and Elizabeth Fearon's daughter Mary.

question. Your visit was so short as really hardly to seem a
reality, and I am now looking forward to the pleasure of
seeing you again shortly, for your advice and experience
would be invaluable in the present state of our affairs.

Major Gascoyne appears dreadfully depressed and
disheartened, especially as no purchaser appears for this
place, and having expended all his capital we are falling
deeper into debt until we can dispose of some of the land.
All my endeavours to send Charlie and Amy to school, when
money is so scarce, are useless, but I try and do the best I
can with their lessons at home.

Charlotte and Caroline are standing beside me and desire
me to send their best love for the pretty toys you were so
kind as to send them. Caroline was made happy by a doll
and Chatey with picture books. Charlie and Amy also desire
their best love for the German toys (a horse and a goat).

I have only been in Motueka one time since I saw you,
and then only for a few hours. You have won golden
opinions from my friends.

My own affairs continue much as when you were here.
I wish much to pay a visit to Nelson but at present I have
not the means. The great seclusion of this place and the
monotonous life I lead renders a little change now and then
very desirable. I am afraid no change for the better will take
place unless my husband's affairs get a little more clearly
settled and Miss S must remain until I can procure a
substitute.

The Greenwoods continue very unfriendly in their
conduct towards me, but they are the only family that are so
among all our acquaintances in this Colony. I wish much it
was otherwise but I cannot blame myself in the matter

*having always endeavoured to maintain a friendly feeling
between us.*

*When am I to hope to see you? Please do come and see
us whenever you can. Separated from all my Scotch friends,
you can not realize the feeling of delight I feel in your being
a near relation, and one whose judgement I can rely on.*

*Isabelle and the rest of the young people all unite in
kindest regards to you. Let me hear from you on receipt of
this and tell me of Mr. Strang's and Douglas's welfare –
Believe me my kind cousin
Yours with sincere regards
Isabella Gascoyne*

Who exactly was Miss S, and why did Isabella need to
'procure a substitute'? Amelia Sutherland appeared to be a
governess in a million. How could Isabella do without her? At
that time no governess was trained as such: she was a girl, often
very young, who came straight from a usually inadequate
school, offering – for a meagre salary – instruction in 'the
accomplishments' of music, modern languages, drawing, dancing, morals and needlework. If she offered history, arithmetic
and globe work, these were subjects that she rarely understood
herself. But Amelia Sutherland was not one of these girls. Izzy
would later praise her governess as 'a quiet, unselfish, tactful
woman with plenty of good sense, [who] very soon had
unbounded influence over all of us, and was our friend, helper
and teacher.' She also had 'excellent taste in books and she and
my father taught us all we ever knew.'

Miss Sutherland had developed her taste in books at a good
Scottish school in which boys and girls had been taught
together as equals, something still very rare in England. Its boys

frequently went on to Edinburgh University, passing stiff examinations and often entering the Church, while the girls – learned but impoverished gentlewomen – became teachers or governesses. At this school Amelia acquired the almost revolutionary belief that there should be parity in the education of the sexes, and that education for girls was not simply in order to secure them the best possible marriage, but to equip them to support themselves if necessary. Izzy, Mary and Amy always maintained the genuine love of literature which she imparted, and learnt to speak fluent French. Mary progressed so well that despite having never attended school, she became a teacher at Napier District School, and then headmistress of Toitoi Valley Girls' School in Nelson, where she was known affectionately as Gassy.

Perhaps Isabella disapproved of Miss Sutherland's teaching methods. Isabella recorded in her memoirs, with implied criticism of Miss Sutherland, that when she was at finishing school at Oxford House under the man-hating eye of the turbaned Miss Priscilla Brown, 'Our manners, our walk and posture, our accent, how to eat and drink gracefully, how to sit down, how to converse – all these were strictly attended to, along with many other matters which nowadays seem to be totally neglected.'

Charles was on Miss Sutherland's side. An intellectual, a lover of poetry, he also sympathized with Miss Sutherland's views about the equality of the sexes, so far as they went. Charles's grandfather Bamber Gascoyne had grown up in Barking, Essex, where his family had been close friends of their neighbour, the handsome and unconventional Mary Wollstonecraft. In her book *Thoughts on the Education of Daughters*, published in 1787, she advocated not the 'exterior accomplishments' designed merely to render the person attractive, nor useless learning by rote, but genuine 'employment for the mind'. Perhaps the ideas of that pioneering feminist had rubbed off on the Gascoynes. In his will, Charles insisted that his daughters should inherit a share of his wealth equal to that of Fred and Charlie, and that it made no difference whether they were married or not – in other words, they were not expected to depend on their husbands to support them.

However, neglect of the accomplishments was not the reason for Isabella's dislike, since at Pangatotara everyone was working so hard in the house and fields that it was impossible for Miss Sutherland to find time to teach the children at all, let alone to teach them the wrong things. Isabella longed to send the little ones to school because at home they were learning nothing, and without proper schooling were turning into what Mary Hobhouse described as the clichéd image of colonial children whose parents were bad managers: skinny and overworked with elderly faces, and heads empty of childish thoughts or education and full of housework. Even the Greenwood children were suffering, while the Gascoynes' friends the Blundells, who were living in the Waimea Valley, were considered by Mary Hobhouse to be 'very nice people, *but* with a family of *unruly*, *unmannerly* boys and girls growing up round them.'

Isabella could hardly blame Miss Sutherland for this neglect. Its cause was the family's situation: there was no local school, and Charles could not afford to send the children away to board. Meanwhile all available hands were put to work. So the problem with Miss Sutherland was not about education. It seemed to be about her status in the family. Traditionally gov-

ernesses were poor, destined to remain single and to live with
strangers who treated them with insolence. In *Thoughts on the
Education of Daughters* Mary Wollstonecraft was one of the
first to point out what terrible lives governesses led. Not one of
the family, and yet also too much of a gentlewoman to be a servant, she hovered in a lonely void between the drawing room
and the kitchen, and having been a governess in Bath, Mary
Wollstonecraft knew her subject. But Miss Sutherland was not
treated like the despised 'little governess'. It had been impossible to live with this educated European woman in India, the
single other European not only in the household but for miles
around, and not befriend her. Now their new primitive existence had erased any remaining difference of class. They were
all in this together. Yet it appeared that on arriving in New
Zealand, Miss Sutherland had gone one stage further, and was
no longer just 'one of the family'; she was – or so Isabella feared
– rapidly becoming its head. While Isabella was in England,
Charles had given the governess complete control of the household, and she was reluctant to relinquish this role. It was Miss
Sutherland who kept the keys to the cupboards hanging in a
bunch from her waist, 'as Lady and entire mistress of the Establishment', as Isabella complained to McLean. She even took
charge of expenses. For love, the children continued to turn to
Miss Sutherland rather than to Isabella, and they made it clear
that they considered Isabella to be a useless pioneer and mother.
All day long, while Charles and the boys were out in the bush,
Isabella was left to face not only her own inadequacies, but this
other woman, who seemed to have moved in on her life, and to
be taking over.

Miss Sutherland was not alone in being transformed by New

Zealand. Settlers (mostly women) frequently complained of the uppity nature of their servant girls, the way they no longer seemed willing to curtsey and scrape. In crossing the seas to New Zealand they had become cheeky; they answered back. In the new world they seized the opportunity to break out of the old class structures – after all, that was what the colony was supposed to be about. Lady Mary Barker, who settled in Canterbury at this time, wrote that 'the look and bearing of the immigrants appear to alter soon after they reach the colony. Some people object to the independence of their manner, but I do not; on the contrary, I like to see the upright gait, the well-fed healthy look, the decent clothes (even if no one touches his hat to you) instead of the half-starved depressed appearance, and too often cringing servility of the mass of our English population.'*

Isabella wrote to McLean that the governess had gone even further and become 'unbearably arrogant and presumptuous', and her overbearing presence dominated the household. Far from being a comfort to her, 'the person I brought out from Scotland' had become 'quite the reverse'. Isabella's letters show a mounting sense of panic.

Her conduct was mentioned to me on my arrival as most improper by neighbours. I for many years thought highly of

---

* Anthony Trollope, who visited New Zealand in the 1860s, recalled that 'the very tone in which a maid servant speaks to you in New Zealand, her quiet little joke, her familiar smile, her easy manner, tell you at once that the badge of servitude is not heavy upon her. She takes her wages and makes your bed and hands your plate – but she does not consider herself to be of an order of things different from your order. Many who have been accustomed to be served all their life may not like this. If so, they had better not live in New Zealand.'

*her also, though she always had a most violent temper.
Indeed, the Doctor in India said she had a strong tendency to
Insanity, but her conduct since she came to the Colony has
been such as to give me the worst opinion of her principles.
She constantly uses stimulants, allowed it to be supposed she
was a near relative of mine (a sister); has prejudiced my
children and also my husband against me, by every means in
her power, by repeating lies and misrepresentations; she is
most extravagant in her habits; insolent in her manners to me,
taking possession of my property as her own, of the best
bedroom, furniture etc etc in the house, locking up every
thing in her own charge and refusing me access to, or control
over, any thing in household matters etc etc. Surely no wife
could patiently endure such daily – hourly – insults and trials.*

Isabella was distraught. On Christmas Day 1856 she left the
family festivities – if such they were – and retreated to a private
place to pour out her heart.

*Pray destroy this letter when read.
My dear Cousin,
I was very glad to see your handwriting again for I really did
not know what to think of your long silence.*

> *When I last saw Mr. Tudor he told me that he expected
you would come by the next steamer as your presence was
required to settle some native question regarding land, so
that I trust I may have the pleasure of seeing you sooner
than you anticipated – and most anxious am I to see you on
several accounts.*

> *Every thing goes on very quietly here outwardly – and I
never take any notice of any thing I see or hear. But the fact
is, I have endured such persecution and suffering ever since I*

joined my family, all more or less connected with the person
who controls the whole house – and is in fact my mistress.
For practically I am nothing more or less than entirely under
her control, both from dread of her temper and her influence
with my husband and children, that I am only waiting to see
you to consult upon what course I must pursue.

I am so completely isolated from all friends that I trust
you will forgive my thus troubling you for advice in my
affairs for otherwise I am helpless and hopeless.

But to live on as I have been doing, even for my
children's sake, I could not. It is positively ruination for
them as regards all domestic virtues and their duty and
affection to me.

Either I must leave my family and earn my bread, which
thank God I am perfectly able to do even in New Zealand
with all its hard work, or E [sic] Sutherland must leave my
family, one or the other. Major G has settled £100 on her for
life – and at present she has carte blanche as far as his means
go – while I only have received for my individual wants 10£
the first year, 5£ the second year, and 5£ this year from my
husband. My Godmother left me 300£ which I lent to Major
G on the understanding that I was always to have the
interest whatever it might be for my dress etc, and in India I
always got it. Since I came out here, he says he cannot afford
to give it to me. The interest here would be 30£ – ample for
my small wants. I feel so much never having a shilling to lay
out or to give the younger children.

Frederick and Isabelle have both been very kind and
dutiful lately. Indeed they would always be so. Mary is a sad
trial – but her conduct is also very much the effects of mis-
management.

Major G's peculiarities of temper and eccentricities often

fill me with a vague feeling of alarm for his mind. He has
been so totally changed, so completely the reverse of what he
was formerly in every way, that I do not know what to think.

Mr. Tudor and others can tell you a great deal when you
come that they have heard from others, not from me. But if I
was as silent as the grave regarding my family, the very
stones would cry out I believe. I assure you were it not for
my trust in an overruling Providence, and my own
consciousness of endeavouring to do under all circumstances
what is right, and of having been innocent of any sufficient
cause to my husband for having acted towards me as he has
done, I should have lost my reason.

This is a sad egotistical letter, and were it not that on
both sides of the home you have Dunstaffnage blood in your
veins, I should fear my wearying you. But I never yet met
with coldness or unkindness from one of my own relatives –
thank God – except my poor uncle [Alexander Campbell]
and he only took my money when he had lost his own.

But now I must close my letter in hope of seeing you by
return of post, but if that cannot be – pray – pray write and
tell me at once.

I hope Mr. Strang and Douglas are well. I should be
completely happy keeping house for them with my two
youngest children with me, and I am sure they would soon
give me that regard I am denied here.

Farewell my dear cousin. May your prospects in life bring
gladness from year to year, and may God's blessing be upon
you and all dear to you. Accept of all the kind wishes of the
season and believe me always
Your affectionate Cousin,
I.A. Gascoyne
Panga Totara – Xmas day 1856

Despite Charles's 'prejudice' against having servants in the house, by now they had a couple named Margaret and George Cranford living-in. The Cranfords helped about the farm and in the house, and while they relieved the physical burdens, they also (and this may have been what Charles feared) spread gossip about the goings-on at Pangatotara. Tongues were wagging about such 'unusual domestic arrangements', hinting at something more between Charles and Amelia than the usual master–governess relationship. Rumours of scandal were spreading downstream to Motueka, and across Blind Bay to Nelson. People were whispering behind their hands. Isabella, in need of company and longing to entertain friends in her new home, invited the Blundells and Richmonds to visit, but while these friends – in fact everyone in Motueka and Nelson, including all the old acquaintances from Fell & Seymour's Glass Case except the Greenwoods – sent kind invitations for Isabella to visit them, to Isabella's mortification they declined to enter the Bungalow themselves while Miss Sutherland was in residence.

Was there truth behind the rumours, or was this terrorizing witch who was stealing the affections of her children and her husband a figment of Isabella's jealous imagination? Certainly, there are frequent references to Isabella's 'nervous fears', her 'illness', her 'irritable temper'. Her collapse after Caroline's birth may have been a post-natal depression severe enough to require her removal from home (and from her baby), then for her to be sent back to Britain. Isabella may even have suffered from something more extreme, a post-natal psychosis which may have had symptoms such as anxiety, mood changes, confusion, even delirium and hallucinations.* Faced with the additional stress of poverty, and the immense task of setting up and running a household in the bush, it is hardly surprising that Isabella felt unable to cope. This put her marriage under terrible strain. But did this also mean that she invented what was going on at the Bungalow? Had she created the crisis in her family, and was that why the Greenwoods were so hostile to her? After all, if there was a love affair going on between Charles and Amelia, as Isabella hinted, why did the upstanding Greenwoods, and Izzy, support Miss Sutherland?

Whatever the truth, Isabella could stand this ménage no more and longed to escape. Her confidant was Thomas Tudor, a popular red-faced blue-eyed Welsh deacon who thought nothing of walking up to Pangatotara in all weathers. According to Mary Hobhouse, with whom he later went to lodge in Nelson, he was not clever but he was practical and efficient, and he had a natural frankness and sympathy which encouraged Isabella to pour out her heart. Mr Tudor urged her to leave Pangatotara and go to Mr Strang in Wellington. But Isabella could not leave; she was imprisoned by her lack of money. As a Victorian husband Charles controlled her finances – 'what's yours is mine,

---

* Around 10 per cent of women become severely depressed in the first few months after delivery. In Isabella's case this could have had the physical trigger of an infection, all too common in those unhygienic times, or an emotional trigger such as prolonged distress caused by the death of her two older children. By 1851, when Caroline was born, post-natal psychosis had long been recognized, but Dr Pierson would have known little about it; the condition was rare (c. 2.2 per 1,000 deliveries in 1858) and the medical profession showed little interest in it until the 1870s. The remedy in Isabella's day was to apply 'stimulating medicines and blisters', while by 1875 it was recognized that 'tonics and a change of scene are useful'.

and what's mine is my own'. Even if he did not wish his daughters to suffer such dependency, Charles was quite willing to inflict it on his wife. Legally Isabella had no right to keep her own small legacy, and what Charles had given her in India was out of the goodness of his heart. Without money, she was beholden to him.

This was a role Isabella knew she ought to have accepted dutifully. The bestselling *Domestic Habits of the Women of England*, published in 1846, was in effect a hugely popular marriage-guidance manual that expressed the mores of the day. 'In her intercourse with man, it is impossible but that woman should feel her own inferiority, and it is right that it should be so . . . she does not meet him on equal terms. Her part is to make sacrifices in order that his enjoyment may be enhanced. She does this with a willing spirit, but she does it so often without grateful acknowledgement. Nor is man to be blamed for this . . .'

Isabella was tormented. By staying at home she condoned what she hinted to be a gross immorality, which offended her conscience and which tore apart her heart. By leaving she would escape the torture caused by Miss Sutherland's overbearing presence, but she would fail in her duty as a wife.

Isabella begged McLean to help, but each steamer from Auckland arrived without a reply. She understood that he was busy with the land question, and had now also become Native Secretary, with responsibility for all native affairs under Governor Gore-Browne, but that did not stop her hoping for news of him and little Douglas and Mr Strang. 'When will you find or make time to come to see us?' she wailed. 'I almost fear it will always be put off – and put off – to an indefinite period.'

Ironically, she felt she was coping better on the practical side. 'I seldom leave home even for a day,' she told McLean. 'But,' she added bravely, 'I am now getting *used* to living alone, and to manage other things which were once great trials.'

The family's worldly prospects continued 'very unpromising'. Hursthouse had written that 'there is probably scarce a farm in New Zealand that would not now fetch double what it had fairly cost to create,' but he was wrong. Nobody wanted to pay a penny for the Bungalow. Charles was in debt to Fell & Seymour for £700. The interest was a cruel 10%. Charles's pension was only £130. This left him with £60 – today's £2,640 – for a family of ten. As they were earning very little from their farm, the Gascoynes were clearly desperate. Alfred Fell on the other hand was doing so well that he was able to retire at the age of forty-two, and return to England for his children's education. On leaving, he transferred his business to his chief clerk, Nathaniel Edwards, who continued to pester Charles for the interest payments.*

Isabella derived some comfort from the fact that they were not the only family to suffer. Prospects that had looked so promising had turned out to be a mirage, and other neighbouring farmers had lost almost everything. McLean had lent Isabella £5 and this she felt compelled to give to a neighbour even less well off than herself. The Gascoynes' nearest neighbours were the Jennings family, who owned two hundred acres on the opposite bank. The lean-faced and thickly moustached

* Edwards became a member of the House of Representatives (1867–70), and did so well from his business that he added a wing to his house in Nelson with twelve bedrooms, three turrets, a conservatory and a tall tower with a ball-room.

David Jennings was a solicitor turned 'grazier and agricultural-
ist', as he styled himself on the Nelson electoral roll. Too poor
to plough and sow his bumpy land, and without any help except
from his young sons, Jennings was attempting to hoe the tan-
gled roots of burnt scrub to clear the land in order to experiment
with different sorts of grapes with the mad idea of using them
to feed his sheep. Despite his hardship, he neglected his farm
and his children's education to steep himself in Isabella's problems, along with those of the rest of the neighbourhood, which
he found far more absorbing than his futile attempts at agriculture. Although Isabella considered him eccentric, he was nevertheless a worthy gentleman and a good man, thinking rightly
and honourably on all points. His wife endured her poverty and
her husband's peculiarities uncomplainingly, and became like a
sister to Isabella.*

Even that paragon of settlerhood, Dr Greenwood, was
having difficulties. He had set up a sawmill in the Brooklyn

---

* In her letters home, Mary Hobhouse disguised David Jennings as Mr XY, an
example of a failed pioneer. 'I do not think they would be prominent people
but for the restless activity which carries Mr XY always into the thick of everything that is going on and unfortunately in so doing carries him away from the
farm that he ought to be cultivating and the children he ought to be educating.
He really has a strong sense of duty and makes himself of use to his neighbours
in their moral and spiritual interest by his watchfulness over public affairs, but
when a man with 7 childn [sic] to feed off a bare hillside and no one but himself and his boys to put a spade into the ground it seems doubtful whether he
ought to spend his time and wear out his shoes by attending every Board Committee & meeting within 30 miles. He has been one of our most constant
visitors at Nelson which he reaches usually not by boat but by a 30 mile walk,
occupying 1¼ days. His old eveng [sic] coat, short-waisted and half buttoned,
in which, as his fullest costume, Mr XY usually arrives at our door, is one of
his most prominent characteristics, together with a lean face and large mous-
taches, a black stock and cotton gloves full of holes.'

Valley in Nelson, run by his son John, but it had failed and was up for sale. Having wasted three years of hard labour, the well-educated John was forced to go to the Wairau as a shepherd, in the hope of getting the chance to buy a run. Isabella told McLean that as a result of John Greenwood going away, his marriage had to be put off 'to an indefinite period, which is another source of anxiety and trouble'. Why should this have worried her? The answer is that the bride-to-be was Izzy.

Aged twenty-one, not beautiful but pleasant-looking, with a long face and wide, gentle mouth, Izzy was lucky to find an educated young man to marry. There were not many in the bush. On the Nelson electoral roll John Greenwood described his profession as 'gentleman'. Sarah Greenwood's portrait of her son in 1848 shows him poring over a book with a sensitive face, his nose and chin narrow, lips thin and prim. As Bishop Selwyn's secretary, he had joined the Bishop on two voyages around New Zealand, which took him four hundred miles into the Pacific to the remote Chatham Islands. He spoke not only fluent French but also numerous Maori dialects. He was upright, cultured and refined.

Isabella was concerned for Izzy's sake that the wedding had been postponed, but for her this marriage was not an enticing prospect. The Greenwoods were, she wrote, 'all very cordial with Major G and other members of the family but continue to show me marked coldness and discourtesy, which I regret on their own account as well as mine, as their having done so made them many enemies among our neighbours and mutual acquaintances'.

Another source of concern was the relationship between Charles and Fred.

*Something must be done about Fred at once. I feel uneasy
every day lest there should be some trouble between him and
his father. Their dispositions are so very opposite and
altogether I am most anxious that the poor boy should be
put in a way of doing something for himself and learning
some way of livelihood.*

*He is a good dispositioned, honourable, well principled
boy, but he has a hot hasty temper. You can do much with
him by kindness, but he resents being driven and always
being found fault with.*

*As far as I know the boy, he is as yet perfectly free from
all vicious propensities, but he is so unhappy here that I
dread his taking to any. Of course all this I say to you in
confidence and depending on your kindly interest in me and
mine. For never did any one want a friend's advice more
than I do as regards myself and my children. If Fred could be
of use to your brother Alex or to you in any way, and just
gain sufficient for his food and clothes, he, poor boy, desires
me to say he should be only too thankful.*

*Oh do, my dear Cousin, for the sake of the same blood
that runs in our veins, do something for my son – anything
to get him away from home (such a home) for a time.*

McLean had bought nine thousand acres in Hawke's Bay on
the North Island, where he planned to create a sheep run to be
managed by his brother Alexander. Isabella asked if Fred could
join him as a hand: he knew how to lamb and dock and card,
and cut timber for fences. Fred already knew not to shear in wet
weather if he wanted to avoid getting boils between his thighs
where he gripped the wet sheep. As the farm at Pangatotara was
not productive enough to support the whole family, Fred's

absence would ease his father's burden. His place could be taken by little Charlie, who was now able to do as much work as an average man, and was particularly handy with an axe.

More importantly, Fred would be removed from Miss Sutherland's malign influence, which Isabella felt was poisoning the very air of her home. She described Miss Sutherland as an incubus, although she actually meant the demon's female form, the succubus, who descends on a family and oppresses it like a nightmare, and has sexual relations with the men in their sleep. Was she implying that Fred had also fallen under Miss Sutherland's spell?

Isabella yearned to cut out this sickness, but Charles refused to support her. 'On this point Major Gascoyne has certainly acted as if he were not in his sound mind.' Perhaps the physical and mental stress of pioneer life, the battle against the bush that he seemed to have lost and his sense of failure, had sent him out of his mind. But when one neighbour remarked that they feared this might be the case, the reply was that it was more likely that Charles wished to drive Isabella out of hers. Was this the same Charles who, in Isabella's words, was 'the most perfect gentleman in manner and appearance generally that I ever knew'? Was this the Charles who was 'courtesy itself to womanhood, whether young or old, rich or poor'? The Charles whom his mother and wife found it impossible to help worshipping?

Isabella felt that the only possible end to ruin and disgrace was to sack Miss Sutherland since, by law if not in reality, Miss Sutherland was still her servant. She plucked up courage and with Dr Greenwood as witness gave Miss Sutherland notice. Rather than leave her destitute, Isabella allowed her to remain in the house as a visitor. This was not only kindness; had Miss Sutherland left, everybody in the neighbourhood would have believed that Isabella gave credence to the 'dreadful scandal which the arrangements and attentions she receives from my husband give rise to.'

Isabella told McLean that Miss Sutherland responded by attempting suicide. Fear of destitution? Desperate love for Charles? Cynical blackmail? Isabella does not reveal what form the suicide took, or how it was prevented from being fatal; in fact she mentions it almost in passing. Perhaps it was simply not true. It is hard to equate Isabella's Miss Sutherland – an insolent, ungrateful, lying, controlling, drug-taking, suicidal fiend – with the woman Isabella's own daughter loved and described as quiet, unselfish, tactful and 'with plenty of good sense'. If Isabella invented this suicide attempt, perhaps she did so because she feared that her jealousy and humiliation were not sufficient cause to summon McLean to her aid. If Miss Sutherland did attempt suicide, what motive could Izzy have for pretending that her governess was so unselfish and sensible? Loyalty to her adored father, perhaps? Either way, the Bungalow seethed with hatred. Miss Sutherland was soon back in power as ruler of the roost and, according to Isabella, as extravagant as ever.

Charles refused to discuss their financial affairs, but Isabella gathered that he was still hugely in debt to Fell & Seymour and, having paid the interest on the debt, labour costs on the farm and Miss Sutherland's expenses ('for dress etc and £15 a year sent home to her family') had nothing left for the children or Isabella. 'I can see only ruin before us, and yet my husband brought upwards of 3000£ into Nelson [£147,000 today], which I believe is all gone, never to return.' She blamed Miss Sutherland for joining Dr Greenwood in encouraging Charles to farm in this way, rather than buying a run, on the back of which their contemporaries were now making a fortune.*

Later Isabella was told by a neighbour that Charles was not in fact in such deep debt to Fell & Co. as he made out, that he had mortgages to cover everything and that he had exaggerated the debt in order not to give her money. He had a small flock of sheep, thirty head of cattle, ten acres in cultivation and thirty more laid down to grass for the cattle, to be gradually extended to 60–80 acres, which was enough to keep his head above water – just. Isabella, inclined to believe her neighbour, suspected that Charles had been lying about his financial problems, hiding behind a debt he possibly never had and thereby causing her acute anxiety, so as to be able to shower Amelia Sutherland with gifts, including a settlement of £100 a year.

When the *Oliver Lang*, a vast 1,224-ton Black Ball clipper, docked in Nelson, Henry Seymour of Fell & Seymour decided to return in her to England. Isabella begged Donald to come by the next steamer to help her accomplish 'what is the first wish of my heart', which was to get 'that person who has exercised such a wrongful influence over my family' sent back to England with the Seymours as chaperone. Of all the people in New Zealand, only McLean commanded enough respect from Charles to be able to intervene and to shame him into acting decently.

---

* In just a few years Samuel Butler doubled his capital on a vast Canterbury sheep station of 8,000 acres, the story of which formed the basis for *Erewhon*. He wrote to his father, 'As for farming as we do in England, it is universally maintained that it does not pay; there seems to be no discrepancy of opinion about this. Many try it, but most men give it up.'

*I know it is an unpleasant duty I am asking you to undertake
– but alas for the cause – my natural protector is my tyrant
and persecutor . . .*

*Oh pray do come, and I am sure a blessing will follow
you for helping me to do what I know is right and my duty
as a Christian wife and mother. All our neighbours here
except the Greenwoods have expressed themselves as
approving of it, and willing to aid me were it in their power.
But you and Mr. Tudor, who is too timid to act alone in the
matter but who says that with you he will do all in his power
to assist, are the only men who from position etc are entitled
to interfere in the matter.*

*I can do nothing until I see you, though I know I have
but little claim on you, my dear cousin. Do come and see
what you can do to assist me in getting rid of this woman.
Major Gascoyne will, I know, say that he has not the means
of sending her home. Could you advance the funds necessary
– and I will repay you out of a legacy of 300£ which is at
present in Major Gascoyne's hands. You know not how I feel
in asking this favour, the first of the kind in my life, but I
think you will have pleasure in assisting me thus if necessary.*

McLean was in Nelson – again extinguishing the last claims
of the Ngati Toa tribe – but he did not reply.

The disappointment, and the 'anxiety of mind I have under-
gone for some weeks past', seriously affected Isabella's health.
She tried to comfort herself with the fact that McLean had been
away somewhere with the Governor, or that some accident had
prevented him from replying; she was sure that he would not
willingly slight or add distress to one 'so already overburdened

as I am'. He could have no idea what she had endured since his last visit, what insults had been heaped upon her.

Far from removing the governess, Charles had, Isabella believed, adopted a system to try to oust his wife. Such was Charles's cruelty that Isabella was forced to admit both to herself and McLean that his 'weakness for this woman' was nothing new, but had been going on for seven years. She had tried to deceive herself for as long as possible, but his recent conduct made further concealment impossible – '*facts* speak for themselves'. Until recently, Isabella explained, she had contradicted all the scandalous reports, but now could conceal it no longer. 'It is impossible to hide the fact that Major Gascoyne invariably treats me with utter indifference and neglect in the presence of others – that he shews the utmost solicitude and minute attentions on all occasions to Miss S – that she is liberally supplied with luxuries while my wardrobe has not been renewed since my arrival in New Zealand.' Charles had selected the best pieces of furniture, pictures and clocks in the house and given them all to Miss Sutherland. Neighbours commented on Miss Sutherland's presumption and arrogance of temper, and on Charles's 'naughty and wicked conduct' in upholding Miss Sutherland in her assumed authority over the family.

Isabella was too delicate to spell it out, but she implied that Charles had been in love with Miss Sutherland since 1850, since before Caroline's birth, since before Charles wrote such passionate letters to Isabella when she was recovering in Almorah, and again when she was in England. Had his sentiments been false? Was he a hypocrite and liar, or did he still love Isabella, even though he had betrayed her for someone else?

If Isabella was aware of their relationship in India, it is hard to understand why she left for England in 1853, and thereby allowed Charles and Amelia sixteen months of liberty together. She now revealed to McLean that she would rather have remained with her family, but that Charles had insisted on her going 'for the sake of her health'. Looking back, she must now have wondered if he had ever been concerned for her health, or if his single aim was to get rid of her so as to leave him time alone with Miss Sutherland.

A neighbour informed Isabella that Charles had never expected her to come to New Zealand, and had not wanted it. Evidently he had hoped to start a new life in the new colony with a new 'wife'. She finally understood why he had made no arrangements to pay for her passage, leaving his brother John to borrow the money for her. Isabella now realized that, having returned to England in the knowledge of Charles's 'weakness' for Amelia Sutherland, she should have acted with more worldly wisdom and remained there. Charles's family had urged her to stay for at least another year, but she had fondly hoped that by showing him that her affection for him was unchanged, she would win back his heart.

As a 'gentleman' in New Zealand, a respected major, Charles's cavalier attitude towards propriety is astonishing. Everyone in the community, however widely dispersed, was interested in what was going on; all the neighbours took sides. Again and again Isabella praised her friends such as David Jennings and Thomas Tudor for the way they behaved so rightly and honourably, and as *gentlemen*. But Charles didn't care. He contemptuously defied all the increasingly puritanical conventions of the day, disregarding, as Isabella put it, the 'decencies of domestic life'. Having struggled free of the straitjacket of the cavalry and Anglo-Indian society, he apparently intended to live as he chose.

In February 1857 Isabella declared that Fred's eyes were at last opening to the truth, whatever that was. He did not necessarily take Isabella's side; in fact she criticized him for being 'undutiful'. He and his father were also not getting on, but despite their differences, and even though 'no boy could have a more unliked home', Fred did behave respectfully to his father. Hoping to escape from both parents, Fred took Isabella's advice and went to Nelson to meet McLean to try and get work on his run.

March 8th 1857

My dear good cousin,
Anxiously have I been looking for a letter from you – but not a line has reached me since you left Nelson. But I dare say you have been very much occupied. Do however, if possible, let me have a few lines on receipt of this. I know I have no right to claim your friendship or advice beyond our relationship which some people might think little of – but separated as I am from all my own family and bereaved of my brother who was always my guardian and protector while he lived, your warmhearted interest and kindness have made me look upon you in the light and in the place of a younger brother.

I have suffered much since you left. No wife or mother could be placed in a more cruel or unjust position, utterly neglected and set aside in every domestic arrangement – yet God knows I have studied in every way I could derive to conciliate my husband and win him back to the right and only road to happiness for us both – either here or hereafter.

But the poor children are fearfully misguided. My influence as a mother has been undermined and set aside and their moral and religious training is totally neglected. Isabelle is much at the Greenwoods and Fred and Mary have both given me much cause of unhappiness by their undutiful conduct, but pray do not mention this to them as they would only threaten and upbraid me in consequence. Fred did so on his return from Nelson declaring you would not have spoken to him about being dutiful to me had I not complained of him.

Were it not for the kindness and sympathy of the Campbells and Mr. Tudor I do not know what I should do – but I am not permitted to ask any friend to come and see me (I do not like to visit much at Motueka.) The Greenwoods – I mean Dr and Mrs. G – have acted throughout most unkindly and indeed unjustly towards me. They constantly invite every member of my family including Miss Sutherland to visit them for a little change when agreeable, excluding me, which as Isabelle is so much with them I regret, as I should like to accompany her, as this place is infinitely more miserable to me when she is from home.

What is to be done I do not know. I feel that the last two years have wrought a sad change in my health and spirits, already sufficiently tried by the cares of a large and young family in India during those fearful years of war and anxiety, my many voyages and journeyings all over the world nearly for 20 years – and now – but I must try and not murmur at God's will – He gave me happiness in my family and He has seen right to withdraw it.

I can not sustain such a load of sorrow alone. Poverty, loss of station and friends, disgrace and slander – all these my husband has brought on me and I could bear these evils I

*think without a murmur were his affections and my
children's left me also. But I fear nothing but a miracle could
soften my husband's heart. If my husband insists on the
arrangements remaining as they are I must go and seek a
home by my own exertions, but I must have my two
youngest children with me. The little one is now completely
placed with Miss S and her affections weaned from me. Amy
is also sadly changed from what she sees around her. The
only chance of doing her or Charley any benefit is by sending
them to a good school but this, from want of funds, their
father declares impossible.*

Pray excuse this long letter about myself and my sorrows.

*I hope dear Mr. Strang and Douglas are quite well and
the latter thriving in every way.*

*When can I hope to see you? God bless you my dear
Donald, and believe me your
Attached Cousin
Isabella Gascoyne*

McLean upbraided her for imprudence in discussing family
affairs with all and sundry, and urged her from then on to
refrain from mentioning them. Isabella replied that her mind
had been weakened by the terrible revulsion of feeling she had
experienced on her arrival in New Zealand, by the coldness and
indifference of her family. She knew she should have held her
tongue, and not sought sympathy from strangers, but she felt
so desperate, and the more she needed her family's love, the
more she felt them withdraw, while her rights in the household
were steadily usurped by a woman she herself had nurtured and
befriended. Having admitted to herself what was going on,

Isabella's unhappiness poured forth like a flood, drowning her discretion.

In April 1857, after much consideration and prayer, and consultation with Mr Tudor, Isabella decided that as she could not live under the same roof as Miss Sutherland, she had to go. 'Where? No matter! Go from my home, my children, my husband, after being for twenty-two years a wife and the mother of nine children, and live and die destitute among strangers.' She was not permitted to take any of her children with her. Her brain reeled.

Isabella packed her few belongings and left her family. She moved to Motueka where she became a lodger in 'Northwood' with Mrs Fearon, 'a truly kind and worthy lady'.* Here Isabella lived quietly. She was invited to stay in Nelson by the Blundells and Richmonds but she couldn't face being amongst relative strangers. She just wanted to lick her wounds in private, mourn her children and hide her shame until McLean arrived and helped to bring back Charles's good feelings and open his eyes to the truth.

---

* Mrs Fearon doubtless welcomed not only the extra income but also the companionship, since Captain Fearon, who had retired from the merchant navy, was often away on the vast sheep station he owned in the Awatere Valley, or in Nelson, where he represented Motueka and Massacre Bay on the Nelson Provincial Council.

TEN

Exile

Isabella complained that Fred, although 'a fine, good lad', had recently given her much cause of unhappiness, for which she blamed Charles and Miss Sutherland. 'Everything has been done to mislead him and to pervert right and wrong in his mind where I am concerned.' The good news was that he was to be removed from these pernicious influences by McLean, who had agreed to take him on as a cadet. McLean also lent Isabella the money to buy him some decent clothes to leave home in, something Charles claimed to be beyond his means.

Fred was nineteen: strong, tough, a shaggy-bearded pioneer about to begin his own adventure. It was May 1857. Armed with a letter of introduction from Isabella, he spent ten days with Mr Strang in Wellington – though this became a cause for concern when Isabella heard there was smallpox on board one of the ships in port ('I hope dear little Douglas is vaccinated', she wrote anxiously to McLean). Unscathed, Fred set off. McLean's run lay two hundred miles north, beyond a range of forested mountains. Fred could have travelled there by coach – a narrow dray track to the Wairarapa wound up a gorge and then precipitously down the other side – but at that time of year it was riven by gales and awash with mud and landslips. The best way was by ship, but Fred had no money. Instead he shouldered his swag and walked to Maraekakaho. He walked for fourteen days.

Rounding Palliser Bay, he edged past Mount Hugh and the black rocks of Cape Palliser, then beneath the Pacific headlands. In the teeth of snapping autumn winds he forded the myriad of east-coast rivers that forked into waist-deep deltas as they reached the sea, and while waiting for the tide to recede enough for him to wade across, he slept on the track or in caves, wet, tired, often hungry. He tramped over sand of such softness that his feet blistered until he could walk no further, and had to rest for three days at Akatio. Sometimes he reached a shepherd's whare or the outstation of some nascent run where any company was welcomed, and he was given a rough meal and an empty wool pack to spread on the earth floor; he wrapped himself in his plaid blanket and used his swag bag as his pillow.

Fred was met at the coastal settlement of Clive by Alec McLean,* Donald's brother and run manager, who lent him a horse and rode with him to Maraekakaho. The homestead was a primitive shack with a shingled roof and lean-to veranda stuck on the front. Fred was directed to one of the tiered bunks slung with sacking which lined the living room. At the far end a mud-brick chimney dangled with hooks from which cauldrons hung over an open fire, and from these cauldrons Alec's wife, Catherine, dished up a wholesome meal of mutton and potatoes.

Many of the local Maori chiefs had long been clamouring

---

* In his obituary in the *Wellington Independent*, Alec, known as the Waka Maori, was described as ever-welcoming. 'Visitors to Maraekakaho, rich or poor, ever experienced his kind hospitality, and his door was never shut against the weary and hungry traveller.'

for pakeha to settle in Hawke's Bay. As one chief said, 'The pakeha himself will be ample payment for our land, because we commonly expect to become prosperous through him.' The Maori chiefs who signed the Waitangi Treaty had been content – eager even – to sell tracts of unused land in exchange for a few pakeha of their own who would provide them with tobacco, blankets, clothes and, above all, muskets with which to conquer other tribes. To have a pet pakeha – and the more the better – boosted not only their coffers, but also their mana, their prestige. In turn, the pakeha needed the Maori for their potatoes, watermelons, pumpkins, fish and land. Beyond the new British settlements the Maori led independent lives, well armed and, although they were British subjects, largely beyond British law. They maintained a polite trading relationship with the pakeha and there was little overt friction, largely because they rarely met.

Donald McLean came to Hawke's Bay in 1856 and on behalf of the government bought about half of the available land, while the Maori leased out the rest to the smallholders, pastoralists and traders who edged north from Wellington. One section of thirty thousand acres called the Maraekakaho Block* was bought for £1,000, and worked for a while by three settlers, but they were defeated by the roughness of the terrain, the low price of wool and the wild dogs and pigs that slaughtered their stock. They persuaded McLean to take on part of Maraekakaho himself: nine thousand acres of swamp and undulating hills covered with high tree ferns and manuka.

As at Pangatotara, the task was immense. First Fred and his

---

* *Marae* meaning gathering place, and *kakaho* the pampas along the riverbank.

fellow cadets had to raze the tree ferns, but when they sowed the newly cleared land it proved so sour that many acres failed to germinate; then when they drained the swamps they discovered the remains of ancient forests which made ploughing impossible until they used bullocks to drag out the stumps. Nevertheless, unlike Pangatotara, Maraekakaho was a success. Within sixteen months, in September 1858, Fred was able to write to McLean that despite a shepherd being gored in the leg by a cow, which meant that Fred had to do the shepherd's job as well as his own, things were going well. 'We have a good many acres in cultivation, about 4 in wheat, 2 in grass and clover, 1 in oates [sic] and several ploughed for potatoes. The sheep are lambing at present and have dropped a great many twins, they are in good condition and few lambs have died, the horses are all right but my mare is not in foal. I am working on bullocks, now having broken in a pair lately.'

Outstations were established, each with its permanent staff with cooks and good quarters for the cadets. Some lived in temporary camps of two-roomed whares on wheels and skids which could be drawn by horse teams wherever they were needed, along with cook houses, fowl houses and pigsties. The run became vast. By 1860 there were 5,070 sheep, and during the next few years more land was bought, until by 1873 McLean owned an astonishing 28,000 sheep. The wool was taken by bullock dray to Clive, a journey of three days, and from there by surfboat out to the sailing ships to be sent to England. Fred had helped turn Maraekakaho into one of the most profitable estates in New Zealand.

Fred enjoyed the work. Because the McLeans hailed from Tiree most of his fellow cadets were Highland Scots, so Gaelic was the common tongue, and of an evening bagpipes were played. The rest were Maori, and Fred, who had not inherited Charles's love of scholarship but did have his facility for languages, soon learnt Maori too. He admired the Maori's bareback riding, the way they manoeuvred so light-heartedly – Fred was still a would-be cavalry officer at heart.

Thankful to have escaped the febrile atmosphere of home, Fred rarely wrote to Isabella. A useless correspondent, his handwriting still childishly unformed, months went by without him sending word, although to Isabella's distress he did occasionally write to Charles, and also to Izzy (and of course to McLean). Isabella feared that Fred's affection for her had been undermined by 'falsehood and a father's influence'; certainly Fred's autobiography, written in old age when all this was over, makes no mention whatsoever of his mother. Fred preferred to be with Alec and Catherine McLean, who, unlike his parents, were resourceful and uncomplaining. They became his lifelong friends. Although Isabella felt wounded by being ostracized by Fred, she was still thankful that Donald's brother was so kind to him and that he was 'removed from bad influences at present'.

Isabella, in her lonely exile in Motueka, was dismayed that the rest of the children did not visit her. Charles prevented the younger ones from doing so, while Izzy, Mary and Amy, who were considered by their father to be old enough to take sides, joined forces against her. They accused her of having exposed them to scandal. Whilst Isabella remained at Pangatotara the facade of respectability had been maintained; by leaving she gave credibility to the rumours. What was going on at the Bungalow was now openly discussed throughout Motueka, as if it was public property, and the girls lived in a house of shame. The stigma was such that they feared they would never be able to escape into marriage – except into the Greenwood family.

Isabella, more cynically, accused her older children of 'dishonouring their mother' through self-interest. She did not say this directly to them for fear of their anger, in fact she never once upbraided them, but she told McLean that she believed they knew which side their bread was buttered, and upheld 'that wretched woman' because they understood that their comfort and welfare 'depended both with their father and the Greenwoods'.

As soon as Isabella left Pangatotara, the Greenwoods had made a point of showing Miss Sutherland every attention. They never called on Isabella. When Amy and Charlotte visited Woodlands, the Greenwoods prevented them from seeing their mother who was not far away and was longing for them. Isabella had to send for them several times before they were permitted to visit her.

Sarah Greenwood declared in public that Charles was justified in his treatment of Isabella because of her temper, which had provoked the same scenes of quarrelling and discord between them ever since they married. Isabella vehemently denied this, claiming that many of her old friends in India who she had known for twenty years, far longer than she had known Sarah Greenwood, were mystified by Charles's behaviour, having always considered Captain and Mrs Gascoyne one of the happiest couples in the regiment. As proof, Isabella showed over two hundred of Charles's letters to Mr Tudor. He was moved by them and urged her to send extracts to Donald McLean since her cousin had not known her in India – they

were still comparative strangers – and might need convincing
that contrary to Sarah Greenwood's claim, she and Charles had
indeed been 'happy in each other'.

In justifying herself and her marriage and opening herself up
to Donald McLean, Isabella made herself painfully vulnerable.
As she sat in her spinsterish bedroom at Northwood with her
sheets of rough cream paper, reading and re-reading the letters
to choose the extracts, she was reminded of what once was, but
had been stolen from her.

Camp, Army of the Sutledge, January 1846

My most dearly beloved wife,
I have been reading of you in the last chapter of Proverbs –
truly you have been a most prudent and wise wife and have
saved me more money than the virtuous lady of old made
with her wool and her maidens – I wish to make some gifts
and first to thee, my best beloved, on the 11th anniversary of
our marriage, marking the happiest years of my life – by far
– far the happiest, and each happier than its predecessor till I
think no man living happier than myself. In thee my fondly
loved wife I have enjoyed all of earthly happiness that can
fall to the lot of man. Under certain and particular trials you
have proved your worth and excellence shown at all times,
and I have really and from my heart to say it, no fault to find
with anything you have said or done since our marriage – I
am satisfied that no man living was ever happier in his wife
than I have been – in everything we seem so peculiarly well
suited to each other and next to my salvation, you my
Isabella are the Lord's richest gift to me . . .

Isabella would not have needed to check the reference to

Proverbs; she knew her Bible, and knew what Charles meant. 'Who can find a virtuous woman? For her price is far above rubies. The heart of her husband doth safely trust in her, so that he shall have no need of spoil. She will do him good and not evil all the days of her life. She seeketh wool and flax, and worketh willingly with her hands. She riseth also while it is yet night, and giveth meat to her household, and a portion to her maidens.'

On the eve of the Battle of Sobraon Charles had written again. 'My wife, my own dear wife, you never have known – you never can know – how dearly I love you. My fondness for you almost exceeds the degree of love permitted to a fellow being . . .'

A few days later, 'Isabella, my dear loved wife, God bless you. You have been and are dearer to me than words can give out. Your very faults seem dear to me, and your ever-tender affection far far, far greater than I deserve. And yet, I never – God knows – loved a woman as I love you. No, never with half the tenderness, purity, and true affection I have ever felt towards you. I have been guilty of faults towards you – but I know you forgive them whatever they are. I will not enumerate your good qualities. I feel and appreciate them. But I believe there never existed in this world a woman whom I could have loved more tenderly than you.'

Isabella was convinced that on the eve of battle, in the face of death and of his Maker, Charles would surely write the truth. The letters showed how drastically he had changed, but they were not enough to persuade McLean to come, and in September 1857 she wrote to him again.

Exile

My dear Cousin,

I have now been for the last six months an inmate of
Captain Fearon's family, having been desired by Major
Gascoyne to live apart from my family. You must be aware
that thus being separated from my children I have lost
ground in their affections (I mean particularly the little ones)
and I have also experienced the most unmanly persecutions
from Dr Greenwood.

I know that public matters of business have detained you
from fulfilling your intention of coming to Nelson, had I
been aware of the lengthened period that has elapsed since
I expected your daily arrival – I think I should have endured
my miseries and unkind treatment from my husband untill
[sic] you arrived, but when I left home I expected you in a
week or two. However, now I wish to learn, if possible by
return of post, whether you will be able to come soon – or
not? As in the latter case I should wish to leave this place
where I am subjected to much suffering from my proximity
to the home I am so unjustly deprived of and, if agreeable to
Mr. Strang, pay him a visit until you come to Wellington.

Mr. Greenwood's conduct has been so contrary to all
that is gentlemanly or like a Christian that the whole society
here has taken it up, and in all probability a requisition
numerously signed will be forwarded to the Bishop
requesting that his continuance in offices of trust connected
with the church is detrimental to its true interests. Mr. Tudor
has acted like a brother to me – may God reward him and
also Mrs. Fearon.

I will not go into any details at present but would
implore you if possible to hasten your presence here – I can
do nothing to regain my rights until then. Pray let me have a
line by return of post as you may suppose that I have already

suffered from months of anxiety and suspense, but I know so
well that I have right on my side that I put my trust in that
power who can and will protect the innocent and the
oppressed.

Hoping to hear from you in reply at your earliest
convenience,
Believe me my dear Donald
Your affectionate cousin
I. A. Gascoyne

I have had most affectionate letters from the
Dunstaffnage ladies, expressing much grief and indignation
at my husband's conduct and regretting that I am not near
you for help. Major Gascoyne's family also write in the
kindest manner, saying they cannot understand the total
change in Major G as they knew and had seen his devoted
love for me for so many years. All my friends here are
looking forward with impatience for your arrival, as they all
seem to think you alone can set matters right.

The situation deteriorated further. Dr Greenwood joined his
wife in publicly disparaging Isabella's conduct as a wife and
mother. Claiming in front of a gathering of all the 'gentlemen
in our neighbourhood' that Isabella had written him a letter, he
implied some impropriety on her part which she vehemently
denied as a '*tissue of falsehoods*'. Dr Greenwood also insulted
Mr Tudor, insinuating that the deacon had sordid motives in
supporting Isabella, and criticized his ability and character as
a clergyman, solely – Isabella believed – because he upheld
her cause. Mr Tudor wanted to sue Dr Greenwood, but was
prevented from doing so by 'his office' as clergyman. Isabella
suspected Dr Greenwood knew this would be the case, which

in her eyes made his behaviour even more ungentlemanly, unprincipled and dishonourable. Privately Isabella accused Greenwood of being a liar. 'I only wish I were a man that I might unmask him.' Instead she had to hide behind Mr Tudor, who was unable to explain his own motives (which were no more than sympathy for a parishioner) since McLean had forbidden Isabella or her friends from discussing the matter in public.

Dr Greenwood accused other Isabella-supporters of falsehood, but was forced to retract publicly, and Isabella cringed that her friends had been slandered on her account. Nevertheless Dr Greenwood managed to bias many in the neighbourhood against her and she hated him for the unscrupulous way he used every possible means of winning golden opinions of himself. She feared that she and Mr Tudor were going to see their reputations destroyed.

I can do nothing untill you come. I have been most shamefully and cruelly treated both by my husband and the Greenwoods. My children have been told falsehoods, and taught themselves to state falsehoods as truth. In short they have been lead by precept and example by their own interests to dishonour their mother. They found all their comfort and welfare depended both with their father and the Greenwoods, in upholding that wretched woman and what wonder, considering their long absence from me, that they have acted as they have been instructed.

I have been away from my home now for seven months – suffering all that hatred and bad feelings could inflict on me – not even one of my children allowed to come and stay with me. I shall write a duplicate of this letter for fear of its not

reaching you. Pray forgive all the trouble I give you and
believe me, my dear Donald, your attached cousin
I Gascoyne

Isabella was briefly distracted from her troubles by some shocking news from Bengal. The sowars of the 3rd Light Cavalry who were garrisoned in Meerut (Isabella's 'most delightful station' where she had married Charles), already aggrieved by successive pay cuts and the increasing remoteness of their British officers, were given cartridges for their new Enfield rifles which had to be bitten open and, it was rumoured, were greased with the tallow of the cow and the fat of the pig – one sacred to the Hindus, the other abhorrent to the Muslims. It was a stupid administrative mistake, and quickly corrected – most officers, like Charles, respected the different caste rules of their men – but it ignited a fear that this was a surreptitious attempt to convert them to Christianity. In May 1857, while Fred was en route to Hawke's Bay, the conflagration exploded.

Cities all over north India were besieged, but Isabella was particularly distressed by events in Cawnpore. In the city where she and Charles had blithely begun their married life, and where they had enjoyed the lavish hospitality of the delightful Nana Sahib, over a thousand people, including three hundred and thirty women and children, were besieged in the cantonment for twenty-one days. Their besieger was none other than Nana Sahib himself. Having for years entertained the garrison, now he destroyed it. All but four British officers died, most of them from Charles's brother regiment the 2nd Light Cavalry, while their women and children were taken to the Bibi-ghar, a mud-walled house beside the Ganges, and butchered. Isabella's heart bled at the news of the defilement and massacre of some of her oldest friends, many of whom she had known and loved for over twenty years. Among them were Isabella's close friend Susannah Blair, daughter of Colonel Kennedy of the 5th Light Cavalry, and her children; for fifteen years they had lived in Cawnpore waiting in vain for the return of Captain Blair from Afghanistan. Now their limbs and trunks and severed heads were flung down a well, nearly filling its fifty-foot shaft. 'I am overwhelmed with grief,' Isabella wrote to McLean. 'I have written to dear Mrs Blundell who is the only person who can sympathise fully in my feelings having so many friends there herself.'

British revenge was swift and equally bloody. Town after town was reoccupied, fort after fort stormed. Although the sowars of the 5th Bengal Light Cavalry were successfully disarmed, and only one officer was killed, events consumed the regiment. When the mutiny was eventually crushed a year and a half later, the Indian armies were shaken up and the 5th Bengal Light Cavalry was split into two and renamed the 5th European Light Cavalry, right and left wings. Colonel Kennedy, who had been on furlough during the mutiny, was the only familiar name left on the masthead.* Not only that: in November 1858, it was announced that the East India Company, the greatest commercial and military company that ever existed, was to be swept away and its power transferred to the British crown. Nana Sahib, one of the few princes openly to throw in his lot with the mutineers, vanished into myth.

---

* Forty-seven battalions of the Bengal Army mutinied, twenty were disarmed and only seven (one a Gurkha battalion) remained loyal.

The Indian Mutiny betrayed and killed not only Isabella's friends, but also the world she knew. It shook her not only because of the horror, but because it undermined the whole concept of Empire as a force for good, and stimulated a fear of 'the native'. With this came a loss of understanding and sympathy and a loss of respect that helped to poison race relations not just in India, but throughout the Empire. If such a bloody uprising could happen in India, why not in New Zealand?

Isabella reflected the news through the prism of her own pain. She hoped the dreadful accounts of so many loved friends would influence Charles's heart and bring him back to her. Surely now he would answer her letters, and join her in her commiserations and prayers? Surely he would comfort her in their shared grief? No – he didn't even reply.

McLean ignored her too, and Isabella began to suspect that Charles and Dr Greenwood had ordered him not to come. She was in despair. She had done as he asked, and not discussed her affairs; the result was that she had become an object of ridicule and slander, from which she was prevented from defending herself. She had done as Mr Tudor advised, and not returned to Pangatotara while Miss Sutherland remained; the result was that she had lost her home and her position as wife and mother. Abandoned as a child, she now felt abandoned as an adult; deprived of her parents, she was now deprived of her children. All her brothers were dead, many of her friends were dead, the East India Company was dead: she had no one to turn to except Donald McLean, and he seemed to have abandoned her too. She beseeched him not to delay any longer. '*I want my children. My husband is dead to every right feeling I believe, but still what right has he to deprive me of my little ones? I am almost*

heartbroken. Oh for mercies sake – come and give me your
advice and assistance – and I shall ever be grateful to you.'

In October 1857 Charles, encouraged by Dr Greenwood,
declared that nothing would induce him to part from Amelia
Sutherland. Instead he wanted to separate from Isabella for life.
If she refused to submit to the separation, he would cease his
subscription to his widow's pension, and leave her penniless.

Isabella vowed she would never agree. Charles had not
accused her of anything wrong in her behaviour as a mother or
a wife. His complaint was that her 'disposition and manners'
were now displeasing to him. One thing was clear to Isabella:
she might have lost her husband's heart, but nothing on earth
would separate her from her children. They were, she warned
McLean, her only tie to life.

Her children did not return her affection. When she met Izzy
on the street in Motueka, her eldest daughter rudely turned the
other way. Izzy had always adored her father. As a five-year-old
in Clifton, she had once returned from a walk and seen Charles
and his mother descending arm in arm from the drawing room.
'I have a vivid recollection of this,' Izzy wrote later, 'for I thought
they looked so loving and beautiful, almost like angels. I cannot
remember a time when I was not passionately fond of my father
and did not admire him immensely. He was the handsomest of
men. Grandmama was beautiful too, her expression making her
most lovable, and father was like her.' Izzy's memoirs included
no such eulogy to Isabella. In fact, she mentioned her mother
only once, and then slightingly and in passing. Her childish
ambition, she revealed, was to be like her grandmother, 'whose
goodness and kindness to those less fortunate than herself made

her beloved by everyone.' The implication is that her mother did not share these qualities.

Mary also 'disgraced herself by her open disregard and undutiful conduct to me'. The Greenwoods snubbed Isabella too, passing her as strangers, and Charles ignored her, except to send a blank envelope once a month enclosing a cheque for £8 for her board and lodgings.

Isabella was cheered briefly by the arrival of John's sons, Fred and Arthur Gascoyne, from Clifton. Charles had invited his nephews, offered them a home and to set them up in the new world, but now refused to do anything for them, and would not even have them in the Bungalow. Isabella was ashamed. She thought them very fine, honourable lads, and invited them to stay with her at Mrs Fearon's house and, despite her own limited funds, was able to spare a few pounds to start them off. They soon left for the Wairau Valley to seek work as shepherds, leaving Isabella alone again.

Another bleak Christmas passed – the Fearons' six children a poignant reminder of Isabella's – but in January 1858 Donald McLean came at last and took her away to Auckland.

It was a happy interlude. More distanced physically and mentally from the source of her torment, she was able to enjoy McLean's company, and by the time they parted her mode of address had evolved from 'My dear Mr. McLean' to 'My dear cousin', 'My dear good cousin', 'My dearest cousin', and now to 'My dearest Donald', by which time she was signing herself (rather cloyingly) as 'your affectionately attached Aunty'. She also made lasting friendships with McLean's brother John and his wife Jessie, who were on their way to farm in Christchurch.

Isabella still grieved for her children, and was not allowed

respite from her pain. She was pursued by three letters from
Charles, each proposing a separation on the same grounds of
dissimilarity of disposition, and Isabella's nervous irritable
temper – as shown, he stated, at various periods of their
married life but especially when at sea, and towards several
individuals, namely the captains of vessels during storms, and
native servants on several occasions. His main reason for sepa-
rating was because of her dislike of, and wish to rid her family
of, the presence and influence of her former servant, Amelia
Sutherland.

> *On appealing to my husband, he replied that I was totally*
> *unfitted for the management of a family in the Colony, and*
> *that it was his will and pleasure that this person should*
> *retain her position as, in all respects, a member of the family,*
> *as a Lady and entire mistress of the Establishment, no one*
> *being invited to the house but by her permission, and that*
> *he would not permit the smallest interference on my part.*
> *I must, he states, agree to these arrangements, or to a*
> *separation – moreover threatening me that if I returned home*
> *without submitting to these arrangements, he would restrict*
> *my personal liberty, allow me no intercourse with any*
> *neighbour, or Mr. Tudor, and that he would leave me*
> *pennyless at his death etc etc.*

Isabella fought back. She knew Charles's means were too
straitened to provide her with a home as comfortable as the one
he deprived her of in favour of 'this woman', and that to drive
her forth homeless and childless at her time of life, after being
his wife for twenty-three years, was the act not of a Christian
gentleman but of a tyrant. She declared that his long residence

in India had led him to adopt certain views regarding the absolute power of the husband over the servile submission of his wife, views she regarded as more suitable for a Muslim than a Christian.

Although she had committed no crime that could justify her expulsion from the family, Isabella admitted to having been bad tempered during their last years in India, and while she attributed this to nursing a large family in a hot climate, it is true that Isabella was not the meek passive little wife that Charles might have preferred. It was generally known, even by the Roads Board in 1874 when there was some dispute over a route across her land, that Mrs Gascoyne was 'not one to take difficulties lightly'. She even managed to have 'quarrels and *scolds*' with McLean during her stay. Nevertheless, she insisted that now she was better than she had ever been. She felt she could cope at the Bungalow. 'I am no longer so nervous or irritable, and I have acquired so much Colonial information now, as would enable me to manage my family as well as other ladies do – provided the present bar to our peace were removed and I have a fair chance of showing what I can do.' Miss Sutherland's presence was, she considered, 'most improper', and made her uneasy and unhappy, and that ought to have been sufficient cause for Charles, as her husband, to remove the woman. Isabella was willing cheerfully to do her utmost to fill Miss Sutherland's role, to work hard, to carry out Major Gascoyne's wishes in all things, 'and to imbue the children with ideas suitable to Colonial Life – to contribute as far as possible to their comfort and welfare in the country he has chosen to adopt as his home.'

Charles was unmoved. Isabella begged McLean to write on

her behalf, 'trusting that God, who alone can give wisdom, may direct and bless your endeavours with success.'

My dear Major Gascoyne

I intended some time ago to have paid you a visit at Motueka, in the hope that I might settle some of the differences between yourself and my cousin, but my duties in this Island have prevented me from going.

I need not say that my cousin's position, estranged as she is from her family, is a most painful one, and I very much trust as there are no doubt faults on both sides, that the past may be forgotten, and that matters may be so arranged as to provide harmony and close relations in your family.

I shall not dwell upon the consequences of allowing children to grow up in a state of alienation from their mother, although I deeply feel that they cannot be otherwise than deplorable. I trust therefore, my dear Major Gascoyne, that you will duly consider the course to pursue in the present instance. I feel confident myself, that on mature reflection, you will perceive that it will be a clear matter of duty on your part, to restore Mrs. Gascoyne to her proper position in her family, as I cannot discover that she has done anything either as a wife or a parent to forfeit that position.

The state of unhappiness and suspense in which my cousin is placed induces me to make one request which I trust you will comply with, and that is, to come up here on a visit yourself, when I have no doubt we can settle all differences – I shall be delighted to see you, and may be of some assistance to you in devising plans in reference to your future prospects. In any case I trust that I may soon hear from you.

*Of course you are aware that Mrs. Gascoyne is at present
on a visit to me.*

I am, my dear Major
Yours very truly
Donald McLean
Auckland May 13 1858

Charles took two months to reply. He may have felt guilty,
but he had also been busy with a wedding. On 21 May 1858,
Izzy married John Greenwood. Isabella suffered in the knowledge that not only had she been excluded from her daughter's
marriage, but that the loathed Greenwoods were now part of
her family.

Charles's handwriting had become a mad sprawl, with single
words lolloping the whole way across a page. Sometimes even
the horizontal of a crossed 't' strode across an entire sheet. The
characters were loose, the ink blotted, the words without shape
or rhythm. It could not have been more different from the beautifully formed copperplate in which he had written to Lord
Salisbury thirteen years earlier. Those letters had suggested a
cultivated and well-organized man; now it looked as if he had
lost control.

Nelson, 31st July 1858

My dear McLean,
I received your letter of the 13th May – a few days since.
The subject on which you write is a painful one and
approached by me with great reluctance. All reflections
thereon still lead me to the same results, namely that it is
better that Isabella and I live apart.

I prefer it because I consider it best for them that the

children continue with me – until they attain seniority, the
age of fifteen, after which it will be optional with them to
reside with either parent.

If the allowance I offer appears small, my income must
be considered. My pension amounts to £130 per annum –
besides this I have ewes – eight hundred of them on Mr.
Morse's run, on terms, and a few cows in my fields, but
beside these I have no funds of any description whatever.
I have with me six children, (the eldest eighteen years of age)
to feed, clothe; and care for. Should my means increase I
should certainly increase the allowance in proportion. At my
death it will have more than doubled.

Believe me – my dear McLean
Sincerely yours
Charles Gascoyne

My dear Major Gascoyne,
I received your letter of the 31 July enclosing a cheque for
17.6. which I have duly handed over to Mrs. Gascoyne.

It cannot be a pleasant subject to either of us, to refer to
the unhappy differences that have occasioned an estrangement
between yourself and my cousin, but it is nevertheless a duty
that devolves upon us as men and Christians to have such
matters amicably adjusted and rectified.

For my own part I am truly anxious that this should be
accomplished and I have written to Dr Greenwood as an
intimate friend of your own, to request that he will confer
with you on the subject.

To urge separation where no sufficient cause can be
assigned for it appears to me quite out of the question. With
reference to my cousin, the alleged fault it seems is that of
unstable temper. I am unable to offer an opinion on this

subject, as I cannot say what her temper may have been but of this I feel satisfied that grief and unhappiness have so far covered up what may have been faults of this description that I feel assured there is no possibility of a recurrence of them. She feels most painfully a separation from her family and her case is certainly one of peculiar hardship.

I am really in hopes that the difficulties on this subject have now subsided and that you will calmly reconsider the decision you have formed about living separately. It occurs to me that the present differences can be easily disposed of by dispensing with Miss Sutherland's services – for my own part I am desirous that this question should be settled either by arbitration or by any other fair and impartial mode of adjustment, that may be decided upon. To let matters continue in their present state must be exceedingly disagreeable to all parties concerned.

I remain

. . .

Signed Donald McLean

The Auckland party broke up. John and Jessie McLean were travelling south to Christchurch, and Isabella accompanied them as far as Wellington where they all spent a happy Christmas with Mr Strang and dear little Dougie. Donald McLean boarded HMS *Iris* to join Governor Gore-Browne at a great korero in Taranaki, where discontent was again brewing between the settlers, the Maori landowners and each other.

When they said goodbye, Isabella, overwhelmed with gratitude for all his kindness, was unable to thank Donald with words, 'but I am sure you know me well enough now to *feel* that I understand and appreciate your large and warm heart.'

They were, she believed, firm friends for life. She was touched by the generous way he slipped a £5 note into her hand, but determined to risk hurting his feelings by returning it as soon as she received a remittance that she hoped was awaiting her in Nelson, 'as I think you have already been at quite enough trouble and expense for my visit to Auckland'.

After Isabella and John and Jessie McLean boarded the SS *White Swan,** Isabella remarked that 'We all felt very dull last evening on parting from you, and so did you I daresay, though you would not acknowledge it.' Nevertheless, she was buoyed up by her Auckland interlude, and loved the journey south, relishing the companionship of her fellow passengers. Almost for the first time since she arrived, she was distracted enough from her problems to be able to enjoy New Zealand's landscape. She walked in a wonderful kauri forest, and while other passengers climbed a mountain she and Jessie McLean stayed at the bottom and sybaritically ate peaches. Although afraid to land in New Plymouth because the sea was so rough, she was entranced by conical snow-peaked Mount Taranaki, 8,000 feet high. This had been her first ever view of the colony, in the frontispiece of *Hursthouse's New Zealand*: curvaceous hills, bucolic cows, a settler's pretty homestead and towering over them – not

---

* Four years later, in June 1862, the SS *White Swan* was holed by a rock while travelling south from Napier to Wellington, and the captain was forced to run the ship aground to save the passengers, who camped on shore or in a nearby homestead for three days before being rescued. It was a shipwreck that nearly sank the entire government, because on board and travelling to Wellington for the first meeting of the General Assembly outside Auckland were fifteen members of the House of Representatives and four members of the Legislative Council, including the Prime Minister, William Fox, the Colonial Treasurer, the Chief Justice and the Attorney General.

menacing but spectral, almost angelic – the snowy peak of the volcano. How could Hursthouse have known that his vision of rural bliss would seduce Charles and destroy his family?

On leaving Wellington and bidding farewell to Mr Strang, John and Jessie McLean and dear little Dougie, Isabella suffered new pangs of parting and loneliness. Douglas had temporarily sated the craving she felt for her own children; she loved him as if he was her son, as she did McLean (even though he was only a few years younger than she). As for Jessie McLean, Isabella felt she could happily live with her for the rest of her life, if she hadn't had other ties. 'I miss dear Jessie every hour in the day. For the last few months she has so completely occupied my thoughts and affections that I feel quite a blank. John too was so kind and affectionate and until I said goodbye I did not know how much of my heart he had gained.' When Jessie, by now in Christchurch, suffered a miscarriage, Isabella longed to go and take care of her; instead she felt she ought to remain within reach of her own family, who wouldn't allow her anywhere near them.

This was made painfully clear when Isabella was greeted off the ship in Nelson by Arthur Gascoyne, one of her Clifton nephews. He bore bitter-sweet news: sweet that Izzy had been 'safely confined of a little girl', bitter that Mrs John Greenwood, as Isabella now referred to her eldest daughter, had given birth to her first grandchild and none of the family had seen fit to notify her, let alone invite her to share their joy. In a sympathetic letter to Isabella, Jessie McLean expressed a total lack of comprehension as to why Izzy should not want to be with her own mother at such a time – and such a loving mother! – and why Isabella should be treated with such deliberate heartlessness. 'But I am not singular in that it puzzles wiser heads,' Jessie wrote.

Arthur Gascoyne also brought news from Pangatotara. Having some business to discuss with his Uncle Charles, he had visited the Bungalow a few days earlier, and could report that Amy had become a very sweet-looking girl, while the two little girls had improved in both looks and manners. 'Alas,' Isabella wailed to McLean, 'that I who could feel most happiness in their improvement and welfare am denied all participation in it. The children are all forbidden ever to mention my name!'

Because she made her situation worse by continuing, despite McLean's admonishing, to discuss her private affairs with all and sundry (this was one source of 'all our quarrels and *scolds*'), McLean begged Isabella not to return to Motueka but to remain in Nelson for the two months until he arrived. After only one night Isabella risked McLean's anger by disobeying. Although she dreaded returning to the place where she was scorned as her family's – and society's – outcast, she argued that it would look very strange if she did not go back to the Fearons, and everybody would gossip that her former friends had thrown her off, or that McLean had thoughtlessly abandoned her to strangers. So by January she was back at Northwood, both she and Mrs Fearon having solemnly promised that they would not allude to family matters, and would confine their conversation to 'indifferent subjects'. In any case, Isabella said, she had no plans to go anywhere or see anyone, and if Mrs Fearon was asked about Isabella's intentions, she was instructed to say that she did not know.

That Sunday for the first time in ages Isabella braved church, the main social gathering of the week. On her return Mrs Fearon

told her that Mary had been sitting in the seat next but one to
Isabella. Thankful not to have seen her because it would have
caused her such distress – to be so close and yet so far – Isabella
vowed not to go to church again until Donald came to Motueka
and could accompany her. Meanwhile she had heard nothing
from Fred for four months. As for Charles, she was told that he
had got into a morbid unhappy state partly because of his financial difficulties, and partly (Isabella hoped) from self-reproach.
She was worried he might do something 'prejudicial to the
family'. He had become indifferent to everybody but Amelia. She
begged McLean to persuade him to go on a trip to see his run:
'Unless I get him away from home I have no hope of any
improvements in his conduct to me which is most unkind.'

Isabella lived a quiet life reading and working, or riding
along the beach where she was sure of meeting no one. She saw
Izzy only once, but her daughter cut her, and Isabella feared she
was now a Greenwood, and the link between mother and
daughter broken forever. John Greenwood made no effort to
breach the rift between his wife and mother-in-law. He did not
once call on her, and when he saw her in a shop in Motueka he
turned his back. Isabella was not invited to see her granddaughter.

Then McLean came at last.

> *My dear Mr. McLean,*
> *If it be your intention, as I hear, to visit The Bungalow on*
> *matters of a domestic nature, I have particularly to request*
> *that you will come alone.*
> > *Yours sincerely*
> > *CM Gascoyne*
> > *20th Feb 1859*

McLean visited Charles – alone – and tried to reconcile the warring Gascoynes. Charles gave McLean a friendly welcome which led McLean to hope that Major Gascoyne's better nature would prevail. He was wrong. Charles proposed that Isabella should go back to Clifton, taking two children with her. This meant the family would be sundered, and Isabella would never see her other children again. Isabella declined this proposal out of hand. Instead, McLean suggested she moved to Nelson, and be allowed to have at least one child with her at all times. Charles refused.

Nothing was achieved. Isabella was sincerely grateful for McLean's trouble, and for cheerfully undergoing so much disagreeableness on her behalf, but she sensed that Dr Greenwood and Charles had swayed him, and that his sympathy for her was running dry. 'I could see, during your short visit, that *even your* sense of right and wrong in this matter had been influenced by Mr Greenwood's statements and also by Major G's.'

Mr Tudor now told Isabella that rather than part from Miss Sutherland, Charles planned to sell up and return to England or the Continent. He threatened to take the children and go from place to place so that Isabella could never find them. If she tried to follow he would withdraw her allowance and widow's pension, leaving her penniless. Not only penniless, but shamed, abandoned.

It was the last straw. Isabella was so devastated that she decided to confront Charles herself and ask if it was true. In July 1859, after more than two years' absence, she defied Charles's ban on her coming to Pangatotara and rode the six miles home.

Isabella must have felt tremulous as she arrived, unsure of

her reception. Little had changed on the farm, just a few more sheep. Amy heard the horse's arrival and came to the door, but when she saw her mother she turned angrily away. Isabella called out that she wanted to speak to Charles, and Amy ran back inside, returning to tell her that Charles 'declined the interview'. Mary appeared, and the two of them bitterly upbraided her for leaving home and causing them so much misery and exposing them to scandal. Then at last Amy threw her arms round her mother and entreated her for their sakes to return, promising that if she did so, she and her siblings would do all they could to show their love and gratitude.

Isabella retreated to Northwood, but was followed by a letter from Charles saying he would permit her to come home to the Bungalow provided she complied with certain conditions. She was to sign a declaration that Miss Sutherland was driven only by Christian motives, nothing more, and had been so during the whole of her stay in Major Gascoyne's family; that Isabella would in no way interfere in his domestic arrangements with Miss Sutherland; and that she would see nobody at all – except the Greenwoods.

Isabella accepted that McLean could or would do nothing more for her. If she wanted to avoid destitution and separation from her children she had no alternative but to accept. Rather than retaliate she would put her faith in God, and bear and forbear.

In November 1859 Isabella wrote to McLean and for the first time for two and a half years headed her letter 'Pangatotara'. For better or worse, she was back, although not as wife or mistress of the home. Any lingering hope she had of Charles feeling less vindictive towards her had soon evaporated. 'Until some change takes place my life must of necessity be one of constant suffering and humiliation, which for the sake of the children is doubly to be regretted.' Permitted to educate the children for four hours a day, she had in effect swapped places with Miss Sutherland.

My dear Donald,

I have just recd. a few lines from Mr. Strang, telling me that you had been suffering from Rheumatic fever on the Coast, which had grieved me very much. As he only mentions this much, I am in ignorance whether you had good nursing and medical attendance but I know you always make the best of everything and your spirits would carry you through what could prostrate most men. I had been so long without hearing of or from you that I wrote to him, to enquire about you and Douglas, who seems now quite out of my reach, until he can write letters for himself. Dear boy, I often miss him very much, with all his wild spirits I never knew a more loving child. I hope his Grandpapa will be gratified with a sign of him soon.

I am, as I last wrote to you, employed all day and every day teaching the children, and making them clothes. To all enquiries why I returned, whether I believe all the reports etc, I now invariably give the same answer: that I particularly wish to avoid all references to the past, and that though when away from my husband I felt obliged for sympathy etc, now as I reside under the same roof I never allude to the subject of my own affairs in any way.

I find Amy a great comfort. She continues her lessons very steadily though engaged to be married, I think I mentioned to you, to Frederick Greenwood. He is the best of

the family I think, and treats me with courtesy. They are not
to be married for a couple of years.

I occasionally go to Motueka to church on Sacrament
Sunday but otherwise seldom leave the valley for a day. I feel
very lonely at times but I have peace of mind in
endeavouring to benefit the children, and they are improving.

Pray send my love to dear Douglas when you write to
him, and believe me with every kind wish,
Yours affect.
Isa Gascoyne
Pray remember me most kindly to Mr. Strang, I will answer
his letter shortly.

ELEVEN

Rough Water

If McLean sometimes appeared to have heartlessly abandoned Isabella, this was because he was steeped in and distracted by native affairs. New Zealand's race relations were deteriorating, particularly in Taranaki where land was, as ever, in dispute. Despite McLean's efforts, the Maori still owned most of it, but left vast acres untouched and apparently unwanted. Settlers argued that by refusing to sell this land, the Maori were preventing them from expanding their farms and building towns and roads. They argued that the Maori owned five-sixths of the land in the North Island, but while the Maori were dwindling away, the number of settlers was spiralling. They complained too of being subjected to extortion by the few Maori who remained, and of living under the rule of the tomahawk.* The settlers were hungry for what they considered to be surplus land, starving for it, and they had run out of patience.

Many Maori chiefs had welcomed the pakeha when they first arrived, but soon the Maori found that where British surveyors

---

* Settlers referred to Maori weapons as tomahawks, using the Native American term, but the Maori weaponry included not only the tomahawk, which was introduced by the settlers along with axes and firearms, but also their traditional long- and short-handled clubs, mostly made from greenstone (jade or nephrite) or whalebone.

came and measured up the land, British rule invariably followed. The Maori in the South Island were few, but in the North Island every extension of white settlement saw the Maori being pushed out. As towns grew, the Maori chiefs began to realize that the pet pakeha was really a cuckoo outgrowing its parent and its nest, covetously demanding more and more land, and forcing the Maori deeper and deeper into servitude. The cuckoo had also brought with it a bewildering array of European influences that were destroying tribal unity, community and the chiefs' own authority. Where once their rule was paramount, now it was derided by increasingly demoralized Maori, many of whom had turned to drink and prostitution – the familiar companions of the white man. Maoridom was already under threat from tribal war and imported diseases, but from the mid-1850s many chiefs realized that succumbing to the immense pressure to sell more land could all but finish them off.*

As opposition to land-selling grew, Maori chiefs from a number of different tribes got together for the first time to form

---

* Maori numbers were dwindling dramatically. By the end of the 1850s there were 60,000 Maori, and when the new Governor, Sir George Bowen, took up office in 1868, he ordered his Minister for Native Affairs, J. C. Richmond, to make a survey of Maori numbers, attitudes, customs and health, and discovered that the Maori population had now reduced to 45,000. Some, such as many of the missionaries, blamed this decline on the Europeans' obsession with land. Others, such as Premier William Fox, argued that far from causing Maori decline, the European influence had led to the adoption of better food, better dwellings, better general habits of life; instead the cause of their decline was their 'utter disregard' for essential social and sanitary conditions. Others believed they had wiped each other out in tribal warfare. The Maori with their fierce clan loyalties had always fought each other, but guns provided by the colonists had raised the stakes; it was for guns that many Maori had eagerly sold their unwanted land.

a confederation. In 1857 McLean attended a vast korero along with two thousand Maori and a throng of missionaries, traders and government officials, at which the Maori elected an old but much-respected chief, the splendidly named Potatau Te Wherowhero, as king. He was chief of the Waikato, a swathe of wild mountain and forest bordering Taranaki, which few pakeha had managed to penetrate; by 1855 only three hundred pakeha lived here, all in remote, isolated settlements. At this stage the aim was to govern Maori affairs through a peaceful union of chiefs under the masthead of this pro-pakeha Christian king.

While Isabella was moving back to Pangatotara, McLean rushed away to another crisis in Taranaki, probably relieved to have Isabella off his hands. Her private dispute was mirrored by a much larger one that demanded all his time and diplomatic skills. Conflict was growing over six hundred acres whose ownership was disputed. One chief wanted to sell, another did not, but Governor Gore-Browne nonetheless proceeded to send in the surveyors. It was a huge blunder. McLean was not actually present when this sale was agreed, but as Native Secretary, answerable directly to the Governor, he took the blame.* A bitter little war followed in 1860. The 'Kingites' joined the fray; these were followers of King Potatau's son and heir Tawhiao. Dismissed at the time for being weak and a puppet of his king-making generals, Tawhiao, whose tight face swirled with

---

* New Zealand acquired self-government in 1852, and by 1856 enough differences of opinion had been shelved to make it workable. But largely to protect the Maori from the settlers, Governor Gore-Browne reserved for himself, as representative of the crown, the management of native affairs, with McLean as his minister.

tattoos, was in fact hugely influential as a symbol of Maori confederation and independence. Gore-Browne hoped to give these
'rebels' a short sharp shock and check their growing independence, but instead the government suffered a succession of
defeats. Although McLean managed to negotiate a ceasefire in
1861, this was the start of the Maori Wars that would rage
sporadically for the next thirteen years, and suck down the
Gascoynes – and most of the country too.

Back at Maraekakaho another McLean brother, Archy,
replaced Alec as manager. He and Fred took an immediate dislike to each other, and the hasty-tempered Fred decided in 1860
that the change in management 'made him want a holiday'.
Charles and Isabella wrote independently to Donald McLean
with concern that Fred had left his establishment several
months earlier without giving them any idea where he had gone.
Charles was anxious that Fred might not be 'living in a
respectable manner', while Isabella heard that her son 'talks of
going to the Feegee Islands', adding disparagingly, 'I hope he
will lose this silly notion.'

Eventually in late 1860 Fred returned to Nelson, but rather
than going back to Pangatotara, he kept his distance from his
parents, and indirectly declared his allegiance by choosing to
work with his brother-in-law, John Greenwood. The Greenwoods' sawmill had been withdrawn from sale and Fred joined
John on the two hundred acres of wood and open land where,
beneath a rough canvas roof, a huge water wheel turned belts
and pulleys to power a circular saw that planked the flitches. It
was strenuous, skilled work. The business failed to flourish. A
bush fire that spread from a farmer's burn-off destroyed many
of the trees, and more setbacks followed when John's ship the

Nautilus, built specially to transport the timber, was wrecked not once but several times, and after being stolen by the captain was finally sold at a heavy loss. Far worse still, John's frail younger brother Charlie Greenwood joined them at the mill, but found the work so arduous that it killed him. The whole venture was a disaster.

Fred was unemployed, and broke. All the time he was hearing talk of gold. Particles had been found on the Aorere River as early as 1842, and by 1857 the *Nelson Examiner* reported that gold worth £70,000 had been found near Collingwood during the previous twelve months. Diggers flocked from all over New Zealand and Australia and even straight off immigrant ships from England. In March 1859 Isabella had written to McLean from Motueka that 'the only piece of news I know of is that gold has actually been found about three or four miles from this place on the banks of the river. About twenty men are there at present and some pieces upwards of 1 oz in weight have been positively found. Should it prove a fertile gold area the whole scale of things will shortly be changed hereabouts.'

In 1861 gold was found on the West Coast and another rush began. A procession of men tramped through Nelson, Californians in tall boots and cowboy hats, and long-haired Australians fresh from the Victoria goldfields, swigging from bottles of grog. Hard on their heels came suppliers herding bullocks over the dangerous passes, and behind them the card-sharpers, prostitutes and thieves. Everybody was on the move, everyone knew someone who knew someone who had made their fortune, enough to set themselves up in style. John Greenwood's brother Graham had an alluvial gold-mining claim near Collingwood, where he was so successful that he was able to invest in a sheep farm in Motueka (where he lost the lot). Like a pied piper, gold lured away the men, leaving behind the women, the elderly and the infirm, but as fast as the men flocked, so others returned disillusioned and hungry. Fred chose not to notice their despair. He had witnessed the excitement in Melbourne six years earlier, and now he too was stricken by the feverish anticipation of riches. He caught the disease.

Nearly all the diggers had a mate. You needed a mate not just for company, but also to help with the work. Fred persuaded one of his Gascoyne cousins – another Fred – to go with him.

They began in Collingwood, where the gold rush had started. Overnight this swampy peninsula had been transformed into a shantytown of stick-and-canvas hotels, brothels, grog shops, banks and mining offices. By 1857 there were 2,500 diggers in Collingwood, a fiftieth of the total population of New Zealand. Four years later, when the two Freds arrived in 1861, the place was unexpectedly quiet.*

Presuming the miners were out on their claims, the two Freds wasted no time joining them. They trudged with their picks and shovels, pans and cradles and sluice boxes up the bullock track bordering the Aorere River. Along the banks the scrub had been uprooted, trees felled, the ground pocked and plundered. The rush looked as if it was over and nothing remained but the detritus of the abandoned claims – old sacks and boxes, broken tools, ends of rope, old bottles, piles of wash

---

* During the previous year most Maori miners had returned to Taranaki, where they were fighting against the settlers and each other. Many of the European women and children fled the war to take refuge in Nelson, thereby temporarily filling the labour shortage created by the gold rush.

dirt: the remnants of the heyday when gold sprang out of the ground and brandy was brought up to the celebrating miners in buckets rather than bottles. Now the place was silent. Had the two Freds left it too late?

After wading across the Slate River, they begin a perilous climb towards Moonlight Flat, Brandy Point, Chinaman's Flat and the One Ton Claim. The names were memorials to their predecessors' adventures; maybe one day there would be Gascoynes' Claim commemorating their own stupendous find.*

As they climbed they heard above the churning of the river the reassuring noise of grating and groaning and chinking. The grating was the sound of pebbles rocking back and forth in cradles, and the squeaking and groaning was the windlasses turning to speed up the extraction of the dirt. The chink was of picks on rocks. Bearded scarecrows squatting on the shingle looked up glassy-eyed from their dishes, and waved briefly then returned to work, frightened of missing a flake. Others emerged blinking in the sun from cock-eyed hovels or makeshift dwellings under projecting rocks, and shouted ribald greetings.

The Freds pressed on. They wanted to reach the bush line and probe into the backcountry where no one else had been before. By nightfall they reached the tip of a creek. Was this the best place to peg out their claim? What if they marked it out just one inch from the gold? Too bad: they were too exhausted to go on.

There was a tiny patch of flat land on which to erect their

---

* Much of the river was barricaded with cliffs, which they had to edge their way along. Above Brandy Point they had to negotiate Jacob's Ladder, Precipice Walk and Break-Neck Steps. Later this year (1861) the river was bridged for the first time, making the Freds' lives easier.

tent and collapse on the hard ground. The next day they prepared their living quarters. This was dead work, and Fred was
frustrated by how much time it wasted when he wanted to dig
out his fortune *right now*. But they had to be systematic: first
they had to cut down trees, saw the trunks into planks and build
a weatherproof shelter hard up against the cliff, roofed with
flax, with a separate bush chimney made of bits of old iron
clamped together. They had to build slab beds, slung with sacks
as mattresses. They had to gather dry sticks for the fire, dig a
latrine and build a rat-proof store and fight off the sand flies
and mosquitoes.

Only after the dead work could they start panning. It took
a few tries to get the hang of it, using a deft twist of the wrist
to swirl the dish underwater, slipping the sediment over the edge
and leaving a few handfuls of fine gravel. Gold, which is heavier than gravel (and one and a half times as heavy as lead),
would sink to the bottom. One day the final swirl left a few
glints of colour clinging to the outer edge of sand and pebbles.
The cousins' shouts of jubilation could be heard down the
creek, and a few miners climbed up to see. Their disappointment was palpable: just a few grains! An ounce, worth $8, was
about a thimbleful, so they had a long way to go. But the Freds
were undaunted: they had a show, and every shovelful now had
its promise, the promise of prising precious metal out of the
earth.

They made enough only to cover their expenses, no fortune.
When they ran out of tucker they lived on a repulsive porridge
called burgoo, and when winter came the river turned icy.
While thawing out at the bush tavern at Washbourne's Flat

they discovered that no one else had been lucky either. One miner had died in a rock fall, another had caught bronchitis.

There was one standby for prospectors down on their luck: the Baton goldfield. This lay south of Pangatotara, not where the Baton River flowed into the Motueka River but further upstream at the junctions of the Skeet and Ellis rivers, where the Salisbury brothers had a farm.* It was one of the first goldfields in New Zealand to be consistently worked. The Freds shouldered their remaining swag and decamped.

The Baton tumbled over rocks and boulders, a fast-flowing stream with steep drops to the river below. The Gascoyne cousins built a dam using sandbags and rocks, and diverted the flow through their sluice boxes. It was mid-winter and the snowmelt was freezing, but day after day they were rewarded with a film of gold left on the ridges of their sluice boxes and on the sacking floor.

One night in June 1863 it began to rain. The men crouched in their wooden hut while drips from the roof snaked down their backs. The ground outside turned into a myriad of rivulets and swampy pools. The river's flow became a swirling sucking whoosh and it rose, then rose again, a turgid yellow force tossing flotsam on its angry crest. The two Freds piled rocks and spare sandbags on top of their dam, but the current forced them back, and the sacks they had laboriously filled with shingle were

---

* The Baton River was named after a runaway sailor boy named Baton or Batteyn Norton who worked on the Salisburys' land in the 1850s. The Salisburys and Baton Norton found gold on the beaches where the Baton joined the Motueka, and soon hundreds of diggers had arrived. They did not bother the farmers, but their dogs harassed the sheep, so the Salisburys sold their valuable farm for a pittance.

thrust aside and the river spewed through, vomiting itself downstream, taking with it not only the remains of the dam, but all the sluice boxes, and all their gold.

When the deluge subsided they saw the devastation. Hunks of timber from other people's claims higher up, shreds of clothing swept from other people's huts, sandbags from other dams. Of their own stuff, little remained. After two years of toil, filth and wet, they were ruined.

A neighbouring digger clambered over the debris with some mail. Fred's letter bore an official-looking stamp and he opened it gingerly. It was an offer of a commission as a lieutenant in the newly raised Colonial Defence Force, Hawke's Bay squadron. The New Zealand government had decided that in view of Maori unrest, local forces would have to be raised, and the Colonial Defence Act of 1862 authorized the formation of the first regular force, a five-hundred-strong body of mounted troops. Fred was to be one of them. It was a lifeline, just as he was sinking, and what he'd always wanted – not the Honourable East India Company, to be sure, but soldiering none the less. His cousin was equally delighted to get an ensigncy in the Waikato Militia.

The two Freds hastened downstream, pausing at the Bungalow to say goodbye.

TWELVE

Holy Water

The North Island was sliding deeper into chaos. While Fred was on his way back to Pangatotara, Isabella wrote to McLean to express concern over the increasing unrest, and her dread that the South Island might go the same way. She begged him, 'Do write and tell me what you think of Maori affairs.'

Gore-Browne had been sacked as Governor, and Sir George Grey returned. To McLean's fury, he proposed restoring to the Maori the disputed land in Taranaki that had caused the 1860 war. In a puzzlingly contrary way Grey also punished those so-called Maori rebels who had fought against the government by seizing their land – a massive three million acres – and handing it over to the pakeha for settlement.* His justification for this confiscation was that it was the traditional Maori punishment for those defeated in battle, so was something the rebels would understand. One aim was to cripple burgeoning Maori independence; another was to supply settlers with land. It seemed a good idea at the time and McLean thought so too.

The Maori chiefs were so enraged by the land confiscations

---

* The New Zealand Settlements Act, passed in December 1863, entitled the Governor to declare that any land owned by any tribe who had, during the previous twelve months, been 'engaged in rebellion against Her Majesty's authority' would now be appropriated for settlement.

that by the time Isabella wrote so anxiously to McLean, many had declared their support for King Tawhiao. The King not only vehemently opposed all land sales and confiscations, he also encircled the King Country in a pale that no pakeha was permitted to cross without the King's permission, on pain of death. The Auckland settlers feared an attack from the King Country at any moment.

Meanwhile the settlers were alarmed by reports of a new religion named Pai Marire, or Hau-hauism. They had reassured themselves that most Maori had forsaken cannibalism and slavery and polygamy for monotheism, humility, forgiveness, churches, European clothes, houses and a cash economy. Now they were terrified by an image of fiendish tattooed 'Hau-haus' garbed in flax cloaks, with feathers protruding from their top-knots, gripping their clubs, thrusting out their tongues, dancing around Niu posts like flagpoles, chanting, '*Hau! Hau!*' and then tucking into a hearty meal of human flesh.

In fact Pai Marire meant 'the good and the peaceful', and mixed some traditional Maori beliefs (not necessarily cannibalism) with the Maori version of Christianity and its founder's own millenarian beliefs. But – and here the settlers were right to be afraid – Pai Marire also totally opposed land sales or confiscations. Although it was committed to non-violence, it was a force of passive resistance, and not all the faithful were pro-peace. It also had the attraction of being independent of the missionaries who many Maori believed were as greedy for land as the rest of the settlers. Pai Marire spread like a burn-off. Soon almost every Maori village in Taranaki had a sinister-looking Niu pole at its centre. King Tawhiao rejected his absurd baptismal name of Methuselah, and was converted.

In 1863 Grey built a military road leading straight to the King

Country. 'No words', Isabella wrote vehemently in June of that year, 'can be too strong in condemning Sir George Grey's policy.' She was right to criticize the Governor. Despite his promise to return the disputed land in Taranaki, in 1863 some disgruntled Taranaki Maori, threatened by Grey's manoeuvre and encouraged by one of King Tawhaio's henchmen, killed nine colonial soldiers. On 4 June 1863, a British commander ordered his 870 troops to retaliate and 24 Maori were killed. Sir George Grey decided to invade the King Country and finish off this unacceptable Maori rebellion once and for all. By supporting their King, the Maori were deemed to oppose the exercise of British sovereignty. If the settlers' motive was land-hunger, Grey's was the desire to enforce Queen Victoria's rule over all those who, since the Treaty of Waitangi, were considered to be British subjects. Grey intended to govern not only in word, but in deed.

While this cloud of war was massing over New Zealand, and a cloud of rain unleashing itself over Fred's claim, Isabella told McLean that the cloud which had darkened *her* home had been lifted. Fred arrived to find, to his astonishment, that his family was happily reunited. What had brought about this reconciliation? The answer was God, who had come to in the valley in the form of James George Deck.

James Deck had disembarked in Motueka the same year as the Gascoynes and bought land nearby. His beard flowed like an Old Testament prophet's and his handsome face had a look of benign determination. He had been brought up in Bury St Edmunds by a passionately religious mother, who always prayed with her children before punishing them. In 1824, two years before Charles joined the East India Company, Deck had taken up a commission in the 14th Madras Native Infantry, during which time he became so convinced of his own sinfulness that he drew up a code of good resolutions and signed it with his own blood.

Deck's aim was to distinguish himself in India, before returning home to enter parliament. God had other plans. When Deck returned to England on furlough he was stirred by a rousing Church of England sermon, married the daughter of an evangelical clergyman, and dedicated his life to winning not seats but souls. Back in India he converted several fellow officers, but he felt that his beliefs clashed with soldiering so, in 1835, he resigned his commission, intending to become a clergyman in England.

It was while his father-in-law was christening his baby that Deck first had doubts about the Church of England. The Bible made no mention of infant baptism, which had evolved because of the high rate of infant mortality, and the fear of having to bury an unbaptized baby in unconsecrated ground and thereby consigning it to Hell. Since James Deck believed that what was written in the Bible was the test of everything, by not following the word of God, the Church of England failed that test. In fact he found no justification in the written word for most of the practices of the established Church, including the very existence of the priesthood. Could not all men transmit the word of God? Deck came to believe that all ministers, whether Episcopalian, Presbyterian, Baptist, C. of E., or anything else, were a denial of the scripturally based priesthood of all believers, and interfered with the guidance of the Holy Spirit. He abandoned not only the living he had been offered but the Church altogether. Without job or home, he and his large family subsisted, according to a descendant, by 'looking only to the Lord to supply their temporal wants, a trust never disappointed'.

In Devon and particularly in and around Plymouth he met

others who shared his anti-clerical views. People were abandoning the established Church in droves. Isabella described James Deck as belonging to no sect of Churches, but that he and those who thought like him were generally termed Plymouth Brethren.

In 1843 James Deck settled in Wellington, Somerset and then in Weymouth where he won souls from what he scorned as the 'godless' High Church. The movement mushroomed. At this time Deck wrote over a hundred hymns. Simple, direct, earnest and tender, many of them were so popular that they were included not only in the earliest Nonconformist hymn books, but in Church of England hymn books too – and are still sung today. Until then hymns were rare. Congregations had to sit through the interminable droning of metrical psalms or to an unruly band scratching away in the church's west gallery, and the High Church Anglican clergy often derided hymns for their vulgarity and sentimental doggerel, or for their unseemly arousing quality which could lead to all sorts of licentiousness. The Church did not officially sanction the singing of hymns until 1820. It was Dissenting congregations like Deck's who first lifted up their voices in song.*

James Deck's hymns were a success, but his purpose was always serious: to praise God and His creation, to convert

---

* Charles Wesley is said to have written an astonishing 6,500 hymns, and his brother John compiled the first major denominational hymn book in 1780. With their catchy tunes and rhythms and stirring or touching lyrics, they were the pop songs of the day, sung at all occasions – open-air ceremonies, matches, rites of passage, around the piano in the parlour, births, marriages and deaths. They were one of the main things that lured congregations away from the Church of England. It was not until *Hymns Ancient and Modern* was first published in 1860 that the Church of England, alarmed by the desertions from its ranks, really caught up.

sinners, sustain the righteous, comfort the sad, to educate and to help the faithful to express their faith.

Divisions were growing between the more sectarian Closed or Exclusive Brethren and the more ecumenical Open Brethren, who allowed non-brethren Christians to take part in their meetings. Deck tried to mediate between them but failed, and after being partially paralysed by a stroke in 1852 the doctors prescribed a long sea voyage and an immediate end to preaching. Deck emigrated to the 'other' Wellington, and thence to Motueka.

Tragically, only three months after landing, his wife, mother of their eight children, died. 'Alas!' Deck wrote, 'the past, the present makes more drear; the house remains, but gone the inmates dear.' His own health recovered, he remarried, had five more children and, ignoring his doctor's advice, quickly set about 'witnessing for his Lord and Saviour' among the settlers. At his home in the Moutere hills outside Motueka he held the first ever Brethren meeting for breaking bread in New Zealand.

Isabella was ripe for conversion. Not only had her own Nonconformist beliefs taken root on the *Broxbournebury*, but she was also immediately attracted to this sensitive, warm-hearted man. With McLean so far away, and Thomas Tudor having left for England in 1861, perhaps Deck could meet her need for a father figure, even though they were the same age. Charles too was drawn to him; as well as sharing his experiences of the East India Company, Deck was a charismatic preacher, a leader (though not an authoritarian one) and a linguist literate in Latin, Greek and Hebrew, and fluent in French. In short, he was someone Charles could respect.

One core of Brother Deck's teaching was that there was no

hierarchy: everyone could transmit the word of the Lord. The other was that infant baptism was meaningless: only adult baptism was sanctioned by the New Testament, since first you had to show that you believed.

Fred discovered that while he was further upstream seeking gold, the faithful of Pangatotara had gathered on the banks of the Motueka River and three members of his family were led into its cool waters. Charles wore a white shirt and trousers, while Isabella and Amy wore long white shifts. They sang some of Brother Deck's hymns, then each in turn was permitted to speak. In front of their fellow believers, they described their sins and humbled themselves before God. Maybe Charles admitted publicly that he had treated his wife cruelly, and had 'walked in lasciviousness' and committed adultery – if indeed he had. Maybe Isabella admitted that she had not borne her new life in the colony with fortitude, that she had been jealous and angry. Maybe Amy confessed to her disrespect towards her mother. Their hearts acknowledged the depths of their own wickedness. As James Deck put it, 'Many of us have drunk, and deeply too, of Babylon's intoxicating cup: we have lived long in the "far country" and eaten of its dainties and husks.' Then each described how they had gone astray like lost sheep, but how the teachings of Mr Deck and his family had led them to greater light and knowledge of the Truths of the Gospel, and now they acknowledged the Lordship of Christ in their lives.

Too young to be baptized, Charlie, Charlotte and Caroline watched from the bank as their parents and sister waded into the river. The spotless white clothes billowed as the water deepened, then Brother Deck plunged them beneath the surface. He did not make the sign of the cross over their foreheads, but simply offered prayers to God. They rose gasping from the river to a new life dedicated to Christ, leaving their old life of sin to be swept out to sea. This was not simply a cleansing process, but a watershed, a birth. They were resurrected, dead to the world of sin, born anew in the Lord. 'Nicodemus saith unto him, How can a man be born when he is old? Can he enter the second time into his mother's womb, and be born? Jesus answered, Verily, verily, I say unto thee, Except a man be born of water and of the Spirit, he cannot enter into the kingdom of God.' (John 3: 4–5.)*

Isabella's spiritual journey mirrored her earthly one. The river, which carried her to Pangatotara nine years earlier and deposited her on its ferny banks to begin her new life as a pioneer, was the very river that now bore her into a new life free from sin.

This life, however painful, was merely a path towards the ultimate joy not of death, but of Christ's own rebirth, his second coming. Every moment of anguish was assuaged by the anticipation of this great event.

Meanwhile Fred had been up to his knees in a tributary of the same river, waiting for a second coming of his own.

Isabella marvelled to McLean that 'Mr Deck has been instrumental in working a most wonderful change not only in our family but among all the neighbours of the valley, who now with only a few exceptions have become totally changed char-

---

* James Deck was more inclined towards the 'Open Brethren'. Exclusive Brethren believe in household baptism, in which all members of the household, possibly including servants, are baptized in the bath.

acters. Those who were notorious as Drunkards, as bad sons or husbands, and as most quarrelsome bad neighbours, have become quite opposite characters'. The drunken husbands gave up the drink; the prodigal sons returned; the quarrelsome neighbours sought reconciliation.

Pangatotara was no longer the valley of darkness. The sheep and lambs that grazed around them in pastures green, beside quiet waters, were daily reminders of their own rebirth as lambs of God, 'without blemish and without spot'. (1 Peter 1: 19.) God was their father and their shepherd, and they dwelt in Sion.

These reformed souls were so convinced of the truths Deck preached that they erected a simple timber meeting room beside the river in the Gascoynes' front paddock. Here beneath plain white walls, unadorned with a crucifix or any other decoration, they met to emulate the brotherly love of the early Christians. On Sunday mornings they sat on rough wooden benches arranged in a circle, as the Lord gathered his disciples, around a central table on which lay the Bible, James Deck's hymn book, the bread and the cup. Whoever was leading the service proposed one of Deck's hymns, which they sang unaccompanied, then came a prayer followed by another hymn. 'Jesus I rest in thee, In thee myself I hide; Laden with guilt and misery, where can I rest beside? 'Tis on thy meek and lowly breast, My weary soul alone can rest.' There was no service sheet or prayer book; they simply recalled the Lord's words in an informal liturgy, and remembered their own sins, and that Christ had paid the price for those sins and commanded them to remember Him. Then came the key moment not only in the service, but in the week. Brother Deck stood to give thanks and break the loaf of bread, which was handed from one to another around the room in silence, followed by the wine in a silver cup. Then the plate was passed round, and the collection redistributed to the needy among them.

Despite men and women being equal in the eyes of the Lord, in his letters St Paul instructed women to keep silent in church, and to aspire to woman's 'meek and quiet spirit'. The Brethren followed this literally, but it was subtle: the women participated in the meetings, but *silently*. Although it was against Isabella's nature to keep quiet about anything, she cherished this stricture since it was written in the Epistles. It was God's Word, and to have a Word to obey was reassuring. The regulations of the East India Company had found their substitute in a system that governed every aspect of life, both material and spiritual, in the wild backbush of New Zealand.

One rule Isabella tried hard to follow was St Peter's first Epistle (3: 1), in which he exhorted wives to subject themselves to their husbands, and acknowledge themselves to be the weaker vessel. Sister Gascoyne, as she was now styled, found solace in this self-abnegation; she was a Victorian wife, longing to worship her husband in a way she had been prevented from doing. Although she was subject to her husband, most Brethren households were, however, matriarchal – the Brethren said of themselves that the man was the head, but the woman the neck. In domestic matters Isabella ruled, a role she had sought to retrieve for years. Plymouth sisters were not doormats; she subjected herself to Charles willingly, and therefore empowered him, but it was she who gave him that power. Besides, she may have seen her subjugation as conditional, since he had to follow the scriptural injunction to honour and love his wife, something he may have found difficult.

The Bible also exhorted 'ye younger, submit yourselves unto the elder.' So Isabella's undutiful children were brought back into line, and the family regrouped in its traditional hierarchy. The Brethren believed in the sanctity of the family as a symbol of the great family of believers, and after Isabella's years in exile this was balm to her soul.

Before James Deck left for New Zealand, he had written a touching little book called *Joy in Departing*, and this gives an insight into the intense, passionate religiosity of the Deck household that the Gascoynes now tried to emulate. The book described the death of a beloved foster son in Wellington, Somerset in 1845. When Augustus Clarke first joined his family, Deck had been forced to chastise the child 'with an aching heart' for his exceeding sinfulness, and required him to purge his conscience with self-denial and subjection to the Word. Aged only ten, Augustus wrote to his parents in 1841 of his sense of his own vileness. To Deck's joy the child was converted, and Jesus washed him in his precious blood, and made him one of his own dear lambs, and when the child accidentally stabbed himself in the eye, he died joyful in the knowledge that he was going to a happier place.

Fred returned from the godless and lawless goldfields to find his family home a scene of equally devoted asceticism. Every detail of life, however humdrum, was now devoted to the Lord. As Brother Deck put it, 'A true home on earth is a type below/of the home in His house of love.' The day began with family prayers. Of an evening Charles still read aloud to the assembled family, but Walter Scott or Shakespeare were now considered

salacious or romantic and were strongly rejected, 'For to be car-
nally minded is death; but to be spiritually minded is life and
peace.' (Romans 8: 6). Charles would have chosen something
more elevating such as a devotional work, or accounts of meetings held in Belfast or Bristol, or gospel tracts sent out by the
Weekly Tract Society in London. With more prayers the day
ended, early.

Grace always preceded meals. The meals themselves were
always frugal. On very rare occasions wine was permitted since
the Brethren were not excessively teetotal – moderation in all
things – but fresh water was preferred. The Brethren disapproved of bandwagons so there were no temperance meetings
or pledge-signings, but Fred found that an enjoyable evening
sharing a drink with friends, or singing secular songs, was now
condemned by his family as deeply shocking and ungodly.
Christmas was now derided as a heathen festival in which the
papist word 'mass' was appended with gross profanity to
Christ's name. At the Bungalow there was no roast turkey or
Dashwood pheasant, no plum pudding, no 'excess of wine, rev-
ellings, banquetings, and abominable idolatries'. (1 Peter 4: 3.)
Christmas Day, which had in any case been a miserable one for
Isabella since she came to New Zealand, was now no different
from any other.

Fred found that far from complaining about the primitive
conditions she suffered in Pangatotara, his mother now welcomed the lack of luxury as an absence of temptation. For years
she had been forced to dress simply; now that simplicity was
praised as a lack of corrupting self-adornment and vanity.
Cakes, parties, society, the garrison life Isabella had so enjoyed
in India – their absence was joyfully celebrated, and instead of

longing for a trip to fashionable Nelson, she avoided it at all costs since its pleasures could lure her heart away from the Lord. What did it matter if Miss Sutherland occupied the grandest apartments in the house, with all the best furniture? What did it matter if she had a handsome dress allowance while Isabella was still in the clothes she brought from England? Isabella had the comfort of virtue.

Separation from the secular world, easily achieved up this remote valley, was essential for the soul. 'Come ye out and be ye separated,' said the Lord.

However ascetic, Isabella's new life within the greater family of believers was also a companionable one. There were countless social events to look forward to. On week nights in the simple meeting room there were prayer meetings at which Brothers stood up to pray extemporarily, or Bible Readings in which they studied the Holy Scripture in detail and drew godly thoughts from the text, whether practical or doctrinal. It was a scholarly exercise; they knew the scriptures intimately but often vehemently disagreed about their interpretation. Amy had serious academic inclinations and enjoyed these discussions, even if she was not permitted to join in. The climax of the week was the Lord's Day. After Breaking the Bread in the meeting room in the morning there was Sunday School and Bible Reading, then an evening of Gospel preaching at which hymns and prayers were followed by a reading of the scriptures. The unconverted were invited to attend, and if they responded positively they were gradually absorbed into the weekly rituals.

During the 1850s the colony's total population had more than doubled, and in June 1863 Isabella told McLean joyfully that the valley was now 'thickly populated with *twenty* families', who included several well-heeled Indian Army officers who had fled the Mutiny and bought large plots of land on which they were building houses. Most were gathered into the Brethren fold. John Salisbury became a preacher taking the Word of the Lord to the godless goldfields of the Aorere River. Sadly the Gascoynes' nearest neighbours, Captain and Mrs Wright (to whom Isabella was deeply attached), were so shocked by the family's fanaticism that they refused to speak to them ever again. Evidently Charlie did not join his parents either, because he later married the Wrights' daughter Mary, and celebrated their marriage in the Anglican Church in Motueka.* No doubt attempts were made to convert Fred. For all the joy of Deck's conversion of little Augustus Clarke, a conversion of a child was far less profound than that of an adult who had already experienced the temptations and delights of sin. But Fred's rumbustious character could not have been more unsuited to his parents' asceticism, and he managed to resist.

Fred found that all attempts to sell the Bungalow had been abandoned, and life on the farm ticked along with Charlie, now eighteen, doing most of the work, while Mary (twenty-three), Charlotte (seventeen), Caroline (twelve) and the beautiful Amy (twenty-one), helped with the housework. The rift with Izzy had been healed: although she and John Greenwood lived in Nelson, Isabella declared blithely to McLean that 'some of their

---

* Charlie's marriage to Mary Wright was memorable because after the ceremony the newly-weds found the gate out of the churchyard locked; undaunted, they mounted their horses and leapt over it.

children were always visiting Pangatotara'. The Greenwoods senior had departed for Nelson where Dr Greenwood had become headmaster of Nelson College, and happily for Isabella, though perhaps not so for her daughter, Amy's engagement to Frederick Greenwood was broken off. Isabella told McLean that 'Major G', now fifty-seven, owned 120 sheep, but they were mostly out to terms so required little attention. There was something affectionate but faintly denigrating in the way Isabella described her husband as 'amusing himself with carpentering', and otherwise occupying his time as adviser and friend and doctor among his poorer neighbours, but Isabella enjoyed being able to talk of 'us' and 'we'. She wrote proudly that 'Major Gascoyne and I will both be most happy to have a visit from you, my dear Donald. Now that I have a happy home to ask you to visit us in, I hope you would enjoy seeing us all again.'

The icing on the cake (if cake wasn't too frivolous a metaphor) was that Pangatotara was to have a suspension bridge over the river and a *real road*. In addition Nelson, officially designated a city in 1858 (New Zealand's first) even though its population was still less than five thousand, now had steamers plying between New Zealand and Home, so while Isabella herself rarely used them to go anywhere, they whisked letters back and forth.*

The cloud in Isabella's life had not literally gone. Miss Sutherland remained at the Bungalow, but either her power had

---

* By the 1860s new iron hulls and screw propellers made steam ships lighter and more stable, faster and able to use far less coal, which meant that they did not have to stop so frequently to refuel.

dwindled in the face of God, or Isabella simply rose above it. Perhaps Isabella managed to follow St Peter's instructions to lay aside all malice, and all guile, and hypocrisies, and envies, and all evil speakings. (1 Peter 2: 1.) Perhaps she would be able to live with her governess happily ever after.

THIRTEEN

Te Kooti

Fred left his family in their state of grace, and retraced his steps to Hawke's Bay to join his squadron, just as the North Island again disintegrated into war. Sir George Grey persuaded the British government to send ten thousand troops to invade the King Country. The result was a clash between the British army and not just one or two Maori tribes, but a collection of fifteen of the twenty-six major North Island tribes, plus warriors of other tribes who, for the first time, fought together as a single entity under the flag of King Tawhiao. This was the first great force of Maori nationalism.

The Queen's army, many of whom were experienced veterans of the Crimean War, hugely outnumbered the King's two thousand men, but although the imperial troops dealt Tawhiao some major blows, they did not manage an outright victory. Many British troops sympathized with the Maori and saw their role as protecting the natives from the colonists who, they suspected, were exploiting them to help the settlers acquire Maori land. In turn, some colonial politicians despised the British army for its apparent weakness. When the war was deemed to have ended, the New Zealand government announced that it could no longer afford to contribute towards the cost of imperial troops, and proposed a 'self-reliant' policy, whereby they would depend entirely on local forces and Maori auxiliaries. The cost-conscious Colonial Office readily agreed that from now on the colony could defend itself, and withdrew all but one regiment. Shrugging its collective shoulders, the army erected a memorial to the fallen Maori, and went home.

On the other side of the North Island, Fred was being bullied into shape by Major (later Colonel Sir George) Whitmore. Small and wiry as a terrier, Whitmore had resigned his commission in the Queen's army and stayed on when the rest went home, buying a sheep run in Hawke's Bay which he worked with a vengeance as he did all things. He drilled his recruits relentlessly, with square bashing and bayonet practice, and although Whitmore was disliked, the Hawke's Bay squadron was soon the best-drilled militia in the colony. As far as soldiering was concerned, Whitmore was the real thing and Fred respected him – for now.

McLean, who had recently retired as Chief Land Purchase Commissioner and Native Secretary, was also in Hawke's Bay running Maraekakaho. Far from settling down, however, he had become not only agent for the government for the whole of the East Coast (from Napier right up to the Bay of Plenty and inland to Lake Taupo), but also Superintendent of Hawke's Bay province, and would soon be Member of the House of Representatives for Napier.

Concerned about the fighting in the North Island, and the possible danger to both her cousin and son, Isabella wrote to McLean, 'Do the natives around Napier look on you as a friend? Or otherwise?' The answer was that unlike the Maori in Taranaki and the King Country, the Hawke's Bay Maori were mostly contented. Despite McLean's strenuous efforts to persuade them to sell, and to prevent settlers from renting, they had hung on to much of their land, and leased it out at excellent rates. That year, 1863, their leases yielded £9,000 (£432,000 today), and by 1872 the leases would yield £26,000 a year – the equivalent of just over £1 million today – with more to be made from mills, timber, crops of wheat and maize, and earnings from shearing and other labour. Often the dapperly dressed pastoralists seen trotting past Napier's prosperous shops were not pakeha but Maori, and when they arranged to meet in town, the venue was their own Maori Club. Their chiefs, the distinguished Tareha and Renata, drove about their estates in coaches, dined frequently at Maraekakaho and entertained McLean with champagne in their own comfortable English-style houses. They owed much of their wealth to Donald McLean: it was to him they had sold the land that lay beneath the streets of Napier. This was not just about money, however: Chief Tareha had been a signatory of the Treaty of Waitangi, while Renata – powerful and ugly (even more so after he lost an eye in battle) – had been freed from enslavement to another tribe by Christian missionaries, with the result that his loyalties lay more with the pakeha than with his own race. McLean's power and charm enabled him to amass a network of such allies. In fact he could boast more influence over the province's chiefs than any other European in New Zealand. He was uncrowned king of the East.

While the Hawke's Bay chiefs were contented, unrest was spreading among the Ngati Porou further north on the East Cape. In 1865, Hau-hau missionaries had travelled over from the King Country, and the East Cape settlers were terrified to hear that as proof of the seriousness of their intent, they had brought with them the head of a blond pakeha soldier, Captain Lloyd of the 57th Regiment, who had been decapitated during a recent battle.* Many Ngati Porou chiefs were converted, and sympathized with King Tawhiao. Although too independent to submit to his rule, they shared his desire to stop all sales of Maori land. Factions for and against Queen Victoria broke out – Kingite Hau-haus versus Queenite Christians – and the latter summoned McLean and his Hawke's Bay Militia to their aid.

Silently embarking and disembarking his troops in the pitch dark, signalling, creeping through jungle, leading his men in 'skirmishing formation' and getting 'warmly engaged': here was Lieutenant Fred Gascoyne, in his element at last, doing what he had been waiting for ever since he was seven years old. After a few setbacks, the Hau-haus were crushed and the 'rebel' Ngati Porou rounded up and forced to swear the oath of allegiance to 'Kuini Wikitoria'. They were allowed out on parole under a thirty-strong guard commanded by Fred.

The battle was not over, however. Many of the Hau-hau had fled south to Poverty Bay, where they barricaded themselves into a formidable-looking pa. McLean followed, and persuaded the pro-government Ngati Porou chiefs Ropata Wahawaha and

---

* The Governor of New Zealand, Sir George Bowen, delighted in comparing the Maori with the clans of Scotland. The fate of Captain Lloyd echoed a description in Lord Macaulay's *History of England* in which a band of Macgregors cut off the head of an enemy and carried their ghastly trophy in triumph to their chief, whereupon every member of the clan laid his hand on the dead man's scalp and vowed to defend his slayers to the end.

Hotene to bring 250 of their best warriors to fight on the government's side.*

Poverty Bay, which lay between the East Cape and Hawke's Bay, was a beautiful crescent on the Pacific, ringed by a fertile plain and then a half-moon of forested hills that rose in the distance to the peaks of the untravelled and secretive Urewera Mountains. The tiny Anglo-Maori settlement of Gisborne pimpled both sides of the yawning mouths of the rivers Waimata and Taruheru. Originally a whaling station, on its swampy banks shanty-like European buildings had been flung up beside thatched Maori huts. There were stores selling all and sundry, a hotel, courthouse and post office, and two military redoubts, one an old Maori pa. Unlike Napier, eighty miles south, Gisborne looked as if it had only just begun. It was a sketch, waiting to be coloured in.†

Poverty Bay had a warm English climate, and the plains – six miles long and four miles wide, light, dry, fertile, well watered, dotted here and there with small patches of bush –

---

* Known as 'kupapa' by the Maori and 'friendlies' by the settlers, these pro-government warriors were not so much turncoats as allies, fighting against opposing tribes for reasons of their own. They earned good wages, and received government protection for their own tribal lands. All the battles of the Maori Wars involved kupapa. Their help was essential, not only because of their numbers, but because they understood both enemy and terrain in ways that the pakeha could not.

† Poverty Bay, known by the Maori as Turanga (and its port as Turanganui), was the place where Captain Cook first landed in New Zealand in 1769 – almost exactly a century earlier. The natives had been hostile, and six of them were killed. Cook's companion in the *Endeavour*, the naturalist Joseph Banks, was shocked by the killings and described it as a black day, the most disagreeable in his life. Cook named it Poverty Bay 'because it afforded us no one thing we wanted.' Turanganui was renamed Gisborne in the 1870s.

made excellent sheep country. But the Maori were not keen to give it up. The few settlers who had managed to get hold of land, mostly by marrying Maori women, had established sheep and cattle stations but these were on nothing like the scale of Maraekakaho or the great runs of the South Island.

A tight community of about a hundred and fifty whites and five hundred Maori, in Poverty Bay everyone knew everyone, even if they didn't like each other much. Now they abandoned their homes and fled to McLean's camp for safety, and in their absence some homes were looted. Meanwhile more Hau-haus were gathering inland and McLean feared they would descend on Poverty Bay and attack the Europeans. When the Hau-hau chiefs in the pa failed to surrender, a combined force of six hundred English and kupapa laid siege, and after six days the pa fell.

The Hau-hau prisoners were rounded up, but instead of being allowed out on parole under guard, as before, a stiffer sentence was imposed. They were loaded onto a ship and transported five hundred miles east into the South Pacific to a remote archipelago named the Chatham Islands.

In the prisoners' absence, preparations were made to confiscate their land.

Fred believed that it was only thanks to McLean's decisive action that Hau-hauism was contained. Others blamed McLean for rushing into battle, and thought this was the 'hinge of fate' that would bring death and barbarism to Poverty Bay.

In October 1867 the worst of the fighting was thought to be over, so the Colonial Defence Force, including Fred's Hawke's Bay Militia, was disbanded. It was replaced by a force under Whitmore's command of about six hundred Armed Constabulary, who were to combine military duties with manning redoubts, patrolling unsettled districts and carrying out public works like road- and bridge-building. They were given a smart blue uniform with a white belt and forage cap. Nearly all Fred's colleagues, many of them junior to him in both rank and length of service, transferred to the new force, but to Fred's fury, his name was not included. He had been sacked. His military career was dead.

Fred blamed it on a feud that was growing between Whitmore and McLean; Fred was punished for being McLean's cousin and friend. It was also true that Fred was, in Isabella's words, 'hasty-tempered'. He often considered orders ridiculous and made no attempt to hide the fact. Whatever the cause of his exclusion, this was the moment that Fred fell out of love with Whitmore. He would come to loathe him.

Humiliated and at a loose end, Fred loitered in Poverty Bay. He had no intention of returning to Pangatotara. Although fond of his family, he had little in common with them anymore. He enjoyed a swig of whisky and a ribald song, not Gospel tracts and other humbug. Fred was the very essence of pioneer: he had been a farmer, sawyer, gold prospector and soldier. Robust and vigorous, he wasn't going to spend his life on his knees.

Instead he hung around with some of his former fellow lieutenants who had fought with him on the East Cape. Promoted to captain in the Armed Constabulary and then major, Reginald Biggs was now appointed the government's agent in charge of confiscating Maori land, and also resident magistrate, running the settlement under the wider authority of Donald McLean. James Wilson, handsome and mutton-chopped, also made the

rank of captain and settled with his family nearby in Matawhero, while Charles (now Captain) Westrupp began a sheep
station not far away at Te Arai. While peace reigned they busied
themselves with farming, and Charles Westrupp also bred birds
for sale on behalf of the Acclimatisation Society. With the
'rebel' Maori who were blamed for the problems in Poverty Bay
safely exiled to the Chatham Islands, ordinary life in the nascent
settlement got underway.

For Fred there was also the attraction in Napier of a young
woman named Marion Carr. She was the daughter of old
friends of Charles and Isabella's from India, a robust sort of girl,
ideally suited to the life of an officer's wife. Now that life was
lost to him, and he had no means of keeping a wife, but there
was no harm in remaining nearby.

The only event of interest was when Sir George Bowen, the
genial and energetic new Governor, paid a vice-regal visit to
Poverty Bay and Hawke's Bay in June 1868. At a dinner in
Napier given in his honour by Superintendent McLean, Bowen
told the assembled company that a friendly chief had warned
him not to attack King Tawhiao. The King, the Maori chief had
said, was like a single tree left exposed in a clearing, and that
if he was attacked with iron and steel he would fall on his
aggressors and crush them, but if left alone, he would before
long wither and die. There was no point in war, not only
because over ten thousand British troops had already failed to
establish British law throughout the island, but because the
Maori population was in decline while the Europeans were
increasing. It was, Bowen argued, more politic and humane to
outlive than to fight the Maori. Bowen quoted a Maori chief

who had told him, mournfully, 'Our race is gone, like the moa.'*

Mr Richmond, Bowen's Minister for Native Affairs, replied to a toast from his fellow guests by asserting sanguinely that the clouds which had darkened the colony were now beginning to pass away. Thanks to the Maori Representation Act, which McLean had piloted through its various stages, the Maori had been given the vote in 1867 and four native members of the House of Representatives, who included local Chief Tareha, were due to take their seats for the first time the following month.

Bowen and McLean did not share Richmond's confidence. Notwithstanding his remarks about King Tawhiao, Bowen believed the Hau-hau were well aware they had not yet been conquered. Far from being at peace, the country was in a state of armed truce. The flame of discontent was smouldering, and could at any moment burst into a conflagration.

Three weeks later Isabella opened her copy of the *Nelson Chronicle* to read some startling news. The Poverty Bay Hau-haus on the Chatham Islands had, after two years' exile, captured a ship, made a brilliant escape and landed back at Poverty Bay. She read that 'the ringleader of the miscreants', named 'Koatee' or 'Kooti', had led these fanatical Hau-hau to capture not only a ship and its cargo, but all the arms from the

---

* A huge flightless bird, like an ostrich, which the Maori had eaten to extinction before the pakeha arrived.

Chatham Island garrison. They had rifles, double-barrelled guns, revolvers, pistols, swords, powder, cartridges and toma-hawks, and were no doubt keen to avenge their exile and the confiscation of their land. Naturally, Isabella's first thought was for the safety of her son.

Fred's first thought was for action. Swallowing his pride, he reported immediately to Major Biggs – once his colleague, now a superior officer – and offered to assemble a force of civilian settlers and 'a few friendly natives' to recapture the prisoners.

Few hard facts are known about Te Kooti: his birth date, place of burial, even his real name are disputed. No portraits or photographs have been proved to be of him. Born around 1832, it is known that he attended the Anglican mission in Poverty Bay in the early 1850s, where he acquired his detailed knowledge of both Testaments. At one point he even tried to become an Anglican minister, but was locked out of church for being drunk.

By 1852 he was notorious as one of a Maori group protest-ing over local land rights. They called it the 'redemption movement', trying to redeem land they had already sold and return the payments – usually horses or cattle. Te Kooti and his gang felt the settlers had cheated them, and in revenge they stripped settlers' houses, stole, drank grog and philandered, enraging not only the colonists but also the Maori chiefs whose authority they flouted, especially those they cuckolded.

When McLean defeated the Hau-hau in Poverty Bay, one of the prisoners rounded up was Te Kooti. He had fought *for* the government, but was arrested by a kupapa chief for being a Hau-hau spy, accused of removing bullets from his cartridges to fire blanks at the enemy.

Te Kooti protested his innocence, but if he was guilty, he was only one of many. While the 'friendlies' from Hawke's Bay and the East Cape were thought to be honest and dependable, Fred did not trust the Poverty Bay kupapa; he always suspected them of double-dealing, passing information to the enemy or firing deliberately above their heads. Many had ambiguous loyalties. Some changed sides, or fought on both sides at once, depending on the context or on old tribal loyalties and divisions; many – including Te Kooti – had family in the opposite camps. The charges against him may have been true.

Te Kooti was released because of lack of evidence but was later arrested again, and even today it is not clear what he was accused of this time. Te Kooti wrote to McLean begging to be brought to trial, but McLean ignored his pleas, possibly encouraged by resident magistrate Major Biggs, who considered Te Kooti a troublemaker, and wanted to get him out of the way.*

The *St Kilda*, a government steamer, was chartered to take the captured 'rebels' into exile. Te Kooti was pushed on board with the Hau-haus. When he demanded to know what he was accused of, Biggs and James Wilson simply shouted at him to 'Go on to the boat, go on to the boat.' Te Kooti was doubly

---

* Some people suspected Biggs was in thrall to 'Trader' Read, a Poverty Bay settler who resented Te Kooti's business competition and wanted his land; others have suggested that Read was willing to give land to powerful colonists such as Biggs on condition that Te Kooti was removed. Read was certainly in close contact with McLean, who took the final decision; Read even gave a party in McLean's honour at this time. It is also possible that Te Kooti's 'crime' was trumped up by a jealous chief whose wife Te Kooti had seduced. Certainly, when McLean arrived in Poverty Bay, his first step had been to seek the chiefs' advice.

incensed when one of the Maori chiefs parroted them: 'Go ona te poti.' Te Kooti would wreak revenge on them all.

The prisoners were deposited on the west coast of the main Chatham Island. It was mid-winter of 1866, and the Chathams were damp, flat and exposed. Trees lay flat, their tops blasted by the prevailing wind. Moors were dotted with gorse, and basalt rocks were worn into weird shapes by the wind. It was bleak until the sun burned through when the light was vivid on the golden grasses, and columnar clouds sent great shadows driving over the scrub to the volcanic cone-shaped mountains.

The prisoners were put to work building their own communal houses of ponga and flax, as well as the barracks, a sod-walled redoubt and surrounding trenches. Their clothing was inadequate, and they had to grow food to supplement government rations, but were not given ploughs for a year and a half, and even then they had no way of pulling them except by yoking themselves like bullocks. Many (though not Te Kooti) were chiefs of high repute; all resented the indignity.

They were billeted at a place named Waitangi. This miserable exile was the outcome of the humanitarian ideals and hopes of prosperity which lay behind the Treaty signed at the place of the same name – Weeping Water – twenty-six years earlier. It would soon lead to more blood and tears.

McLean promised they would return home after one year but their release was postponed. This was on the advice of Biggs, who complained that his efforts to confiscate Hau-hau land were being met, not surprisingly, with almost universal obstruction, and he warned that the released prisoners would exacerbate an already volatile situation. McLean wanted them to return to their old tribal lands – after certain areas had been confiscated as punishment – but the government was obdurate. So now the exiles were faced not only with losing their land,* but also an indefinite imprisonment on this chilly pimple in the ocean. The regime on the Chathams was in fact perfectly tolerable; it was broken promises the prisoners hated, the hope deferred.

Like many of the exiles, Te Kooti succumbed to the damp climate with a lung infection. During his illness he brooded on his misfortunes, and in states of delirium had visions that convinced him he was a mouthpiece of God. As he rallied from his sick bed, he began to preach, quoting from the Old Testament's lamentation of Jeremiah, which dwells on the pain of exile. Baptized an Anglican, Te Kooti had attended a Wesleyan mission, and toyed with Catholicism: now he adopted Judaism. His fellow prisoners liked what they heard, and soon he was holding illicit services in the sand dunes. Reminding his congregations that Jeremiah's lamentation ends, 'But let my heart and my hands be raised up in the search for my God', Te Kooti instructed them to raise their right hands in praise of God. His new faith became known as Ringatu, the Upraised Hand.

While Isabella and the Brethren of Pangatotara steeped themselves in the New Testament, and did their utmost to follow its austere strictures with both body and spirit, Te Kooti claimed the history of Exodus as his own. The settlers were the Egyptians, the exiled Maori the Israelites whose lives were bitter with hard bondage: God heard their cries and their

* There was also outrage amongst the Maori community that a great carved meeting house in Poverty Bay was, in 1867, dismantled and removed, without Maori consent, for display in Wellington – a move organized by Biggs. It is still in the museum in Wellington.

groaning, and saw their oppression. Te Kooti announced that just as God had visited Moses and charged him with the task of delivering the children of Israel out of Egypt, so had God visited Te Kooti on his sick bed in Waitangi and charged him with leading his people off the Chatham Islands and back to the promised land of milk and honey.

Te Kooti was not a chief, so had no authority over any particular tribe; his authority was derived from the power of his personality. He was not tall – about 5ft 9in – but was stoutly built, broad-shouldered and strong-limbed, and his large jaw and chin suggested a resolute will.* His impressive physical presence was boosted by his knowledge, his cleverness and his rhetoric. He also had a fine sense of drama: he would appear dressed in white robes like an Old Testament prophet, then suddenly disappear (through a secret door), and he astonished his congregations by raising his hand in the dark for them to see his palm glowing with an unearthly radiance – after he had painted his hands with phosphorus from match heads mixed with flax gum. Like James Deck, Te Kooti was a prolific hymn-writer (*himene* in Maori), and these hymns inspired his followers.

While Charles and Isabella worshipped God in their little timber meeting house in their paddock beside the Motueka River, Te Kooti and his followers gathered to worship in some

---

* This is according to a settler named Firth who met Te Kooti in 1870 and described his impressions to Donald McLean. Firth added as if with astonishment, given Te Kooti's reputation, that the features of the notorious rebel were 'not repulsive'. Firth continued, 'He has no tattoo; hair black and glossy; wears a moustache and short black beard . . . I noticed that he had lost the middle finger of the left hand.'

small sheds which they had built to sleep in during ploughing time, about two miles from their camp. As resident magistrate Captain Thomas observed ominously, 'it was not the form of worship of the Church of England.'

Fired up by magic and preaching and singing, the homesick prisoners determined to escape. Te Kooti prophesied the date of departure, and declared that if a rescue ship did not arrive, he would strike the sea with a rod and the exiles would walk home on dry land. Te Kooti was infallible: few doubted his word.

Two ships, the *Rifleman* and the *Florence*, landed at Waitangi harbour on the main Chatham Island in June 1868. While some of the prisoners carried out their tasks apparently as normal, others entered the prison guardroom and tied up four constables and the carpenter. Guns were seized and a second group of (now armed) prisoners, posing as workers coming to unload the cargo of flour, boarded the *Rifleman* and began a haka, ostensibly to entertain the crew. As the men dropped back the women came forward, 'shaking their bums' at the seamen; the sailors started to grab at them and were lured into the middle of the group where they were overpowered, all except the captain, who was on shore.*

The *Rifleman*'s chief officer described to the *Wellington Independent* (from where the story travelled to the *Nelson Chronicle*) how the Maori prisoners now swarmed on deck and threatened the crew with death if they dared to move. 'Several of the fellows had swords, which they brandished threateningly,

---

* Te Kooti had ordered that no one was to be killed, but one constable was murdered, possibly in revenge for his molestation of the wife of one of the prisoners. The 'bum shaking' was not mentioned in the New Zealand press, but is recorded in Judith Binney's biography of Te Kooti, *Redemption Songs*.

and also exhibited pistols and revolvers.' Meanwhile other prisoners captured the redoubt, tied up the resident magistrate and relieved him of his money, arms and tools. A third group transferred a cargo of pigs from the *Florence* to the *Rifleman*, sent the crew ashore, and cast the *Florence* adrift. Pursuit was now impossible.

Some 300 prisoners boarded the *Rifleman*. Under threat of death the crew was forced to set sail, but in the face of impossible headwinds had to return to Waitangi harbour. By now the humiliated resident magistrate had been released from captivity by the blacksmith, but he and the *Rifleman*'s captain had neither boats nor arms to do anything except watch impotently from the beach. The chief officer told the *Wellington Independent* that the prisoners appeared to be 'very jubilant over their performance, laughing constantly, and evidently pluming themselves on their outwitting the too confiding white man.'

The next day the *Rifleman* managed to beat out of harbour. According to the chief officer, 'A Maori stood near the helm, armed with a carbine and sword, to see that the proper course was steered.' The crew were not allowed to cook, but were served meat by the Maori and generally well treated. The chief, 'supposed to be named "Koatee" ', was clearly in charge, and he and four other chiefs occupied the cabin.

The storm raged on, so Te Kooti ordered his disciples to throw their greenstone treasures overboard. Many of these had been handed down over generations, and were almost objects of worship in their own right, but such was Te Kooti's power that his followers obeyed without question. When the winds blew as ferociously as ever, Te Kooti sent for his elderly uncle. Te Kooti had worked on his schooner as a young man, and been cared for by his wife when he was sick, but his uncle had informed the Chathams' resident magistrate about the religious services Te Kooti was conducting, which he considered blasphemous, and Te Kooti had accused him of being a disbeliever and spy. 'The unfortunate man was dragged on deck, his hands were tied, and notwithstanding his pitiful cries and resistance, he was pitched overboard, like a dog. He was seen for some time afterwards struggling in the water, but his cruel fellow countrymen did not relent.' The *Wellington Independent* headlined the story 'A FOUL EXPEDIENT FOR FAIR WEATHER'.

After the Jonah's execution the prisoners prayed and sang hymns for two hours, and the storm died away.

The *Rifleman* landed south of Gisborne at a secluded bay. The crew, released unharmed, were given a letter from Te Kooti to the government stating that Jehovah had delivered the Chatham Island prisoners from captivity. 'They are thy people and thine inheritance, which thou broughtest out by thy mighty power and by thy stretched out arm.' (Deuteronomy 9: 29.) They now wanted to be left in peace and not pursued.

G. S. Cooper, the government's investigator into the affair, wrote, 'It is difficult to say whether one's wonder is excited more by the precision, rapidity and completeness with which the enterprise was planned and executed, or by the moderation shown in the hour of victory by a gang of barbarous fanatics who in a moment found their former masters bound at their feet, and their lives entirely at their mercy.' Their amazing haul included tons of flour, sugar, wine, ale, arms and hay, which they used for their beds. The newspaper could not resist a chuckle: 'We have been told that one young lady went to the Chathams to be married; the ceremony was performed, but the

Maori took a fancy to the wedding dress, and it is highly probable that some favourite *wahine* is now disporting herself in this gorgeous robe on the shores of Poverty Bay.'

Major Biggs eagerly accepted Fred's offer of help. It was Sunday morning and Fred found most of the colonists in church at Matawhero. Giving them no time to change or fetch supplies, Fred rounded up about thirty pakeha men and forty Maori, although 'quite half of the last were of doubtful value', wrote Fred, 'for many of the Poverty Bay natives were disloyal at heart.' As for the settlers, they were a ragtag lot, most of whom had never held a gun before coming to New Zealand. Many had emigrated from inner cities in Britain where they had worked in factories or as clerks, and had no idea of soldiering.

They rode to Te Kooti's camp. It sprawled in a pebbly elbow crooked into a niche below a cliff, a beautiful spot strewn with the bleached bones of driftwood, a band of winter surf pounding the reef. Scrubby hills dropped to the bay and here Fred and the settlers lurked while three Maori went down into the camp.* Fred watched from his hideout as they shook hands and rubbed noses and walked amongst the makeshift tents made from the sails of the getaway ship. Children scurried between their legs, and women hunched over small fires. There were, Fred estimated, about three hundred people there. He had never seen Te Kooti before, and didn't now: it was said that Te Kooti ducked out of sight.

Fred reported to Biggs that the prisoners 'did not intend to fight unless they were interfered with'. Te Kooti simply wanted

---

* One of these Maori scouts, Renata Whakaari, was later imprisoned by Te Kooti, and executed.

to be free to travel unmolested up to the forested safety of Ure-wera Country on his way towards the Promised Land.* Later McLean insisted that had he been present, he would have let Te Kooti go: he had proved by his treatment of the Chatham Island guards and the *Rifleman*'s crew that he meant no harm.

Major Biggs was not convinced and hastily called a council of war. He did not trust Te Kooti to go quietly. While Biggs's settler militia was small, ill-equipped and untrained, Te Kooti was armed, arrogant and driven by religious fanaticism – and most Poverty Bay Maori sympathized with him. Biggs might also have remembered that he himself was personally guilty of forcing Te Kooti onto the boat, and that utu, or vengeance, was a potent force for the Maori. For a Jew, which Te Kooti now considered himself, there are few forces more powerful. 'And thine eye shall not pity; but life shall go for life, eye for eye, tooth for tooth, hand for hand, foot for foot.' (Deuteronomy 19: 21.)

Te Kooti's only viable route inland was up the valley of the Te Arai River. Biggs ordered his militia to Paparatu where they could cut the prisoners off.

Fred rode into camp with packhorses laden with provisions for the march just as Biggs was addressing assembled officers, volunteers and natives. Fred overheard him say, 'I will pay £30 [over £1,000 today] to anyone who will carry a dispatch for me to Wairoa.' Wairoa was the next settlement south, between Poverty Bay and Napier. The dispatch was a plea for military

---

* This land of milk and honey was to be beside Lake Taupo, a vast inland sea the size of Lake Geneva which sat like a belly button right in the centre of the North Island, on the fringe of the King Country.

support and reinforcements. Any messenger would have to cross Te Kooti's path. There was silence. Biggs repeated the offer in Maori. No one responded. Fred had a sudden fit of bravado. 'I will take your dispatch, Major, if you will lend me a fresh horse. And of course,' he added proudly, 'I don't want a money reward.'

Biggs looked round, relieved. 'You can have my horse.' Then he muttered, 'I do not like to ask you to do this, as you've been pretty hard at it already.'

Within half an hour Fred was mounted and off on a short cut over the hills. It was a journey of over sixty miles across rough Hau-hau-infested bush.* In the absence of a track, he had to rely on his knowledge of the country, along with his unfailing sense of direction that he had inherited from Charles. He spurred on the horse but knew he had to hold back a little to save its energy in case he was chased.

Early in the morning, twenty miles into the journey, Fred heard gunfire through the frosty air. Guessing that Te Kooti had ambushed the Poverty Bay volunteers, Fred wheeled round to help. Then he remembered he was on special duty and had to get the dispatch to Wairoa as soon as possible. Also, he had more chance of crossing the most dangerous part of the trail while Te Kooti was distracted by battle.

At nightfall Fred reached the bush near Whenuakura. Podocarps dangled lichen in beardy wisps, branches flicked and stung his face and when his horse stumbled over buried tree

---

* Te Kooti's Ringatu faith was different from Pai Marire, but Fred and most colonists referred to any anti-government Maori as a Hau-hau, synonymous for a rebel or criminal.

roots and slipped into leaf-litter and risked breaking a leg, Fred was forced to tether it and continue on foot. Clambering over rotting trunks smothered in greasy moss and ferns, grazing his shins on fan-like tree roots, he realized that unless he found a guide he might break his neck.

The clatter of tumbling water told him he had reached the Hungaroa River. He saw the flare of a fire on the far bank – the kainga at Whenuakura – and although he had no way of telling whether or not the inhabitants were friendly, he had to summon someone to canoe him across the river. He called, 'Coo-ee,' then waited, hunched in the dark, until he heard an echoing, 'Coo-ee.' A man carrying a firebrand clambered down to the river and pushed off in a dugout. Fred drew his revolver and crept to the waterside. When the canoe approached, Fred saw by the light of the firebrand that the tattooed ferryman was Korohina Te Rakiroa, a chief of great mana.

Fred retreated into the bush. Te Rakiroa called out, asking who it was, and why he didn't come to the canoe. Fred replied that he was afraid to move in the dark, and that Te Rakiroa must show him the way down the bank. The old chief growled a little, climbed out of the canoe and scrambled up the bank with his firebrand, whereupon Fred thrust his revolver in the chief's face and ordered him to guide him through the bush towards Wairoa. Te Rakiroa refused: it was late, it was dark, he needed to go back to his kainga to make several rama-rama (torches). Fred had no intention of allowing Te Rakiroa to alert his people that there was a stray pakeha at large, and at gunpoint ordered the chief to get going, adding that there were plenty of manuka branches suitable for torches right there where they stood. Fred promised to pay Te Rakiroa for helping him to find the road and, reluctantly, the chief agreed. 'It was bad travelling', Fred noted drily.

When the bush opened onto ferny outskirts, Fred thanked Te Rakiroa and told him he would bring from Wairoa anything the chief requested. Te Rakiroa was angry at not being paid immediately, but Fred had no money, so he had to accept Fred's word.

After forty-eight hours of non-stop travelling, Fred reached Wairoa, where everyone wanted to hear about Te Kooti's escape and Fred's flight through the bush, before he headed back towards Poverty Bay, pausing first to deliver the promised sheath knife, pipes, tobacco and matches to Te Rakiroa, who was amazed that he had returned.*

Relieved to find his horse still tied up in the manuka scrub, Fred descended into the open country by the windswept Waihau lakes, where he was pitilessly exposed to Te Kooti's scouts. He kicked on the horse at full speed, flanks spraying sweat, until he reached the shelter of the bush. As he eased his panting horse down a bank he met Paku Brown, the half-Maori son of a Poverty Bay trader, who was carrying a second dispatch from Major Biggs to Wairoa. Fred paused just long enough to warn him to race across the flats for the safety of the far ridge.

Two days later Paku Brown's body was found on the track a few feet from where Fred left him. Te Kooti had camped right

---

* Fred later heard that the very next day the old chief joined Te Kooti, taking with him twenty of his men. Te Rakiroa would claim that he had been taken prisoner by Te Kooti but had then chosen to stay with him, although as he had lost land to the confiscations he did also have a grievance of his own. Te Rakiroa fought with Te Kooti throughout the war, and became one of the main architects of his brilliant military strategy.

beside the lakes: he must have seen Fred but chosen to pounce on Paku. Te Kooti's brother was married to Paku's sister, but their kinship did not save Paku. After questioning, he was hacked to death, his corpse left exposed on the path in accordance with the Old Testament, left for the fowls of the air and the beasts of the field. Paku was also left there as a warning to other Maori who might contemplate helping the colonists.

This was the first deliberate execution of the war, and made Te Kooti his first enemies among his own people.

Fred pushed on, horse frothing, until he reached the high ground above Poverty Bay. Below spread the plain of peaceful fields grazed by sheep and cattle, the cosy homesteads and the little white-painted weatherboard church at Matawhero with its green tin roof, innocent of what was to come. He was all but home. Then he heard a whistle, and grabbed his revolver. But it was only James Wilson, a man with side-whiskers and a far-away look lying curled up in the scrub near the track. He had ridden out with Paku Brown but (luckily for him, though his luck would not last) he had been taken ill, exhausted by the retreat from Paparatu. Wilson told Fred that he and the rest of Biggs's volunteers had been routed: two men had died, and the rest fled, abandoning ammunition, rifles and eighty horses. Te Kooti had taken the lot. His strength was growing.

Fred was greeted at Captain Westrupp's outstation by none other than yappy little Colonel Whitmore, who had rushed up from Hawke's Bay. Enraged by the folly of the Poverty Bay volunteers in pursuing Te Kooti, and then allowing him to escape, Whitmore had been berating them as 'cowards and curs', earning their undying hatred. Now he ignored the fact that he had sacked Fred, and ordered him to take two Maori and turn back to pick up Te Kooti's trail.

They crossed ravines and rushing streams full to overflowing, and at dusk hid their horses and crawled through the undergrowth until they became aware, simultaneously, of voices just over a low ridge. They had reached the outskirts of Te Kooti's camp. If they were caught, they would meet the same fate as poor Paku Brown. Silently, they made hand signals to each other, then as they dropped ten feet into a gully Fred strained his left knee so severely that he fainted from the pain. When he surfaced he heard his companions whispering that Fred was dying, and that they had better hide his body and escape. He begged them to keep quiet until midnight, when they could help him to reach the horses, and make their escape. They agreed, even though their own lives were at risk, and at midnight hauled him, passing in and out of consciousness with pain, back to the horses.

As they emerged onto the plain at dawn, they met Whitmore at the head of his column of smart mounted constabulary who had come up from Hawke's Bay. By rights, Fred should have been among them; it hurt his pride to be seen by his erstwhile juniors as an insignificant – and injured – local volunteer. Fred pointed out to Whitmore where Te Kooti's camp was, intending to slip away and ride to Gisborne to see a doctor, but Whitmore stopped him and ordered Fred to ride with him. When Fred explained about his knee, Whitmore insisted that he was indispensable as a guide, and could be carried on a stretcher. This indignity was worse than the pain so Fred trusted himself to his little Ngakahi (the Snake), who could carry him over anything. Today was his thirtieth birthday and he felt like

LONDON
HOUSES
OF THE
XVIIIᵀᴴ CENTURY

No. 71, SOUTH AUDLEY ST.,
The Residence of
Col. the Hon. & Mrs. F. H. CRIPPS.

This Georgian house, in the manner of Isaac Ware, was built between 1736 and 1737, and is remarkable in having preserved its original decoration almost entire

WALKING down South Audley Street from Grosvenor Square, one can hardly fail to be struck by the individuality of this eighteenth century house which stands so boldly at the corner of South Street. With its fine portico built out over the pavement, it makes an undeniable bid for attention in a way that, from their circumscribed position, few London houses can attempt to do. Two centuries have made very little alteration to its exterior, and, what is more wonderful, its interior has escaped the usual changes of fashion. Even fifty years ago, when the eighteenth century and all its works

were abhorred, it was felt to be " a house of a very marked character." So Walford singles it out for special mention, though not forgetting to brand it as " heavy and dull." He adds that it is " by many attributed to Inigo Jones," regardless of the fact that the great architect had been eighty years in his grave before either street or house was thought of.

It is from Hugh Awdeley, the seventeenth century lawyer-moneylender-speculator, who died in 1662 " infinitely rich," that North and South Audley Streets take their name. The tale of his acquisition of the manor of Ebury, which is now the great Grosvenor estate, and of the problem, how he should leave his vast fortune, which the older he grew became more and more difficult to decide, has been told with delightful humour and raciness by Mr. Gatty in his two volumes on the sad history of Mary Davies. When at length "ould Awdeley" did breathe his last, worth no less than £400,000, it was his great-nephew and clerk, Alexander Davies, who, by the last of his many wills, became possessed of the Ebury lands. Of Awdeley's immense estate this old manor, which had once belonged to the abbots of Westminster, formed a comparatively unimportant part, being still entirely undeveloped and, as yet, of no great value. Indeed, Davies, instead of proceeding to build on the property he had inherited, actually bought land for the purpose in Millbank, and by the time of his death, in the year of the Plague, had involved himself in serious financial difficulties. None the less, his little daughter, Mary, was a prize well worth the trouble of catching, as her mother was shrewdly aware. Before she was eight she was sold for £5,000 to Lord Berkeley of Stratton as a match for his son. Failing, however, to complete the bargain, his lordship withdrew, and at the same time asked for his money back. A new bridegroom had to be sought for, and one willing, moreover, to make up the deficit on the £5,000, which, in the interval, had all been spent. Fortunately, it was not long before one was forthcoming, and Mary Davies, at the age of twelve, was married to Sir Thomas Grosvenor. So after the pack had been shuffled and re-shuffled, it was a country gentleman in far-away Cheshire who was dealt the ace of trumps.

Copyright.   1.—THE EXTERIOR   "COUNTRY LIFE."
The house stands at the corner of South Audley Street and South Street

The grand London home of Charles's uncle Isaac Gascoyne, which impressed Isabella and Izzy on their visit in 1842.

TOP: Lyttelton, Isabella's first landfall in New Zealand, from a drawing of passengers landing in 1850 by Sir William Fox, later Prime Minister. ABOVE: The squalid state of Trafalgar Street, Nelson, c.1860.

TOP: Ferry over the Motueka River near Pangatotara, 1910.
ABOVE: Maori group in Motueka in the 1860s.

TOP LEFT: Sir Robert Strang with his grandson, 'dear little Dougie', later Sir Robert McLean, Donald's son, 1860–65. TOP RIGHT: Te Kooti, 1889 or 1891. The portrait thought to be most like him. ABOVE: The Alexandra Redoubt in 1863, commanded by Fred Gascoyne in 1883.

TOP LEFT: Fred Gascoyne.
TOP RIGHT: Donald (later Sir Donald) McLean c.1870.
ABOVE: Fred's drawing of the attack on Ngatapa Pa, 1868.

TOP: Gold miners with their slab huts. ABOVE: Cricket in the redoubt at Pukearuhe, just after the Gascoyne massacre of 1868.

TOP: The Gascoyne whare at Pukearuhe Redoubt, shortly before the massacre. ABOVE: Pukearuhe Redoubt, 13 February 1860.

TOP LEFT: Wetere Te Rerenga with his wife and child in the King Country, 1885. TOP RIGHT: Lieutenant Bamber Gascoyne, 1869, shortly before becoming Wetere's victim. BOTTOM LEFT: James Deck. BOTTOM RIGHT: Chief Ropata Wahawaha, 1871.

an old man. For the rest of his life Fred was crippled, never again able to run fast, jump, dance or – worst of all – play cricket.

Ordered back to Gisborne to hurry up the supplies of provisions, by the time Fred returned Whitmore's proud army was in retreat. The men had been trapped up the gorge of the Ruakaturi River in a brilliantly orchestrated ambush in which Te Kooti had pounced from right and left. After a fierce gun battle Whitmore's army had only just managed to flee, staggering downstream through waist-deep creeks. Some officers of the Hawke's Bay constabulary were killed during the battle; others died from their wounds during the journey back. At the sight of Fred's packhorses the starving, sodden and demoralized soldiers rushed for the biscuit and bacon, and Fred had to use non-commissioned officers to keep them back at gunpoint.*

Fred guided the army through rain and sleet to the shelter of Te Rakiroa's now-abandoned kainga. The next morning Whitmore ordered the entire force on parade, and harangued them for failing to capture Te Kooti, blaming their lack of loyalty and energy. Whitmore then pointed to Fred, and announced to the assembled company: 'This is the only man

---

* Fred heard that en route to the gorge, the Poverty Bay volunteers had reached such a nadir of exhaustion and hatred for Whitmore that they had refused to travel beyond their district boundary. They would go no further. Whitmore responded by charging three of the volunteers with cowardice and, after an impromptu trial by court martial, condemned them to be shot. Their graves were dug; their eyes were bandaged. The terrified men collapsed. Then they were reprieved and discharged with ignominy. Fred wrote: '*As I was absent on despatch duty when this occurred, I set down what is perhaps only a camp tale of this farcical affair. But I never heard it contradicted.*'

who has not failed me since I came into the district.' His compliment did not stop Fred hating him.

Enough was enough, the government decided. The west coast was flaring up again under the leadership of a chief named Titokowaru, who was militarily even more threatening than Te Kooti. Whitmore and his Armed Constabulary were transferred. Despite McLean's protests, the hunt for Te Kooti was abandoned and the Poverty Bay settlers were left to protect themselves.

FOURTEEN

A Fouler Fiendishness

Spies warned that Te Kooti planned to wreak a bloody biblical revenge on the Poverty Bay settlers. Biggs begged the government for help, and was eventually permitted to pay one officer to lead a scouting party. It was better than nothing, but only just. Biggs picked nine trusted men, including several Maori, and asked Fred to lead them, offering him the same pay he had received as a militia lieutenant.

Fred needed little persuading. He was gratified that he had proved his worth and was, almost, back in the fold. He checked his firearms, packed his saddlebags, saddled Ngakahi and set off with his men filing behind. After twenty miles he reached a spot opposite Te Rakiroa's deserted kainga where the road forked to Wairoa and where Biggs's Maori spies had predicted Te Kooti would descend. It was a perfect place to camp. There was a flat of about half an acre, surrounded by a thick shelter of manuka and korimiko with a hill for a lookout. There was grass for the horses by day, and scrub to hide them in by night. The men did not bother with tents, which were too visible, but made bivouacs under blankets and waterproof sheets.

Fred put six men on guard every night, and always stayed awake himself from midnight until daylight. The horses were saddled at all times, and the men slept fully clothed, ready for surprise, ready for flight. They spoke in whispers, and burnt only the driest timber to avoid making smoke, extinguishing the fires hastily.

Each day Fred lay on the hillcrest with his binoculars, scanning the impenetrably forested ranges of the Urewera, ridge after ridge. New Zealand was the size of a small Indian state, but here there was a sense of vastness, and of the impossibility of the terrain. The mountains jutted looming and mysterious, daunting walls of rock and black and red pines pocked by the starburst of nikau palms. The summits were hazy in the early morning, lost in cloud that sagged into the ravines, then the sun burned through and the clouds rose, ghostlike, lifting Fred's spirits with them. Now the whole forest was steaming. Then the sky greyed over and drooped into the valleys, and the trees bowed their heads as if in sorrow.

Each day Fred searched for signs of the enemy on the move. He kept discreetly to the low ground, trying not to expose himself on the ridges, and despite sleepless nights and persistent hunger tried to stay alert to every sound, every twitching branch; each bush could hide a sharpened club, each shadow a gun. But there was nothing. Every few days he rode back to Matawhero to report this absence to Major Biggs, who was growing increasingly apprehensive.

Four months had passed since Te Kooti landed at Poverty Bay. Summer came. The scouts' routines remained unchanged, but tension bristled with the heat. Te Kooti was ready to descend like a wolf on the fold, and word came from spies that the day was approaching. Now Fred forbade his men from lighting fires; they had to be content with bread and cold mutton, and no tea. They were not allowed to shoot their guns. Flies buzzed and hours dragged.

One day, on the track from Poverty Bay, Fred met an elderly Maori who offered his opinion that if Te Kooti were to raid the bay, he would not use the track that Fred was watching but an ancient track from the mountain pa at Ngatapa, a long way from Fred's outpost.

Fred took two of his men to search the edge of the forest further north than he had been before, towards Ngatapa. They penetrated gullies and creeks, anywhere that looked as if it led back into the Urewera, until the next day they reached the Patutahi valley ten miles away. Fred found what the old Maori had described: a deeply worn track so overgrown that it was almost invisible unless you knew what you sought. He battled into its stuffy darkness, fighting the foliage, then stood and listened, and became aware of the stillness, broken only by the whine of mosquitoes, and the rasp of cicadas, and then a bird darting through the gloom. Fred may have remembered being with Captain Lockett in the forest at Lohughat; the same stuffy silence, the same sense of danger, but there the danger had been from tigers: Te Kooti was far more menacing. Fred dismounted and inspected the soil, but the track had not been used for years. He found no evidence of anything but the rootlings of wild pigs. But from a saddle overlooking a stream they saw, about six miles away, smoke rising out of the trees. Fred's companions knew nothing about any settlement there, and suggested the fires had been lit by Maori out hunting pigs. Possibly Tuhoe. Possibly Te Kooti's men.

While the scouts rode back to camp, Fred galloped to Matawhero. In the bleak early hours of 8 November he was knocking at Biggs' door, whispering what he had seen. He asked permission to leave three men to guard the Ngatapa track. Biggs refused. The track had evidently been forgotten and was impassable, and Fred had heard or seen nothing of interest. Biggs told Fred that he knew Te Kooti was getting restless, but his own spies were keeping him well informed of Te Kooti's plans. Te Kooti would advance in the next few days, but he would definitely use the track that Fred was watching, and would try to surprise with the sudden attack of an advance guard. Biggs added peremptorily, 'As long as one or two of you get away and give me the alarm, you will have served your purpose. Now get back to your post, and be sure not to leave it until you hear from me.'

'Sir!'

'And keep a sharp watch every night and scout toward Wairoa every day. If you see armed men or are fired at, you are to gallop to Poverty Bay at once and raise the alarm by scattering your scouts. You yourself are to come to me as quickly as possible.'

They were the last instructions Fred received from Reginald Biggs.

Isabella had heard nothing from Fred for months. Now she opened a special edition of the *Nelson Colonist* that published telegrams from Hawke's Bay, and read what she had always dreaded. If it could happen in India, why not here? 'The dreadful outrages perpetrated on the settlers of Poverty Bay, the cruel butcheries and burnings of inoffensive women and children, and the nameless mutilations, which add a fouler fiendishness to the dark catalogue of savage bloodshed and torture, have created general horror all over the Colony where the news has reached.'

Te Kooti had struck. There was carnage, bayonets and tom-ahawks, children screaming. At least forty people, both pakeha and Maori, had been slaughtered, and the whole of Poverty Bay was ablaze. 'Some particulars untold,' Isabella read with growing dismay, 'are horrible in the extreme.' The newspaper reported that there was no word of Lieutenant Gascoyne and his scouts, but Isabella knew they would have been first in line. Fred was dead – there was no reason to believe otherwise.

The Bungalow became a scene of sobbing and praying as alone in their rooms the members of the Gascoyne family humbled themselves before God for their personal sins and failures, then came together and made united confessions of their sins. They denied themselves things they wanted, begged for forgiveness and beseeched God to be merciful and, against all odds, to restore Fred to them. Despite the prayers, Isabella accepted that whatever happened was God's will. As Job said, 'Though he slay me, yet will I trust him.' All she could do was hope that if Fred had been confronted with death he had embraced it with joy.

On 10 November 1868 a bleak day had dawned in Poverty Bay. A picket alerted Fred that two horses were galloping towards them from the bay. Fred made out two of his native scouts, and before they had even arrived the rest of the men were mounted and ready to go.

They galloped twenty miles back towards the bay. Ahead they saw smouldering houses, not one of them around Matawhero left standing. With any luck, Biggs would have escaped, but that meant he would not be there to give Fred orders. Hoping to get orders instead from Captain Westrupp, Biggs's second-in-command, Fred diverted to Te Arai but found the sheep station deserted. Westrupp, it transpired, had escaped south with a party of women and children.

Biggs' plan had been for survivors to seek sanctuary in Gisborne in the old redoubt on the far side of the river, so Fred decided to go there. Three of his scouts promptly refused to move; they wanted to remain with the other Maori at the nearby pa, and the next day – probably under duress – they joined Te Kooti.

Fred took his six remaining scouts, but realized that he was cut off from Gisborne by Te Kooti's men, who were patrolling across the plain on horseback, rifles at the ready. Fred could see them in the distance plundering and burning the houses. His only solution was to sidle around the edge of the bay, down to a small coastal kainga where, at gunpoint, he commandeered a Maori whaleboat. They had to abandon their horses to Te Kooti, including Fred's cherished Ngakahi, who he never saw again. Then they had to row six miles across the bay.

Fred found Gisborne 'a scene of terror and confusion beyond description'. Survivors who had fled from surrounding districts swarmed down to the beach as Fred docked, almost attacking him in their desperate need for news and help. Some were wounded. Mothers wept loudly for their children, wives for husbands, husbands for wives. Only later did Fred have time to piece together their stories.

Charlie James, a seventeen-year-old servant boy, had been woken at about 2 a.m. by knocking on the front door. He didn't think anything of it, because his employer Major Biggs often worked late writing orders and reports, and was frequently disturbed at all hours by Lieutenant Gascoyne or one of his scouts. Biggs heard the tramp of horsemen surrounding his house.

'Who's there?' he shouted.

A voice – Te Kooti's – answered, 'Open the door and see.'

Biggs shouted at Charlie to get his rifle. The door was forced open and Biggs met a volley of bullets. Stumbling over Major Biggs, who lay wounded on the floor, Charlie fled for the back door and scrabbled under a grating that linked the back door with an outbuilding. Crouching in the dark, he heard Biggs call, 'Emily, dear, make for the bush; the Hau-haus are here.' Charlie then heard the screams of Mrs Biggs.

From his striped hiding place, Charlie saw Captain Wilson's house burst into flames, and heard shouts coming from it. Charlie managed to crawl out and slither into the flax. As he looked back he saw some of Te Kooti's men in Biggs's kitchen nonchalantly eating his food; others had dragged Major Biggs outside, and were beating his head with the butt of his musket. Mrs Biggs, grabbed by several men, was screaming to be let free to go to her husband. Jane Farrell, the nurse, stood helpless, holding the Biggs's newborn baby. According to reports, perhaps sentimental, when Emily Biggs told her to run she refused, saying she would stay with Mrs Biggs and live or die with her.

Charlie fled for Mrs Bloomfield's, arriving breathless at about 3 a.m. He shouted at the Bloomfields' servant boy that the Hau-haus had murdered Major Biggs, but Tommy Newton thought he was joking and refused to get up. Then Tommy heard a shot, and leapt out of bed to wake the family. The recently widowed Mrs Bloomfield was bringing up her three children with only a nurse to support her; she also had a friend from Napier staying, accompanied by her two young children. The women had no time to dress. They flung shawls and cloaks around themselves and the children and fled for their lives six miles across the flats to Gisborne. As they passed the house of Captain James Wilson, they saw it was on fire, but there was nothing they could do. Moments later they passed Captain and Mrs Wilson and their four children lying dead on the trail.

They hurried on as day broke, sometimes along the beach, sometimes scrabbling through brambles and out onto cattle tracks, and reached Gisborne at about 5 a.m., still in their white nightclothes, their hair in curl papers, their bare feet now raw and bleeding. They were the first refugees from the slaughter, and the first to bring the ghastly news.

It dawned on Fred that he was the only officer left alive in the bay. He rose to the occasion. First the safety of the women and children. Two of Captain Read's schooners, the *Tawera* and *Success*, were just beating out of port; the wind was light and they were barely moving so Fred ordered someone to row out and recall them as quickly as possible. At the same time he armed all the men with rifles, and posted sentries along the riverbank. The women and children were herded past the sentries down to the beach and shipped on board the schooners to be taken to safety in Napier. The women cried at being parted from their husbands, who they might never see again, and begged Fred to allow them to come too, but Fred would not permit any man to leave, and posted a sentry at the landing place to ensure none tried; the saddler, who volunteered for the task, was the only man to throw down his rifle and sneak off in one of the boats with the women. (Read also stayed on the *Tawera*, claiming to be going to buy supplies for the survivors.)

There was still no electric telegraph out of Poverty Bay, so Fred gave Read a dispatch for McLean begging for reinforcements of men, arms and ammunition. Meanwhile he ordered the men to fortify the old redoubt. He formed them into a human chain leading down to the beach to pass up buckets of sand, which he got them to pile up behind the redoubt walls. He had slots hacked out of the walls through which to poke the guns.

Most of the Poverty Bay Maori had joined Te Kooti (most later swore this had been under threat of death) but a few friendlies joined the pakeha at the redoubt. Fred sent them to fortify their own pa near the river mouth, and soon he was satisfied with their joint defences. He chose those men he could spare from guard duty and sent them across the river to rescue what they could carry from the township – mostly supplies from Captain Read's stores, which could be protected in the redoubt. (No one bothered to save the goods in the saddler's shop, and when he returned to Poverty Bay he complained about the Maori riding around with gleaming new saddles and bridles. 'Serves you right!' was Fred's response.)

Fred felt distraught at the death of Major Biggs in particular. Biggs would be blamed for not preventing this disaster, yet for all his faults Fred had always been impressed by his courage, prudence and energy. Yes, Biggs had refused to allow Fred to guard the overgrown track, but this was not his fault. Fred considered it the fault of the niggardly policy of the government that would pay for only one party of scouts to defend the settlement when at least six were needed. For of course it was down the overgrown track that Te Kooti had come.

News reached the redoubt of more deaths, and fugitives straggled in. Many had been given up for lost; all were footsore, weary and ragged. There were tales of Maori helping them to escape, and being shot by Te Kooti for their pains. Charlie James was silly with relief at seeing his mother, who had escaped into the bush with her six other children. Her news was confusing. She reported seeing Captain Wilson and his wife Alice lying dead at their garden gate, while their servant John Moran had apparently died in his bed, burnt almost to a cinder – although other reports had him burnt and chopped into three pieces. It was hard to establish what had really happened, but whatever the cause of their gruesome end, the death toll was now thirty-two whites and twenty-two friendlies.

Out on the plain the villages were being plundered. As it says in Deuteronomy 20: 14, 'thou shalt eat the spoil of thine enemies, which the Lord thy God hath given thee.' Flames raged from buildings in all directions. Mrs Bloomfield's mansion was already engulfed; since the destruction was the work of the Queen's enemies, her insurance would be void. She had lost everything.*

The only building left standing in Matawhero was the little kauri hut used as an Anglican church.

On the evening of 11 November Fred received a letter from a friendly native saying that Te Kooti did not intend to attack

---

* Mrs Bloomfield's two-storey mansion was insured with the New Zealand Insurance Company for the splendid sum of £1,200 (about £50,000 today) – far more than any other house in the district. She lost the lot.

the redoubt. Fred was puzzled: Te Kooti had the colonists sitting like ducks on the river. Was he going to let them escape? Perhaps he had some other trick up his biblical robe, some other terrible surprise? Fred could only wait and see.

The letter added that the corpses of Major Biggs and his wife and baby had been devoured by pigs.

Relief came in the form of Captain Westrupp and kupapa reinforcements sailing into port. Fred had found it shattering to bear not only the grief and shock, but also the entire burden of responsibility for the survivors. Now Westrupp could take command.

For the first time Fred's scouts could be spared from guard duty to glean news of Te Kooti's movements. With one party of soldiers prowling to the left, and another to the right, they ventured out of the redoubt. The sun was hazy through the pall of smoke and it was eerily quiet. Stumps of houses smouldered around them. Flecks of grey ash billowed about and aged Fred's beard. Fences had been torn up, and the slaughtered livestock belonging to both whites and Maori lay festering in the fields. After a week, flies sizzled over their rotting carcasses. Harrier hawks wheeled overhead, their mews poignantly childlike.

Two miles from Gisborne the scouts were startled by a dog barking from some low fern. Drawing their revolvers they rode over to investigate, and recognized Flo, a bitch belonging to Paku Brown's mother. Crouching beside the dog was a small barefoot boy, no more than eight years old. He stood up, revealing the remnants of his nightshirt, and raised his hands in surrender. It was Captain Wilson's son, Jemmy.

The boy could barely speak for shock and exhaustion – it was now seven days since the killings – but after being fed and watered back at the redoubt, the bewildered child remembered he had a note in his pocket from his mother, Alice Wilson. It begged for some kind friend to come to her assistance. She had no food or clothing, and was severely wounded – but she was alive.

A rescue party was rushed out. Alice Wilson was discovered in a shed. She had been lying there for days and was in a dreadful state, her chemise saturated with blood. With young Jemmy clinging to her side, she was carried on a litter to the house of Archdeacon Williams, and once the doctor had done all he could, she whispered her ordeal.

Alice Wilson had been in bed while her husband finished letters for the overland mail, which was leaving the next morning. There was a knock at the door, and a voice called out that there was a message for Mr Wilson. Wilson, suspicious, told the speaker to push the letter under the sill. Instead the door was battered with a piece of timber and when it splintered Wilson was summoned outside: something prevented the attackers from coming in. The Wilsons' servant John Moran was sleeping nearby; Mr Wilson called him, and he dashed across the yard as the Maori began to shoot into the house. Three of the children were still asleep upstairs, but Mrs Wilson grabbed eighteen-month-old Jessie from her cot and dived to the floor, while Mr Wilson and Moran returned fire.

The Maori torched the house at both ends and forced the family out, scorching their hair and feet as they fled. Captain Wilson had his revolver loaded, but one of Te Kooti's men promised they would not shoot the family now, and would escort them to safety. One Maori picked up Edwin, Mrs Wilson carried Jessie, Moran carried little Alice and Mr Wilson lifted

Jemmy onto his back. The Wilsons (Mrs Wilson dressed only in her chemise) walked towards their neighbour's house.

They stumbled a few hundred yards through the darkness along a dried-up riverbed, when one of the Maori rushed at Moran, while another bayoneted Wilson in the back. Hearing his cry, Mrs Wilson turned and was stabbed too. Attempting to shield Jessie, her arm was pierced and she was pinned to the ground. Hearing the dying moans of her husband, she turned towards him, and was stabbed in the abdomen. This wound probably saved her life because the killers assumed she was dead; nevertheless they beat her on the breast with their rifle butts before leaving. She passed out with pain, and was conscious of nothing until dawn.

In the bleak morning light Alice Wilson raised herself on her elbow and beheld the carnage. She was lying on Jessie's corpse, while the torn bodies of James, Alice, Edwin and Moran lay strewn around her. All the children had been beheaded except Jemmy, who had vanished.

Mrs Wilson lay there the whole day. No one came, except a Maori who stole her shawl. The following day she gathered the last of her strength and crawled back to what had once been her home. Amongst the rubble she found a teakettle, and she managed to fill it with water from the tank before dragging herself into the charred remnants of an outhouse. She listened to Te Kooti's people, who returned again and again to her house for loot. She waited to be discovered, and finished off.

When Captain Wilson was bayoneted Jemmy was flung to the ground, one arm trapped beneath his father's body. After the Maori had gone, he squirmed out and fled to Captain Bloomfield's. It was still dark, and he curled into a ball on the veranda. While he was lying there he heard Charlie James calling out, then nothing more, and none of the escaping Bloomfields knew he was there.

In the morning he found the place deserted. He wandered about, hiding from time to time under a sweetbriar bush; when he was hungry he crept into an abandoned house and ate something he found there. That night he crept back into the Bloomfields' house, up the stairs and into one of the little boys' beds. Suddenly he heard voices, male and female. He tiptoed to the bedroom door and locked it. The woman came and banged at the door, demanding to know who was in there, but Jemmy cowered under the bed, and eventually she gave up. After helping themselves to things in the house, the couple left.

The next night Jemmy avoided the Bloomfield house, and instead made a nest under a sweetbriar bush. It was a good decision: when he woke, he peeped out from his bush to see hundreds of armed warriors going by, women and children too. Soon afterwards, all the houses, including the Bloomfields', were on fire.

Once the warriors had gone, Jemmy returned to what remained of his home, and saw the bodies of his family in the old riverbed. His mother was missing, so he supposed Te Kooti had taken her away to eat her – but then he found her, crumpled in a heap in the corner of the outhouse.

A few chickens were still clucking about and he uncovered some eggs but had no way of cooking them. He went to an old Maori to ask for matches, but was turned away. Mrs Wilson then said, 'What about getting some fire from the houses that were burnt this morning?' He carried back a smouldering stick and under her direction built a fire, and cooked the eggs. He then went back to the old Maori and was given some potatoes.

Strengthened a little, his mother had another idea. In the pocket of her husband's jacket were a card case and a stub of pencil he always carried. Jemmy returned to his father's corpse, and forced himself to rootle in his pockets until he found them. Mrs Wilson struggled onto her side and tried to write, but both arms had been so wounded that nothing she wrote was legible, and Jemmy hadn't yet learnt to read or write. Hours passed, but despite her agony she managed it, and sent Jemmy on his way. He made several false starts, until he was joined by the dog Flo, who guided him across the open country.

Alice Wilson's miraculous survival became a talisman, a mascot. Where there had been desolation there was now hope. Everyone willed her to recover, but will was not enough, and a month later, on 17 December 1868, she died.*

On 18 November Fred had the most melancholy duty of all. Under cover of a strong picket, he and his scouts set off across the plain to collect and bury the rest of the victims.

Fred found what the pigs had left of Reginald and Emily Biggs. In between lay the remains of their baby, his brains knocked out by a rifle butt or a whalebone club. Two of their servants, a married couple, lay where they had fled from the back of the house, and in a clump of flax bushes about fifty

---

* Alice Beamish, born in Ireland, married James Wilson in 1859. Tall and fine looking with auburn hair, she was thirty-two years old when she died. Jemmy was later awarded the Victoria Medal for bravery. For a while he lived in London with his grandparents and was educated at the North London Collegiate school; on returning to New Zealand he became a surveyor and one of the best shots in the country, representing New Zealand at Bisley in 1902.

yards from the house Fred found the corpse of a half-Maori girl of seventeen or eighteen with a couple of bayonet wounds in her back, probably the Biggs's loyal nurse.

By 6 p.m. Fred had identified and buried twenty-four people. They had all been bayoneted after being shot, in accordance with Psalms 63: 10, 'They shall fall by the sword.' Fred mostly buried them where they fell, in communal family graves. All the murdered Maori had been buried by their own people. Fred brought back a ring or two, a brooch and a few other relics for the bereaved.

Te Kooti assured his people that if they were strong, God would return their land in Poverty Bay. 'Ye shall possess their land, as the Lord your God hath promised unto you.' (Joshua 23: 5–6.) The Old Testament provided him with plenty of brutality to support his case. 'And Israel saw the Egyptians dead upon the seashore. And Israel saw the great work which the Lord did upon the Egyptians.' (Exodus 14: 30–31.) 'And the Lord thy God will put out those nations before thee by little and little . . . But the Lord thy God shall deliver them unto thee, and shall destroy them with a mighty destruction, until they be destroyed.' (Deuteronomy 7: 22–24.)

It was the worst disaster to have befallen New Zealand, and the first time any Maori had attacked a European settlement with intent to kill. Fred might have asked himself: Why? The answer was revenge, land, the voice of God, utu, mana or all these things. The killings appeared to be random, but in fact they were targeted specifically at both whites and Maori against whom Te Kooti bore grudges. Te Kooti blamed Biggs – and therefore all his family – for having refused to let the escaped prisoners go quietly into the hills. He blamed him and Wilson for conspiring to have him exiled. Biggs had persisted with confiscating land, against all protests, in a muddled and tactless way. Biggs had also taken land for himself in Matawhero that Te Kooti had once cultivated. As for the Maori, many in Matawhero shared ownership of land with Te Kooti, and had sold that land without his permission. They had let him down. His killing of innocent children could be explained (but not excused) by the Maori belief in collective responsibility, whereby everyone answered for the actions of their kin, even tiny babies.

Isabella's *Nelson Colonist* howled for revenge, and for imperial troops to be employed at once. An editorial thundered that the butcheries of Cawnpore had woken the sympathies of England to the extent that no cost had been spared to 'draw the fangs of the Indian tiger'; now the massacres and tortures of Poverty Bay required a similar show of force. Downing Street's response was that Te Kooti had a substantial grievance, and the 18th (Royal Irish), the single British regiment to remain in New Zealand, was to continue to hold a defensive position in the garrison towns. The New Zealand government wanted self-reliance, and refused to pay for the imperial army, so the 18th (Royal Irish) would not be permitted to join the fray. This caused outrage in New Zealand. The *Nelson Colonist* blamed events on the removal of the British forces, and despaired that, 'We are being beaten at all hands by the savage.'

FIFTEEN

Cat & Mouse

News filtered through that Te Kooti had retreated the way he came, and was fortifying a position in the Ureweras. McLean persuaded the venerable fighting chiefs from Hawke's Bay to lead 450 of their men against Te Kooti, and Fred was ordered to command them. This was no easy task. Fred had enough experience of the Maori to know that his command was only nominal, since the chiefs were their own commanders. Fred also suspected that their formidable reputation notwithstanding, most of the Hawke's Bay Maori had grown rich and fat, and would rather flee than fight. Fred's technique was to keep his eyes and ears open to avoid mistakes, and constantly to sing the praises of his 'dusky army's' courage and abilities.

If Fred ever had doubts about the wisdom of pursuing Te Kooti, the horror he had witnessed at Matawhero may have dispelled them. For him though, this was not about utu: there was simply a job to do – a job he enjoyed – and a 'scoundrel' to be caught.

On their first day's march they surprised a party of Te Kooti's men, and shot two of them. Although the rest galloped away, this success encouraged the kupapa and they set off the following morning with great determination, but on failing to shoot any more they grew bored with marching. Fred called the chiefs together and persuaded them to go on for one more day, agreeing that if they still failed to find the enemy they would turn back.

By the next afternoon, Fred was in despair: no sign of a Hau-hau. He sat down to rest beside the track at Makaretu while the army tramped past in single file, a loose column that straggled over a mile long. Fred watched the zigzag line of men creeping through the high fern up the valley below him. Some had their hair cropped close in European style; others wore topknots, and many clutched their staffs and had tucked into their belts the carved clubs that could cleave a skull in two. Suddenly there was a yell and a volley of rifle shots from the top of the spur: they had stumbled on Te Kooti.

'Down with your swags,' Fred yelled. *'Kokiri kokiri! Kia kaha, kia kaha!'* Fred scrambled uphill, glancing back to see swag bags flying off to right and left as far as he could see. This was good: it meant quick support from the rear. Urging on those around him, Fred reached the summit in time to prevent his leading men being mown down by Te Kooti's pickets who were posted just over the crest; three of Fred's men had already been killed. 'Fire!' Fred yelled, and gained the ridge that protected Te Kooti's camp. But Te Kooti had a plan.

The wind was blowing towards Fred's army, and the fern on the ridge was high and dry; Te Kooti's men set it alight and flames fanned uphill. Fred ordered a few of the Hawke's Bay Maori to continue shooting through the smoke, while others pulled up the fern along the ridge. The men worked for their lives, the heat blazing in their faces while they hacked at fronds and stems, and after only a few minutes they cleared a firebreak twenty feet wide. It was a critical moment. Fred knew that if his men retreated, nothing could stop them, and Te Kooti would 'harry and punish them' the whole way back to Poverty Bay.

Fred ordered the men to dig a trench, and later recalled that 'digging in the hot ashes with our bayonets, sticks, ramrods, and even our naked hands (for the lazy beggars had left behind all our spades and most of our stretchers), we soon dug a wide, shallow shelter-trench all along the ridge.'

They had rations and ammunition for only one more day. Fred had something else to concern him: water. Te Kooti was down by the stream; Fred's nearest water was where the wounded lay, at the bottom of the gully behind him, too far to lug up a decent supply. It was the height of summer, and after their night of toil in the trenches, the men were dehydrated.

To his relief, a few miles down the track Fred met the pack-horses carrying extra ammunition, and learnt that provisions were on their way. But by now the fire had burnt its way round the hill and was flaming lethally each side of the track back to the ridge, cutting Fred off from his army. Coughing in the smoke, Fred ordered each man to unload every horse, wrap one keg of ammunition in a sack, tie up their own heads in their coats or shawls and mount the packhorses. They would ride them through the flames: Fred led on a fine old packhorse that was more afraid of spurs than fire and slammed blindly into the inferno.

Back on the ridge there was nothing to eat. Anyone who could be spared from digging the trench was sent to dig for fern root. Fred chewed the fern root but couldn't bring himself to swallow it; at least he managed to extract a bit of juice to assuage his thirst. As for sow thistle, this was edible – though it might have been improved with a little salt.

The next day the food supplies failed to arrive, and the next, and the next. Perhaps they would be abandoned here on their ridge to starve to death. Dr Gibbs generously shared a couple of biscuits with Fred, and that was the only food he ate in four days. Fred and his troops gazed hungrily at two packhorses left in camp, but their Maori owner resolutely refused to have them shot.

It transpired that Te Kooti had sent a war party ten miles behind Fred's lines and attacked the supply depot, and got away with all the provisions, plus twelve thousand rounds of ammunition. Again his strength grew.

Eventually replacement rations arrived, and with them the welcome news that McLean had used his famous influence to organize a body of Ngati Porou reinforcements from the East Cape, under the redoubtable chiefs Ropata and Hotene. Ropata was old, but he was tough and ruthless; with the Hawke's Bay Maori so exhausted, Fred decided to await his arrival before attacking Te Kooti. Meanwhile both sides kept spasmodically shooting. At one point Fred glimpsed a man in a black frock coat, thought to be Te Kooti. Fred raised his rifle, brought the sight against his right eye and squeezed the trigger. The man leapt away. It is known that Te Kooti was wounded in the foot at this time and Fred relished the thought that his may have been 'the lucky shot'.

In early December at last chiefs Ropata and Hotene arrived with their 180 Ngati Porou warriors. It was agreed that Ropata – Major Ropata as he became – should come up on the right, with the Hawke's Bay Maori on the left, and as soon as

Ropata's men were in line the whole force would attack Te Kooti. 'It was a beautiful sight,' enthused Fred, 'a line of fire and smoke half a mile long, with both flanks thrown forward rapidly descending the hill: the men closing to the centre as they got close to the enemy's entrenchments on both sides of the river. Our concentrated fire must have been terrible.'

When Fred and his men leaped over the banks into the trenches, they found only the dead and dying. Te Kooti, either alive or dead, had vanished. He had leapt down a fifty-foot cliff into the Makaretu River, and escaped into the mountain fast-nesses of the Urewera, leaving nothing but a small rear guard, giving Fred a pyrrhic victory after all.

A scout made a short pursuit into the bush and managed to capture Nama, one of Te Kooti's most powerful fighting lieu-tenants. Nama was said to have been among the more brutal of the murderers at Poverty Bay. That night the Ngati Porou trussed him up in ropes and dragged him, screaming, through a fire. Then they proposed a cannibal banquet, but the Hawke's Bay chiefs vetoed this, and instead they ate symbolic biscuit around the pyre while the body roasted.*

Before being summarily executed by the kupapa, prisoners reported that Te Kooti was reinforcing an ancient Tuhoe strong-hold on a bluff called Ngatapa. It was said to be virtually

---

* The ropes and fire are from an account written by one of Te Kooti's warriors, while the proposed cannibalism is according to the *Wellington Independent*, 19 December 1868. According to Fred, the scout killed Nama, and he makes no mention of fire or cannibalism. Perhaps he was guarded because the executioners might be open to prosecution; perhaps he considered the story too shocking for his readers; or perhaps it never happened at all. Fred's is the only first-hand pakeha account of the battle at Makaretu.

impregnable, and to loom above trenches and rifle pits. A lozenge-shaped space, it narrowed at the back to a ridge as thin as a knife, which dropped on both sides in sheer precipices. At the front it opened out onto a bald exposed crest. Fred couldn't resist having a look.

Despite the rough broken terrain of rocky gorges and sharp hills, the kupapa were brilliant at moving stealthily through the undergrowth barely causing a ripple. As they slithered on their bellies out into more open flax and manuka scrub, over the tops of the bushes they spied – only seventy yards ahead – Te Kooti's formidable maze of timber palisades. Each post had been sharpened to a spike. There were loopholes every six or eight feet, and through these Fred could make out bullet-proof rifle pits and earthworks. The parapets were between ten and sixteen feet high, and those closest to the summit were topped with flax baskets filled with earth to be dumped on intruders. It was a sight that might have faced Iron Age man – but with the addition of a lethal supply of guns.

There was no movement from the pa. Not a sign of life. Perhaps the pa was empty.

Fred passed word along the line for the men to keep close cover, then crept forward until he was only twenty paces from the outer palisades, in full view of any watching defender. There was no sound, just the rustle of a rat scurrying away through the fern. Everyone held their breath. Fred stood up and walked across the front of the pa. Nothing happened. Then he heard the lightest of sounds and flung himself behind a flax bush just in time to dodge a barrage from the palisade. For two minutes bullets flicked the leaves of his flax bush, until Fred had had enough and slid down the slope back to his men. There, to his disgust, he found himself alone, but for two freshly dead Maori who had been unable to resist peeking above the cover. The rest could be heard stampeding through the bush, fleeing from Ngatapa for their lives.

At last one man, a Scot named Blackstock who had fought with Fred on the East Cape, returned to look for his corpse. 'Every wan of auld Hotene's Maori is running like hell,' he declared, 'and won't stop for anyone.' Racing after them, Fred overtook a staunch old fighting man named Mohi. He tried to persuade him to stop the men. Mohi pushed Fred aside, saying contemptuously, 'Don't you know that it is a whati [panic]?' It was, he said, the result of bad omens which Fred had ignored. There was nothing Fred could do to stop the stampede.

On the track back to Gisborne, Fred was met by the welcome sight of the Armed Constabulary returned from the west coast, including several of his old comrades. Fred was thankful for a good meal, a wash and a change of underclothes. Even more welcome was the news that all had been forgiven, and he had been gazetted captain and sub-inspector in the Armed Constabulary. Fred's jubilation was tempered by the sight of Colonel Whitmore, who was hated in Poverty Bay almost as much as Te Kooti.*

---

* A number of unnamed 'memorialists', prompted by McLean, wrote to Sir George Bowen to protest against Whitmore being sent to Poverty Bay. Whatever his military attainments, he was (they claimed) unfit to deal with the natives, and 'in the highest degree unpopular' with both colonial and native forces. At this critical moment, they wrote, his presence was 'anomalous and hazardous'. What they needed, the memorialists insisted, was united action, and someone the natives trusted and respected – i.e. Donald McLean. But Whitmore came all the same.

While they awaited reinforcements, Te Kooti daringly struck again, killing more Poverty Bay Europeans. On a scouting expedition Fred and his party found themselves face to face with those they supposed to be the culprits, and were very nearly killed themselves.* Accompanying Fred on this expedition was a Captain William Newland, who had come over from the west coast where, the previous November, his troop of volunteer cavalry had lost control outside a place called Handley's Woolshed and in their excitement killed two Hau-haus. Newland was feted in the press for this 'dashing affair'. Only years later during a libel trial in London was it revealed that this dangerous enemy was in fact young children trying to run away. This may have been one cause of the disaster that would befall the Gascoyne children two months later.

When reinforcements arrived, Whitmore began the big push on Ngatapa.

Fred was appalled to see how much the pa had been

---

* Fred rescued one of his own Maori scouts from the gunfire, and as they spurred their horses through fern towards a ridge, he saw that some of the enemy had run uphill and were firing at them from higher ground, while others had followed behind. Fred shouted at the men in front to halt and fire over his head at his pursuers. One overexcited man named Shortt fired his carbine so close to Fred's head that he scorched his face. Years later Fred was having his hair cut in Auckland, when he heard the barber telling a customer how he had nearly shot his officer while soldiering in Poverty Bay. Fred chipped in that this story was true, and that he was the officer. Shortt was so delighted to meet Fred again that he insisted on taking him to sample all the whisky in Queen Street. Frank Short had been part of Captain Newland's attack on the Maori children at Handley's Woolshed.

strengthened since his last visit. A high sod wall, loopholed, had been built right across the front, and a third palisade added on the inner side. The flanks were impossible to scale and as for the rear approach, this was a steep razor-thin edge commanded by rifle pits that could only be reached by climbing the cliff, leaving each soldier a sitting target to the sharpshooters above. The only way in was through the front. Over the next three days the men prepared the attack.

1869: a busy New Year's Day. Instead of roast beef or a haunch of mutton they ate nothing but biscuit. Fred hadn't tasted meat for days, until a Maori friend gave him the gift of a chunk of boiled horse, as big as his fist. It was so delicious that Fred wrapped half of it in paper to keep it clean in his pocket, and saved it for the following day – at the risk of being shot before he rationed himself another bite.

The third day was wet and stormy. That night Fred was ordered to lead thirty men against the fortress, a forlorn hope. Lugging carbines, shovels and axes, Fred and his men crouched in its shelter. It loomed overhead, brutal and impenetrable. By hugging the wall they were fairly safe from enemy fire. No more orders came, so they crouched uselessly in the rain until long after midnight.

Before dawn on the fourth day, through the wind, Fred heard women screaming. He could just make out something about Te Kooti having left the pa. The women seemed to be begging the attackers to stop, crying that only they and their children remained inside, that Te Kooti and his men had escaped down the cliff.

Someone sounded the ceasefire, and as day dawned it transpired that the women had not lied: Te Kooti and his men had

hacked lianas from trees outside the fortress and used them to
plunge from the razor-edged summit of the precipice into an
abyss that Whitmore had considered too steep to bother guarding. It was his greatest mistake. Te Kooti had vanished into the
night, every sound of his flight buried beneath the howling of
the weather. The master magician had outwitted the army yet
again.

Hundreds of Te Kooti's men were captured in the bush.* As
Fred was marching back to Gisborne, he passed thirty prisoners drawn up near the track. He thought they looked a fine lot
of men, but the kupapa said they were to be shot. Fred later
learned that the sentence was carried out on that very spot,
except for one who made a dash for the bush but was run down
in the creek and clubbed to death by a young Ngati Porou.
Around a hundred and twenty male prisoners were executed. It
was a massacre in revenge for Poverty Bay; many of the executed prisoners had themselves been captured by Te Kooti in
Poverty Bay, so were victims twice over. The killings were not
carried out by the pakeha or even sanctioned by Whitmore, but
he felt powerless to prevent them. The aim was to leave no one
alive to seek vengeance.

---

* That morning fresh rations were served. Fred got leave to let his men boil
their billies for tea with their biscuit and cold bacon. While they were eating,
two Maori came over to Fred.
 'Is it true that the government is paying £5 for every Hau-hau head?'
 'I believe so. I think the offer is genuine.'
 The Maori laughed, and one slapped his thigh. 'My word, I get some of that
money.'
 He was back the next day with a sack. It bulged lumpily. Fred drew out by
the hair three bloodied Maori heads. The other Maori produced a second sack
with two heads. (The heads were reportedly dumped in the river at Gisborne.)

Once again Whitmore, having lost the elusive Te Kooti, decided enough was enough. Te Kooti was seriously weakened: two-thirds of his garrison was dead, and for now that would have to do. The east coast settlers and kupapa were again left to face Te Kooti alone. There was only one effective field force, and it was required to deal with another formidable warrior on the west coast, Titokowaru. Whitmore took with him fifty-seven battle-hardened men of the Constabulary, who this time included Fred.

Hostilities in the west had died out in 1866, but dissent was stirred by the way the government continued to confiscate Maori land, almost by stealth. Enter Titokowaru, of the Ngati Ruanui.

Like Te Kooti, Titokowaru had a Christian missionary background, baptized Joe Orton by the Wesleyans.* He was small, dark skinned, renowned for his passionate love affairs and his voice, which was as powerful as a raging lion's, or as high pitched as a shrieking bird's. His most striking feature was the scar that covered the remains of his right eye, which he had lost in battle in 1864. At times he wore a mat of the finest native flax, fringed with green and white feathers, and a cap made from the plumage of a black bird, and in its centre, standing in

---

* This name may ring unlikely bells in modern ears, who would associate it with the bad-boy playwright of the 1960s, but in fact Titokowaru was named after a nineteenth-century dissenting preacher called Job Orton.

front of the peak, a single scarlet feather. At other times he sported a black 'hard-hitter' hat and a European suit.

Also like Te Kooti, Titokowaru was a spiritual as well as a military leader, but instead of steeping himself in the Old Testament, he turned to Pai-Marire. By 1868 Joe Orton had reverted to Titokowaru, Hau-hau warlord and – what terrified the settlers most – cannibal.

While Te Kooti was plotting his escape from the Chathams, Titokowaru was directing his army with a cunning and ferocity never before seen in a Maori warrior. He swept south from the foothills of Mount Taranaki to the outskirts of the town of Wanganui, smashing two superior colonial forces en route, and creating a crisis of confidence in the pakeha. Destitute women and children flocked to the town in search of shelter and food. In September 1868 the Reverend John Whiteley, the much-respected leader of the Wesleyan mission and old friend of McLean, who had lived in New Zealand for over thirty years, wrote to a friend in England that he had 'never felt so desponding as at the present time'. The few colonial troops who had been taken from the east coast to assist in quelling the rebellion in the west would, he warned, soon have to hasten back to fight for their own hearth and homes. Meanwhile farmers had abandoned their land, feeling it was pointless to farm it when they might soon lose it. 'Of course our numbers in this Province are vastly reduced, and if the rebels come here or rise in the neighbourhood we are utterly powerless to stand against them.'

In October 1868 Bishop Selwyn wrote privately to Governor Sir George Bowen, condemning the confiscation scheme as 'a gigantic exaggeration of the mistake which has hampered New Zealand from the first, viz the attempt to occupy more land than we could really govern. The proclamation of sovereignty over the whole island in Governor Hobson's time ought I think to have had no other object than the exclusion of foreign nations. The farce of Provincial Governments professing to govern territory which they had never seen, and people whose language they could not understand, has now been turned into a deep tragedy.'

The danger was not just from Titokowaru, but from the west-coast kupapa who were threatening to defect to the enemy. These Maori allies despised the armed settlers for their weakness, and saw the lack of military support from the British government as a loss of mana, of face and power. Some, such as the Arawa, believed it meant Kuini Wikitoria was angry with the pakeha, and that therefore they should not be supporting them. Without the kupapa, the settlers were doomed.

On 12 November, two days after Te Kooti descended on Poverty Bay, and when Titokowaru had advanced to within ten miles of Wanganui's suburbs, Sir George Bowen left the safety of Government House in Wellington for this Taranaki town. Thousands of Maori gathered at a massive korero on land belonging to the pro-government chief Te Kepa Te Rangihiwinui. Bowen was warned that Titokowaru wanted his head, and planned to parade it among the tribes as a trophy of victory, but he decided to risk his fate to address the korero. Bowen needed to appeal for calm, and for continued Maori help.

Six strong Maori rowed the Governor and his suite across the river. On landing, the stout bewhiskered Sir George was greeted with a volley of musketry, followed by a haka performed with full stamping tongue-thrusting ferocity by 150

Maori armed with rifles.* Time was kept by Te Kepa; known by the settlers as 'Kemp', he was dressed in the full uniform of a captain of the native contingent. After being guided to a seat on the greensward in front of Te Kepa's house, His Excellency enjoyed the usual exchanges of formalities, and had the intelligence to reply in kind, with an equally florid and poetic turn of phrase.†

Then politeness ceased. Chief after chief, including the great politician Mete Kingi, stood up to launch an unprecedented attack on Colonel Whitmore (who was present), saying they would never fight for him again. They blamed him for the entire Maori rebellion, and declared that even if their worst enemy, Titokowaru, was to invade Wanganui, they would not cross the river to fight him if ordered to do so by Whitmore. A Maori woman, an Amazonian creature who fought on the front line, gave Whitmore a piece of her mind, which judging by her gestures was far from complimentary. The atmosphere was tense; most of the Maori – men and women – were armed.

Sir George stood. He reminded everyone present of their joint enmity to Titokowaru, and their joint loyalty to the Queen. 'The Queen,' he declared, 'desires that the Maori and

---

* As Bowen pointed out in his dispatch to the Duke of Buckingham, Secretary of State for the Colonies, this was no mere pageant, because the warriors brandishing their rifles and tomahawks had a few days earlier been fighting a bloody little battle alongside Colonel Whitmore at Ototoku – total killed on the government side nine, total wounded nineteen, missing eight.

† Although the Colonial Office would later acknowledge that Bowen's 'palavers' with the Maori did an enormous amount of good, his dispatches provoked a few smiles up sleeves. The Secretary of State, Lord Kimberley, noted 'the very inflated style of Maori utterances which Sir G. Bowen naturally admires greatly and vainly endeavours to out do.'

the pakeha should grow up together as one people, and that they should flourish as the everlasting green of your native forest.' This eased the tension temporarily.

The Governor and his suite, accompanied by Whitmore and Mete Kingi, retired to Te Kepa's house, where a sumptuous cold collation was laid out in splendid style, while outside fires were lit, and cooks tended coppers and boilers for the meals for the Maori guests. Then gifts of flax mats and greenstone and whale-bone clubs were presented to the Governor by one chief after another, and graciously acknowledged.

The korero continued. Whitmore, his military strategy and his 'hard words' were again condemned. Whitmore, forced to justify himself, complained that most of the Maori force had refused to march because it was wet, and too early in the morning, and had deserted him in his hour of need. The Maori then rounded on the government for weakness and lack of unity; they were also full of recriminations against each other.

Bowen interjected once more to remind the Maori of the debt they owed to the British for the introduction of Christianity. Now, he said, was the time to 'show their sense of that inestimable blessing'. This caused a stir of agreement amongst the Maori; they *did* feel blessed. Bowen seized his advantage and exhorted them to make up a new war party to be called the Governor's taua, with all the young men of the tribes, who would not return home until Chief Titokowaru was subjugated. Te Kepa sprang forward, declaring that he was ready to obey the Governor's commands and lead that taua. Several other brave warriors joined in. 'The korero was very Homeric,' Sir George observed laconically to a friend. 'Kepa is the Achilles, and Mete Kingi the Ulysses of New Zealand.'

The korero was a turning point of the war, but it did not seem so at the time. News of the Poverty Bay massacre arrived, and so did a letter from King Tawhiao announcing his desire to see a general uprising of all Hau-haus across the whole of the North Island. Then Whitmore received a letter from Titokowaru that pithily summarized the Maori point of view.

December 5th 1868

A word of advice. To Whitmore.
A question to you. To whom does England belong? To whom does this place belong on which you are standing? My word to you. In one day the heaven and the earth were both made. In one day man was made and all things contained therein. If you understand that God made these things it is well. You were made a pakeha and England was made for you. I was made a Maori and New Zealand was made for me. You did not recollect that a great division [gulf] was between us, the great sea. You ceased to remember this fact and crossed over from that place to this. I did not cross over from this place to that.

My word to you – move out of my place to your own place in the midst of the sea. Clear out of this town [Wanganui] and all other places. Stand up, be baptized that you may be washed from your sins and call on the name of the Lord.

Enough from Titokowaru.

The obvious logic of Titokowaru's letter made no difference. Fred landed in Wanganui on 16 January 1869, and from there Whitmore drove his rabble army through scrub and brushwood into the heart of the mountains, dragging guns and rockets behind them. By 2 February, Fred was camped below yet another daunting stronghold, Titokowaru's pa at Tauranga-ika, two miles from Handley's Woolshed where the two Maori boys had been murdered. The pa had flanking angles at each corner and two lookout towers, strong double palisading with solid inner banks and earthworks. All the inside quarters were, it transpired, bombproof sunken chambers. Tauranga-ika was said to be the most formidable modern pa ever built.

The Constabulary passed that night in their trenches full of bravado and singing ballads like 'Oh Susannah' to keep up their spirits. Hau-hau riflemen holed up in the pa shouted for more. 'Come on, pakeha, and be food for the Maori,' they taunted. 'Send the fat ones out in front.' It was surely the eve of a great battle.

In the morning the army found the pa deserted. Warriors, women, children: all gone, vanished into the bush. Like Te Kooti, Titokowaru had done a midnight flit; unlike Te Kooti, he hadn't needed to. His pa was almost impregnable; he could have won. Everyone was bemused. Some said that Titokowaru had lost mana through a liaison with someone else's wife; others that Titokowaru was warned of bad omens in a dream. Either way, it was the beginning of the end.

SIXTEEN

During Isabella's sojourn in Clifton in 1853, John Gascoyne had written to Lord Salisbury in despair that although his eldest son Bamber had been given an appointment on the Great Western Railway, 'how to find the means to establish him I know not.' Lord Salisbury, with the merest hint of irritation, had repeated that there was nothing he could do to help. With Isabella's encouragement, Charles wrote to John urging him to send Bamber out to the new world. Aged twenty-two, Bamber promptly embarked in the *Protector* for Melbourne, where he joined the mounted police.

In 1864 news reached Pangatotara that Bamber had decided to leave Melbourne and join Charles and Isabella in New Zealand.

Bamber was grasping the opportunity to better himself. In his mid-thirties, not young, the time had come to start a family, and make something of his life. This opportunity was provided by Governor Grey, who, following the war against the King, had authorized the confiscation of land owned by Maori 'engaged in rebellion against Her Majesty's authority' on which he planned to install hundreds of so-called 'military settlers'. They would hedge in and isolate the King, while simultaneously protecting neighbouring settlements from attack. The arrangement was that these military settlers would bear arms for the country for a certain number of years in return for a few acres of land; they would put down rebellion while also putting down roots on the wild frontiers of Maoridom. Agents were sent into the gold mines of Otago and Melbourne to enlist suitable men, and Bamber responded to Grey's clarion call. He joined the three other officers to take the free passage that was offered on the barque *Brilliant*, landing on 17 February 1864, where he soon found a young wife named Annie.

Land north of New Plymouth had been confiscated, and on its northernmost point stood an old Maori pa, which had long since fallen into disuse. Its palisade rode the crest of precipitous cliffs. Known by the settlers (nostalgically) as the White Cliffs, they were Dover-like in their height and chalkiness, stark above a beach of black glittering volcanic sand. All those travelling south from Mokau could use the beach for part of their journey, but when the cliffs barred the route they had to come inland: the pa commanded the track. This was the gate to Taranaki through which the ferocious Waikato and Ngati Maniapoto tribes had travelled for generations as they plundered the Taranaki tribes to the south. Any of the Kingite tribes now hoping to reinforce the Taranaki Hau-haus, or planning to attack the settlers in Taranaki Province, would have to pass this way. In April 1865 the commanding officer in Taranaki extended his outposts by establishing a strong redoubt here. Bamber was offered a lieutenancy in the Taranaki Militia, and sent to join the garrison. He took Annie with him.

As war receded in 1866, the garrison was steadily reduced in size and by February 1868 had been disbanded altogether, leaving only a shell with Bamber in command. There was a two-storeyed blockhouse pocked with portholes which towered from the midst of impressive palisades and lookout towers. A flagpole rose proudly at one end, overlooking the White Cliffs which plunged eight hundred feet to the sea. Around the blockhouse, nestling in trees, was a scattering of dwellings for the military settlers and their families.

In 1868 a photographer struggled up here from New Plymouth complete with camera, tripod and all the other paraphernalia required to record the scene. The Gascoynes lived in a whare made of raupo, a marsh reed. It was a primitive hut, the floor nothing but dirt. The walls were thatched with bundles of raupo, which were lashed to the framework with flax, and the roof was thatched with layers of different plants. It was ringed by a humble fence made of branches twined with ropes of vines. Annie Gascoyne is framed in the doorway just within the shadow of the room in her full-skirted crinoline – despite their almost Stone Age living conditions, standards were clearly not allowed to drop. She carries her baby Cecil John. His legs and arms are bare, as if he has just been plucked from his cot. Outside are a couple of chairs, the minute sitting room having expanded into the garden. One of them is a high chair, on which sits three-year-old Laura in a white pinafore, and beside her stands Bamber, bearded, in hat and pale-coloured suit; he reaches down a paternal hand in a comforting gesture. A woman in a bonnet, a visitor named Mrs de Webber, sits the other side of Laura, and looks at her, as if also comforting her, as if Laura was frightened by the stranger with the camera and cross at having to sit still for so long in her best dress.*

---

* Laura was named after Bamber's sister, Cecil John after both Lord Salisbury and Bamber's father.

At some point Bamber also had a *carte de visite* made from a photograph taken in a New Plymouth studio, which shows him in close-up. Bearded, uniformed, holding his sword and leaning one elbow on a classical pillar in front of some rich drapery, the intention is to create an image of martial virility. Instead the bespectacled Bamber is slightly hunched, his shoes scuffed and worn down. He looks as if life has not been easy. He looks middle aged.

Bamber had hung onto a few trappings of his past – John's fob watch and chain, and a pair of opera glasses – but Frederick Place with its day and night nurseries, and his spoilt grandfather being fed special luxurious foods, made an ironic contrast with his present existence. Perhaps in humorous comparison with the wealthy town in which he spent his youth, or perhaps from homesickness, Bamber called the area Cliff Town – or Clifton.

News from Clifton England was not good. In July 1868 Julia Gascoyne, Bamber's mother, was living in such dire poverty that when doctors told her she needed to visit the seaside for her health, she was forced to write to Lord Salisbury to beg for the necessary £10 to pay her expenses. Even though his own wife had been godmother to Julia and John's son Cecil, Lord Salisbury promptly wrote to John's sister Mary to ask who on earth this woman was. In November 1868 – while Fred was busy surviving in Poverty Bay, Bamber was commanding the redoubt and Annie was giving birth to a baby they named Louisa Annie – Bamber's father died; two months later Julia Gascoyne wrote to Lord Salisbury again, this time beseeching him for £50 to pay John's funeral expenses. Lord Salisbury sent £30, doubtless hoping this would be the last of her.

News of his father's death in Clifton England reached Clifton New Zealand too late for Bamber.

The Gascoyne family's spiral of descent from riches to rags had been dramatic, but after his allotted few years here Bamber would be rewarded with a handsome acreage nearby. He would continue to bear arms as necessary, but at the same time he would become a farmer of substance. And life at Pukearuhe was not all bad. Bamber and Annie were not lonely: they messed with whoever happened to be in the garrison, such as Edward Richards and garrison cook John Milne, while neighbouring settlers Captain William Messenger, William McDonald, Fred Trent and Edward Gregory, some of whom had been part of the garrison but now farmed nearby, came up for games of cricket, or to take care of the library, play cards or fish from the beach. The distinguished Wesleyan missionary the Reverend John Whiteley rode up from New Plymouth each week to spend Saturday night with the Gascoynes before taking the early service the following morning.

So far, there had been no trouble at Pukearuhe. The fortifications included a trench, then a stockade, and within the stockade the expensively rebuilt bullet- and ball-proof block-house where the ammunition was kept. The sea raged eight hundred feet below, barring the western approach. The top of the parapet commanded views to the beach, and also a footpath down to the creek which was so steep that no one could climb it without stumbling, certainly not if they were laden with weapons. The redoubt both commanded the northern approach from the King Country and overlooked the south for about two miles. To the east rose a wall of wooded hills, but the redoubt was protected from these by a gully, steeper than a moat, which was watchable by day and impassable at night.

Nevertheless, in September 1868 Reverend Whiteley expressed concern for the vulnerability of virtually undefended out-settlements like Pukearuhe. How painful it would be, he warned, if all this English industry was destroyed, and all these families murdered, tomahawked and devoured, with no one the wiser until it was all over.

Later, people agreed that however strong its position, the garrison should never have been disbanded. In 1865 fifty men had guarded the blockhouse, and some would say it needed seventy or eighty to keep it safe. Now Bamber was down to six men, most of whom were often away. How could he have been expected to defend himself?

As Titokowaru hammered his way around Taranaki, support for him grew amongst the Kingites, particularly some of the leading Kingite generals, and in November 1868 two of the most powerful Ngati Maniapoto chiefs seized their chance. The settlers were crumbling, facing disaster: now was the moment for an attack on North Taranaki, which would not only divert government troops from fighting Titokowaru, but would also force the army to retaliate. This would be enough to convince the anti-war factions in the King movement to side with the pro-war camp. The Kingites could then move south to join Titokowaru, and the North Island would be theirs.

The initial attack was entrusted to Hone Wetere Te Rerenga. A minor chief in his thirties – about the same age as Bamber – Wetere lived in Mokau, a Ngati Maniapoto stronghold on the coast on the King Country coast. If he was to head south towards Taranaki, the Gascoynes at Pukearuhe were the first Europeans he would meet.

Wetere was another mission-educated Maori. He had been taught by the Wesleyans, possibly by the Reverend Whiteley himself, who had baptized him Hone Wetere, the Maori version of John Wesley. During an expedition down the west coast in 1845, Donald McLean had met Wetere's father, noting in his diary a rich Ngati Maniapoto chief who had just bought a trading vessel with which to do business with the newly arrived pakeha in New Plymouth.* Wetere's father was keen not only to trade with these wealthy pale-skinned visitors, but also to find out everything he could about them. He passed this curiosity on to his son, who became a noted orator who was empowered by his knowledge of the pakeha world, but soon curiosity turned to resentment; in 1860 Wetere fought in the Taranaki War, then he joined the Pai Marire and became a fervent Kingite. Wetere understood that King Tawhiao himself had ordered this mission, which was largely why he agreed to undertake it.

Warning of a possible attack reached New Plymouth's resident magistrate, who in December 1868 passed it on to Bamber, informing him that the Ngati Maniapoto might send a war party down the White Cliffs, but that it was up to him whether or not to evacuate. Bamber, confident in his defences, stayed put.

---

* Wetere's father wanted to improve his trading prospects by encouraging settlement in the Mokau district, and he made land available for sale, of which his son Wetere was a signatory. Wetere later owned the vessel *Paraninihi* which, ironically (given what was to happen), is the Maori name for the White Cliffs, *pari* meaning cliff, and *ninihi* meaning lofty.

Five days before Christmas, Bamber and Annie were standing on the cliff top looking down to the beach. Annie peered through the glass (perhaps the opera glasses) and saw some natives. She handed the glass to a military settler named Fred Trent. He observed that the natives on the beach were armed; later he realized they must have been on reconnaissance, looking for the best approaches to the redoubt. When Fred Trent left, Annie told him that the next time he heard of her and her children they would probably have been tomahawked. She was only half joking.

In January 1869 a thirty-strong war party of Ngati Maniapoto did set out from the King Country, but was intercepted and forced back by Rewi Maniapoto, King Tawhiao's right-hand chief. Clearly, Kingite factions for and against war were jostling for power. The resident magistrate took the precaution of hiring two native scouts to live at Clifton and patrol the surrounding area, in the hope that with Maori in residence, other Maori would be reluctant to attack. After only a fortnight, however, the danger was deemed to have passed and the scouts were dismissed.

The resident magistrate promised Bamber that if there was any trouble brewing he would be warned well in advance, and was advised to fall back on a garrison manned by friendly natives at Urenui, about ten miles south-west. Afterwards other settlers would condemn this as hopelessly optimistic. The idea of asking frightened settlers to 'fall back' on a post of friendly natives if there was a raid was farcical. Perhaps there would be no warning. The only warning might be the first murder. Could Bamber, with his helpless wife and children, escape from a party of Hau-hau to a post ten miles away, without roads and across two unbridged rivers that might be in spate, with no armed force to protect their retreat?

In early February four Ngati Maniapoto, one the half-Maori Henry Phillip, son of a white man turned Kingite, passed through the redoubt, greeted Annie Gascoyne, then continued six miles south to the banks of the Mimi River, where they knocked on the door of a bush farm. Captain Messenger opened the door. He had built the redoubt and was in overall control, but now lived on his own farm leaving the blockhouse in the capable hands of Lieutenant Gascoyne. Nobody spoke. Captain Messenger noticed with relief that the Maori were not armed.

'What do you want?' Captain Messenger eventually asked. The Maori said they were hungry; they were heading south on a trading trip and had walked that day all the way from Mokau, thirty miles north. Captain Messenger invited them in and gave them supper. He then punted them across the river.

At about 10.30 a.m. the following Saturday, the unlucky February 13th, the four returned, this time on their way home. There had been a lot of rain in the interim and the Mimi River was swollen, but again Messenger punted them across. By now one of them was the proud owner of a double-barrelled shot-gun, but this didn't bother Messenger. He accompanied them as far as his house, and they assured him that everything was peaceful up north now, there would be no more fighting; they were planning to return with some cattle to sell. Messenger watched them vanish along the track north towards the White Cliffs.

These four Maori passed through the redoubt. Not far beyond they ran into the taua of Wetere and fifteen armed Ngati

Maniapoto warriors, who were heading south from Mokau. One of the traders asked where the warriors were going, and what they were planning to do. Wetere replied, 'We are going to kill the whole of the Europeans at Pukearuhe.' The Maori traders thought this a bad idea, and advised Wetere to turn back to Mokau. Wetere refused, and not only that, he ordered the traders to join him. If they resisted he would kill them. The half-pakeha Phillip, he insisted, was to be his interpreter.

The taua halted by the creek at the cliff base. Hiding their guns, along with thirteen of the Ngati Maniapoto warriors, Wetere and six others, including Phillip, climbed up to the blockhouse. John Milne and a military settler named Edward Richards were sitting on stools each side of the fireplace in Milne's cookhouse. They heard a voice shouting outside, saying that Wetere wanted to see them. Milne flung down his book (*Hector O'Halloran*) and emerged, greeting the Maori cordially and shaking hands. There was, after all, nothing unusual about a group of Maori in the redoubt; they often came this way.

'How can we help?' Milne and Richards asked Phillip.

With a deliberately friendly look on his face, Wetere instructed Phillip to say he had pigs for sale. They were down on the beach, and Wetere wondered if Milne and Richards would like to come and look. The two settlers were delighted at the prospect of fresh pork: Milne could cook up a stew, grill some chops, roast a joint and salt the rest for winter.

'Does he have any peaches?'

Phillip translated for Wetere, and Wetere told Phillip to nod and say, 'Yes.'

Milne and Richards, lured by their bellies, scrambled down the cliff path. This was a new track they had only recently hewn from the rock, and it had seemed a good idea at the time: it made access to the beach so much easier for gathering driftwood for fires or for fishing. Suddenly Richards was struck on the back of his head by a *taiaha*, a spear-like staff, causing (according to the doctor at the inquest) 'instantaneous death'. Milne turned at the sound, flinging up his arms to protect himself, but was hit so hard by a long-handled tomahawk that its handle broke off. His nose and jaw were smashed in, and when he fell another Maori clubbed him twice on the back of the head, causing a cross wound from which 'his brain protruded'.

Two warriors were sent to the Gascoynes' whare but found the family out, apparently gone for a walk or working in their potato fields. Wetere sent for the remainder of the taua, who were waiting on the beach, and ordered them to bring up the guns. This group broke into the Gascoynes' house and seized Bamber's rifle, revolver and ammunition. There was plenty of other plunder inside, but Wetere ordered his men to leave that for when their work was done. Then most of them hid, keeping a lookout and waiting.

It was a lovely summer Saturday. Annie and the children were in their nightdresses, although Annie had added a petticoat over hers; it was warm, and these were their lightest clothes. The family strolled back from their fields, Cecil and Laura toddling behind. On seeing the Maori, Bamber called Annie to his side, took baby Louisa in his arms and together they walked towards the visitors. When they reached the blockhouse hill Bamber went forward alone. He recognized Phillip from earlier that day. 'Hello,' he called cheerily. 'Are you back again already?' Bamber greeted the two other Maori who were with Phillip, and shook hands. The story about the pigs on the beach was repeated. Then something made Bamber suspicious – perhaps their weapons. He suddenly hurried towards his whare, probably to get his gun, and was about to open the door when he was struck from behind. The back of his head deeply tomahawked four times, he fell on his face, motionless. One of the Maori grabbed an axe that had been left lying around after chopping wood, and cleaved his head almost in two.

Baby Louisa had fallen to the ground. With a short-handled club one of the Maori almost sliced off the top of her head.

Annie grabbed the elder children and the three of them fled for their lives, crouching paralysed with fear behind a parapet. When a Maori came back to where Wetere and Phillip were sitting, Wetere asked, 'Have you killed the woman?'

'Yes, and the children too.'

'*Kapai.*' Good.

The examining doctor found that Annie had been beaten in the face 'with the clenched hand', suggesting that she had put up a fight; she was then clubbed to death. Cecil was struck on the back of the head, as was Laura who, the doctor added, had 'two tomahawk wounds on the back of the head apparently inflicted with a short handled tomahawk when the child was in a horizontal position.' In other words, she had tripped while trying to escape, or been found lying face down on the ground in terror.

In their frenzy of killing, Wetere's men also tomahawked the Gascoynes' dog and two cats.

Ropes were lashed round the waists of Annie and Laura, and their bodies dragged over the ground to their home where the dirt floor was scraped out to form a shallow grave. The butchered family were piled in one on top of the other, and covered with earth – but not before the third finger of Annie's left hand had been hacked off, and her wedding ring stolen.

Satisfied that the job was done, Wetere gave permission for his warriors to bring the loot out of the Gascoynes' house so that he could divide it up amongst them. As thanks for his work as interpreter, Wetere presented Phillip with a clean white shirt, six boxes of matches and a new pack of playing cards. As for Wetere, he got the fob watch and the opera glasses, which must have boosted his mana no end.

The taua then helped themselves to ham and potatoes in the cookhouse, and rested.

That day the Reverend John Whiteley saddled his old horse Charley and rode the north-eastern route thirty-five miles from New Plymouth to Pukearuhe, where he planned to spend Saturday night with Bamber and Annie before performing the duties of the Sabbath early the next morning. At dusk he paused at Mr Gregory's house four miles south of the redoubt and took his tea there, as he often did. The venerable Reverend was always welcome. Not only was he much respected, but he was also a fount of local knowledge.

At sixty-two, the Nottinghamshire-born Reverend Whiteley was the oldest missionary in Taranaki. He was also one of the first to reach New Zealand, landing in 1833, seven years before the Treaty of Waitangi. After living for years deep in the Waikato with the Maori, he became a renowned preacher in their native tongue, and earned such admiration that he managed to persuade the Waikato tribes to liberate some Taranaki slaves who they had taken as prisoners of war, and allow them to return home. The Taranaki Maori never forgot this. It was one of several times Whiteley intervened between warring tribes

to conciliate and prevent bloodshed. He also intervened to curb
the excesses of the more land-hungry settlers, mostly taking the
Maori's part. However, since moving from Waikato to Taranaki
and becoming a commissioner for native lands, the Reverend
Whiteley was increasingly sympathetic to the plight of the settlers who, it seemed to him, had been abandoned by the mother
country.*

This afternoon the Reverend Whiteley chatted with Mr Gregory about native matters. Although the situation was still
tense, he told his host that he was satisfied with the safety of
the settlers at Pukearuhe. There was no sign that the King
wanted to get involved with Titokowaru, or to send war parties south. The Reverend Whiteley left that evening at quarter
past six, promising to return the next day for breakfast before
holding divine service at nine o'clock at Mr McDonald's next
door.

The weather on Sunday was stormy and the rivers rose, so
when the Reverend Whiteley failed to appear, the McDonalds
and Mr Gregory assumed he had stayed on with Lieutenant
Gascoyne. On Monday morning the McDonald family set out

---

* Donald McLean met the Reverend Whiteley in 1844 when trouble first arose
in New Plymouth over careless land purchases by the New Zealand Company.
The settlers had been forced to abandon their new farms and return the land
to the Maori. As sub-protector of Aborigines, McLean was sent by Governor
Fitzroy overland to New Plymouth via Mokau where Reverend Whiteley was
living in the mission station. McLean described him as 'the excellent Wesleyan
missionary'. McLean carried a letter from Fitzroy asking Whiteley to accompany McLean to Taranaki because of his long experience of the West Coast
tribes, and to use his best efforts to bring peace. McLean stayed with
Whiteley several times on further expeditions along the West Coast. Whiteley
received McLean with 'frankness and hospitality', and was one of McLean's
earliest friends in New Zealand.

to work in their bush farm as usual, but young John McDonald had some business at the redoubt. His horse was fresh and
difficult to catch, so he made up for lost time by riding over at
a brisk pace – so brisk that he noticed nothing unusual until he
arrived.

The previous evening, while Wetere and his cohorts were
dividing up their plunder, one of the sentries warned of a figure
in the distance riding towards the redoubt. Wetere said,
'Whether it is a white man or a native, we must kill him.'

Five men were set to watch. As the horseman approached a
lookout called, 'It's a white man.'

'Let him come.'

Mr Whiteley trotted innocently towards them. The only
sound was his hoofs beating on the dirt road between the poro-
poro branches. He cannot have seen Wetere from that distance,
but if he had he might have shouted a warm greeting to John
Wesley. At the same time he might also have been suspicious:
why was Wetere here, and where were the Gascoynes?

A shot rang out, and the horse fell, dead. The Reverend
Whiteley was flung to the ground, and a barrage of rifle fire
killed him. He was stripped of his coat, waistcoat and watch,
and Charley of his saddle and bridle, and the taua set off for
home, taking the horse and guns and loot and leaving two men
to burn the buildings.

In 1882, thirteen years later, Captain Messenger interviewed
Wetere in Mokau. Wetere claimed that King Tawhiao had
ordered him on this mission, and he maintained that on recog-
nizing Mr Whiteley, he had been appalled: the missionary, well
known by all the taua from when he lived amongst them at the
mission house in Mokau, was the last white man in the world

he would choose to kill. Wetere claimed that on hearing a shot, he ran out of a whare and saw the horse dead, but Mr Whiteley standing unhurt. Wetere shouted '*Hokia! Hokia!* Go back!' The dutiful Mr Whiteley refused, crying, 'I must first see what bad work you have been doing here.' One of the party fired a double-barrelled shotgun, but missed. Whiteley knelt to pray out loud, when someone shouted, 'Shoot him. Dead men tell no tales!' (Or in another version, the more pungent: 'Dead cocks do not crow.') A volley was fired – not, Wetere implied, by him – and Mr Whiteley dropped dead to the ground.

Legend had it that Wetere was then filled with repugnance at what he had instigated. He and his taua knew the old missionary, and they knew how much he had helped their people, so instead of continuing their raid and finishing off all the settlers in Pukearuhe – the McDonalds and Mr Gregory and Fred Trent and the rest – the taua turned for home. In effect Mr Whiteley sacrificed himself, and his bravery saved many lives.*

John McDonald had immediately recognized the body as Reverend Whiteley, and only then noticed that the blockhouse and whares had been burnt out. Panic rising, he wheeled round

---

* In Henry Phillip's confession, made the same year, but for fear of reprisals by Wetere not published until after Phillip's death, no mention is made of Wetere's humanity and sense of shame. Instead Phillip described a bleak and efficient murder. Wetere killed everyone at the redoubt, and once the job was done, he left. In September 1879 a surveyor named Skinner, a friend of Whiteley's grandson, employed two of the murderers to help survey some land in the King Country. Skinner reported that 'The native who had felled Mrs Gascoyne and the infant in her arms was one, and he was an ugly ill-tempered fellow, but a good worker. Other members of the raiding gang, including Wetere, the leader, were in close contact with me during the survey, and care had to be taken in dealing with them, but no trouble arose.'

and galloped home to his father to raise the alarm, then rode to the other settlers to warn them that murder was rife among them. Dreading a repeat of Te Kooti's massacres, the settlers 'fell back' to Urenui, as they had been advised to do.

John McDonald's father rode at once to New Plymouth to raise the alarm. A party of seventy-two volunteers and militia plus a surgeon and a doctor responded with alacrity and boarded the SS *Wellington* to recover the bodies and try to capture the murderers. Everyone in town flocked to the beach to watch them depart – parents, wives and children afraid their loved ones might meet the fate of the Gascoynes. Several families from outlying settlements had already sought refuge on board, and were camped on deck. By afternoon the *Wellington* reached the Wai-iti Gap, the landing place for the White Cliffs about five miles south of Pukearuhe, where they met other mounted troopers who had ridden up to cover their landing.

Even though it was now late, the party travelled the last stretch overland to the White Cliffs, hoping to rescue anyone who might still be alive. They found nothing for the doctors to do, so they camped for the night and in the morning disinterred the bodies and carried them to the ship, where they laid them in the cabin.

The steamer returned to New Plymouth, pausing at the Mimi River to take on board the fleeing Captain Messenger with all his furniture. It was a beautiful evening when the ship arrived. A thousand people gathered on the beach, beneath a new moon that shed a melancholy light on the sand. With the steamer's flag at half-mast, the eight bodies were carried to a shed beside the customs house, where they lay until after the inquest. Speculation was rife. Was this a declaration of war by the Kingites? Would the Kingites combine with Titokowaru, and even with Te Kooti? The superintendent was forced to issue a calming announcement that no one knew who had committed the murders, but that there was no reason to assume this massacre had anything to do with the King. Nevertheless garrisons were stationed in all blockhouses, including the remnants of Pukearuhe.

On the afternoon of 17 February, the stores, bank and all public offices closed as a mark of respect while the coffins, some draped in Union Jacks, were conveyed through the streets. A procession over a thousand strong escorted them to New Plymouth's hilltop cemetery, where the Gascoynes and Reverend Whiteley and the other two settlers were buried with full honours. Their grave was marked with an impressive obelisk. For Bamber it was an appropriate final resting place, given that he had grown up largely in Plymouth – Plymouth, England, that is.

It was five years to the very day since Bamber landed here, full of hopes for his new life.

One month later Isabella wrote to Lord Salisbury.

March 22nd 1869
The Bungalow

My Lord,
Although personally unacquainted with your Lordship, I
believe I am right in supposing that you will take an interest
in the late frightful massacre of British settlers in the

*Province of Taranaki, especially as Lieut. Bamber Gascoyne
was a near relative of your own – your second cousin. I send
by this mail a Taranaki paper containing an account of this
melancholy tragedy. He was a fine gentlemanly man
universally liked, and was struggling with having limited
means to support a wife and children. He has two younger
brothers who have also come out here as settlers but without
any capital – they must sink into poverty. I simply mention
this in case you, as the present head of the family, would
wish to aid these deserving young men in any way. My
application to you is made on my own responsibility without
the knowledge of my husband (Major Charles Manners
Gascoyne, late of the 5th Bengal Cavalry) or my nephews.*

*Our case is a deplorable one. Cast aside by the mother
country and left to our own resources what will become of
us unless English sympathy is enlisted in our favour? You my
Lord can do this by bringing the subject before the House of
Lords, from the fact of your having visited these islands
some years ago (shortly before our arrival from India).
I have every hope of your interesting yourself in this crisis.*

> *Believe me My Lord*
> *Yours very faithfully*
> *Isabella Augusta Gascoyne*

The massacre created an exceptional furore. There would be
more killings, but none that stirred the public so intensely.
There were accusations of negligence that the Gascoynes had
been left undefended, and in June 1870 Bamber's mother Julia
told Lord Salisbury that she even hoped for a pension from the
colonial government because the fort at Pukearuhe had not
been properly garrisoned. (Her claim had been sent to Sir
George Bowen who, she said, had answered encouragingly.) But

the uproar was about more than recrimination and compensation. The missionary was respected by both settlers and local Maori; the children were young and innocent; then there was Bamber himself, a gentleman who had come down in the world but was struggling to raise himself up in the colony. He was Everyman. Every settler identified with him.

None could answer that same question: Why? Was it because the redoubt occupied confiscated land? Was it because it barred the only viable route by which the Kingites could join Titokowaru? No one knew. And why the killing of children, again? Perhaps it because they were pakeha who would grow up to take Maori land. Perhaps they were randomly selected victims, simply in the way of the war party. Perhaps it was vengeance. Fred knew as well as anyone how potent utu could be, and might have remembered Captain Newland and his Kai Iwi Cavalry's slaughter of Maori children at Handley's Woolshed the previous November. Quite often the Maori took that long to exact revenge.

When King Tawhiao saw Annie Gascoyne's wedding ring he recoiled and swore it was not his work. Nevertheless, the deed was done, so he ordered over a thousand warriors into the field. Whitmore received news that six hundred armed Ngati Maniapoto had assembled at Mokau. Everyone feared the North Island stood on the brink of a union of the Kingites with Titokowaru which would plunge the whole country into an abyss of violence.

Whitmore offered rewards of £1,000 each for Te Kooti and Titokowaru, alive or dead, £5 for every Maori rebel brought in alive and £10 for every rebel chief, Wetere included.

Fred continued to hunt for Titokowaru through the worst

of the west coast's swamps and ravines, enduring the most frightful marches and the most difficult campaign of all New Zealand's wars, for which he blamed the hated Whitmore, but Titokowaru slipped away. On the east coast, Te Kooti was still murdering people, and in the absence of what many New Zealanders demanded – a severe military clampdown – some Poverty Bay settlers took revenge into their own hands. New Zealand was plunged, it seemed, into its worst-ever crisis. Outlying regions were ruined, schools and mission stations abandoned, towns overburdened with refugees. Many settlers were destitute, and no one was working the land. The country was virtually bankrupt. The colonial army was condemned as a failure, and the Maori kupapa grew ever more disaffected. There were calls for McLean to return as Native Secretary – he was said to be the only person who understood the situation – and even more strident calls for Bowen to impose martial law.

Resentment against the imperial government reached a crescendo. In a notoriously insensitive dispatch sent too soon after Bamber's murder, Earl Granville, the new Colonial Secretary, implied that the crisis was of the colonists' own making – the result of their greed – and that their internal security was no longer any concern of the British government. New Zealand had asked for independence in the management of native affairs in 1862, and having accepted the responsibility for self-defence associated with such independence, could look after itself. The solution, Granville suggested, was to return the confiscated land. The Colonial Secretary also chastised Sir George Bowen for not having made an official report on the matter of Maori heads; by offering a price on them the colonists would only 'exasperate and extend' hostilities. Bowen replied firmly that many in New Zealand believed that since the British government had declined to take any part in the suppression of rebellion, it no longer had any right to interfere in internal affairs. The price on Titokowaru's head was (in other words) none of Whitehall's business.

Bowen – caught between the colonists demanding revenge, the Gascoyne family demanding justice and his imperial masters in London demanding reconciliation – followed his own liberal instincts and held back.* He argued that both kupapa and Hau-hau would respond less well to a show of brutality than to a demonstration of calmness, common sense and justice. Besides, Bowen argued, the fanatical Hau-haus, 'starving and shivering in sullen seclusion on their hills and morasses', would eventually desire the comforts enjoyed by Maori such as the Hawke's Bay chiefs and would surely abandon the fight of their own accord.

Soon after Bamber's massacre, a trial was held of some of the Maori rebels captured on the west and east coasts. Bowen, ever liberal, argued that blood shed on the battlefield was different from that shed on a political scaffold. It would, he believed, be more useful to seek an end to war than to hang its perpetrators. Consequently only one man, an unusually fearful

---

* Bowen was wary of committing the same error as Governor Edward Eyre, whose case, like a warning, filled pages of his scrapbook. In 1865 Eyre had brutally suppressed an uprising of former slaves in Jamaica, and illegally imposed martial law. 'Rebels' were hanged. His behaviour raised a storm in England, and an inquiry reported that he should not be reinstated. As if to remind himself, Bowen wrote rather pompously in the frontispiece of his scrapbook: 'I am a constitutional Governor, and decline to deal with State questions except in a constitutional manner.'

Maori who was unjustly used as a scapegoat for Te Kooti, was hanged.

In any case, battle was not an option, since far from sending help, the Colonial Office announced the removal of the last imperial regiment. Bowen put his job on the line by intervening personally several times to postpone its departure, but the 18th (Royal Irish) finally left early in 1870.

The debate spread in a blizzard of British press. Lord Carnarvon, the recently resigned Secretary of State for the Colonies, put the case *for* New Zealand when he wrote to *The Times* that surely a small outlay by the home government was ultimately the best economy. The North Island was in dire straits, with property and life endangered; the settlers had now offered to pay towards imperial defence; and their loyalty and affection were not trifles to be thrown away and resumed at pleasure. Thomas Carlyle, who had long championed emigration as a solution to Britain's overpopulation, wrote that he shared the indignation at the treatment of New Zealand, and believed that the government should be taught that it is not permissible to 'cut away the English colonies, and fling into the sea, as useless lumber and encumbrance . . . the most precious possession any Nation ever had.'

When brigands at Marathon in Greece murdered four British tourists, *The Times* called for prompt and severe punishment, and for noble vengeance for the blood of the murdered Englishmen. The New Zealanders were insulted that those deaths received voluminous coverage, while the Gascoynes and Reverend Whiteley were ignored. Sir George Grey wrote to *The Times* that just because New Zealand was further away than Greece, there was no reason for the response to the White Cliffs massacre to be any less vociferous. It raised the question of the status of colonists in the Empire: did they have the same rights as the British, or not? And if not, why stay in the British Empire at all?

People talked of independence, or even annexation by the USA. The Great Pacific Railroad had just been completed, and direct communication between New Zealand and a rapidly expanding San Francisco could reduce New Zealand's dependence on Great Britain. An editorial in the *New Zealand Herald* declared bitterly, 'Our trade will go with our sympathies, and they will avowedly be far from those, who, in their feelings and dealings with us, mingle the love of a step mother with the sharp practice of a petty huckster.' Official visits were paid to the USA, and friendly overtures made by former premier Sir William Fox to the US Consul in New Zealand. When an American steamer, the *Nevada*, called into Auckland in May 1871, its officers were royally wined and dined.

It is unlikely that Isabella elicited much sympathy from Lord Salisbury. The second Marquess had died in 1868 and been succeeded by his son, Robert Gascoyne-Cecil. Although the new Lord Salisbury would become the Tory Colossus who bestrode the expanding British Empire as both Prime Minister and Foreign Secretary (for a while simultaneously), a youthful Grand Tour in 1852 to the Cape Colony, Australia and New Zealand had given him a lifelong disdain for colonists, who he dismissed as 'incorrigible, plausible scapegraces'. The colonists had caused the wars through their rapacious greed, foolish land-confiscation policy and above all what he called their 'nigger-despising temper'. Lord Salisbury did not go so far as the anti-imperialists who would willingly have cut the colonies adrift, but he did share the view that the Maori had been treated unjustly. If the murder of his second cousin was the result, it was a tragedy, but there was little he could do about it.

As a Plymouth sister, Isabella might have felt obliged to turn the other cheek and beg for the forgiveness of her nephew's killers. Not at all. Vengeance may have been for the Lord alone, and faith would triumph over evil, but that did not stop her wanting justice. However, Wetere and his war party remained unpunished and undisturbed at Mokau from where, it was feared, they could at any moment strike out again.

SEVENTEEN

Sailor Prince

Two months after the Gascoyne murders, relief arrived in the shape of Prince Alfred, Queen Victoria's second son. Although he could do little of practical use, he was the perfect person to reignite the flame of loyalty among both settlers and Maori. This was because an earlier visit – the first by any member of the royal family – had been postponed when the Prince, enjoying a picnic in Sydney, was shot through the lungs by a Fenian assassin.* Prince Alfred was rushed to safety, the Fenian caught and strung up and the whole affair turned into a propaganda coup that served to boost public sympathy for the Prince and loyalty towards the royal family. Now fully recovered, the Sailor Prince arrived on his man-of-war, the *Galatea*, the largest warship ever to have visited New Zealand. Her masts riding the waves like the fretted spires of three cathedrals, the *Galatea* was a tremendous symbol of British power. Prince Alfred also

---

* For a while it looked as if the Fenians would be a source of trouble for Bowen too. A Catholic priest and a group of 'seditious and evil-disposed persons', according to the indictment at their trial in May 1868, were accused of spreading inflammatory anti-Queen propaganda, and of exciting hatred of the United Kingdom's government and constitution. The trial was a huge affair, calling into question the freedom of speech, and although the defendants were found guilty, they were imprisoned only briefly and fined token sums. Bowen clearly took the case seriously: it occupies thirty columns in his scrapbook.

brought good will embodied in his fun-loving suite, an orchestra conducted by the Prince himself, his own bagpipe player and even stage sets for his private theatricals. He provided a wonderful diversion in troubled times.

On 11 April 1869 thousands gathered at the wharf in Wellington to greet the Prince, and after exchanges of formal greetings, the procession trouped to Government House where fifteen hundred children sang the National Anthem (and were rewarded with tarts and buns).

Sir George Bowen took the Prince to visit the major settlements. In Nelson the list of those attending the royal levee read like a list of members of the old Glass Case: Henry Blundell, Mr Jennings of Pangatotara, one of the Greenwoods, Nathaniel Edwards, Major Richmond. In short, more or less everyone of note – including eleven Maori – except the Gascoynes. Charles and Isabella were also absent from the 'brilliant ball' in Nelson which was attended by three hundred and fifty people. 'We believe', crowed the *Nelson Chronicle*, 'no ball yet given in the colony ever surpassed this gathering, either in extent of enjoyment, or in the beauty of the ladies, whose presence graced the assembly.' Perhaps the Gascoynes would have been shocked at the very thought of such devilish distractions from the true path of righteousness, or perhaps they were still suffering from the after-effects of their social disgrace, and were not invited.

Prince Alfred's departure from New Zealand was delayed at the eleventh hour – the *Galatea* was about to set her sails – by a government attempt to persuade King Tawhiao to meet the Prince and Bowen. Ignoring those settlers who condemned this as a climb-down, government envoys had been sent into the

King Country to make overtures of peace. Diplomatic negotiations took place with the King's advisers, but they continuously created obstructions until one of King Tawhiao's greatest generals, Rewi Maniapoto, sent this definitive response:

A man had built a small house which he was particularly anxious to keep to himself, free from all intrusion. One cold day a camel came to his door and very politely asked him that he might be allowed to warm himself at his fire.

'No,' said the owner of the house, 'go away, you with the big eyes and ugly head. I do not want you here, I did not send for you; stop outside.'

Then said the camel, 'If you will not let me come inside, let me put my nose inside your door, so that I may smell your fire; that will not harm you.'

The man consented to this; but when the camel smelt how warm was the inside of the house, he soon put his feet there, and when his feet were inside they brought in his body, and the man's house was full. Then the man was angry, and said, 'Go outside, or I will beat you out,' but the camel would not move. The man then seized hold of the camel, and beat him.

'Do not beat me,' said the camel, 'you are hurting me.' But he did not go out, and the man beat him again, but the camel would not leave. He then proceeded to beat him with all his strength; then the camel lifted his leg, and kicked the man so severely that he died, and the camel stayed in the house.

Rewi added:

The pakehas are like the camel in my story, they come, they are the nose; more pakehas follow, they are the feet; let once

*the feet inside and you will have no end of them, and if you
get angry they will kick you out and take possession of your
place.*

Negotiations with the King collapsed and Prince Alfred
departed, but all was not lost. It transpired that the attack on
Pukearuhe had come too late: King Tawhiao had already withdrawn his support from Titokowaru. Meanwhile the British did
not retaliate as the Ngati Maniapoto hoped, and the war fizzled
out. Although Titokowaru was not actually defeated, he came
to be seen as a sinking ship, and his army floated away.

Fred was sent back to the Urewera, where Te Kooti
remained a threat. There was more hard marching, more starvation rations, more killing of both settlers and friendly natives
and more skirmishes in the bush, in which some of Fred's closest friends died. Te Kooti remained, as always, one step ahead,
but support for him was dwindling too, particularly when most
of his followers were captured. Eventually – to Fred's disgust –
the government announced that Te Kooti and his remaining
men were to be arrested without bloodshed. As Fred knew this
was impossible, he gave up, and Te Kooti travelled past him
unmolested to the King Country. The hunt was over.

Whitmore was shunted aside (to Fred's relief) and McLean
left Maraekakaho to return to the fray as Minister with the
double brief of both Native Affairs and Defence, a post he
retained for seven and a half years, no matter which party was
in power. He adopted a firm but conciliatory policy; to many
settlers' outrage, the pragmatic McLean refused to punish
Titokowaru by confiscating his land in central Taranaki, and
instead returned it to him in the understanding that Titokowaru

would otherwise take up arms again.* At last seeing the folly of encouraging settlement on confiscated land, McLean agreed with Bowen that any further settlements on confiscated land should be opposed, and together they undertook tireless visits to the major settlements and clans. McLean became the first minister to cross into the King Country to open negotiations with the King's henchmen; he hoped to persuade them to hand over Te Kooti, stop sending out war parties and mutually to strive for peace. The korero was a success and at the end several Maori rushed forward to shake hands and rub noses with their old friend. Rewi Maniapoto, King Tawhaio's leading chief, declared that 'Light was now peeping out like the dawn; it would soon spread.'

Isabella had scant news from Fred, but she read in her *Nelson Chronicle* in the summer of 1870 that Prince Alfred had returned on a private visit and was being taken by Sir George Bowen on a tour of the central North Island. This was brave – perhaps foolhardy – since no Europeans lived here yet and Te

---

* McLean was partly right: in 1881, four years after McLean's death, Titokowaru again tried to prevent the creeping confiscations by Taranaki settlers, but this time through non-violent resistance. He joined a prophet leader named Te Whiti in carrying out monthly raids ploughing up settlers' land. Fred was transferred back to the west coast and arrested Titokowaru and sent him to jail in New Plymouth. He was released after eight months, and became a wandering prophet of peace before embarking on further non-violent protests. Fred arrested him again, along with Te Whiti, but they were bound over to keep the peace and released. Titokowaru died a free man in 1888. The onward march of the land-hungry had proved impossible to resist.

Kooti had only just slipped away ahead of them. Isabella read that their strong guard of honour, a native contingent of Arawas, was commanded by none other than Captain Frederick Gascoyne.

Out in the bush, Fred and his troop had found their clothes disintegrating so they had taken to wearing sacks split lengthways as shawls, which they wrapped around their waists like kilts. Prince Alfred was so charmed by this novel style that he and his friends adopted it. Be-kilted, the royal party travelled under Fred's guard to the Hot Lakes of Rotorua, and the celebrated pink and white Rotomahana Terraces.* While the Arawas performed a fearsome haka on the shore, the guests bathed in the warm sulphurous water. When they undressed, Fred was astonished to see that although Queen Victoria's son seemed a shy and awkward man, his arms, legs and chest were smothered in flamboyant Japanese-style coloured flowers, birds and dragons. His friend, the powerfully built Lord Charles Beresford, was even more elaborately tattooed all over his body in nautical emblems, anchors, ships and dolphins.

Prince Alfred presented Fred with a signed photograph and thanked him for all the arrangements for his comfort, protection and amusement. On his return to Scotland in 1871 the Prince wrote to Bowen to report that his passage home was very long and tedious, and added, 'I shall always look back to our trip to the hot lakes as one of the pleasantest and most successful trips I ever made.'

---

* These would be smothered by a terrible earthquake in 1886.

With Te Kooti gone, Fred and his Maori troops were sent into the bush to hack out roads. McLean and Bowen believed that roads would open up the interior and leave no place for rebels to hide. Bowen reminded the Colonial Office (at some length) that this was a scheme that had worked well in the Scottish Highlands after the Jacobite rebellion, and had forever destroyed the independence of the Scottish clans – McLean's included. To hasten that day, Bowen invited Wanganui chief Mete Kingi aboard the vice-regal yacht for a voyage to the major South Island settlements. It was a propaganda exercise designed to demonstrate the glories of modern British civilization. Bowen pictured the future British Empire as a federation, like the United States. Great Britain would cease to be an island off the coast of Europe, but would be a great homogeneous people of one blood, language, religion, law and constitution, dispersed over boundless space. That civilization would naturally be British. According to the press, a suitably impressed Mete Kingi duly reported back to his people the wonderful light that burns without oil (gas), and the melting of iron until it runs like water and the great hammer that kneads iron like bread. Bowen's attitude was despised by Lord Salisbury as a form of racism, but Bowen meant well.

To prove that peace (or was it conquest?) was a reality, Bowen mounted his horse, and in April 1872 rode the length of the North Island from Wellington to Auckland, across the Ureweras. It was a brave gesture, and he survived unscathed even in those places which until very recently were seething with hostile Hau-haus.

At the same time, a change of Colonial Secretary brought a

new conciliatory tone from Whitehall, and £1 million from the British government. Loyalty towards the Mother Country was restored.

EIGHTEEN

The Deluge

Peace had come to New Zealand and, after years of domestic strife, to the Bungalow. Charles and Isabella were photographed in a Nelson studio; not as a couple (perhaps that was asking too much) but at least at the same time and place. Both are seated, Charles bearded, still handsome with his thick head of hair, albeit now white, and that one quizzical eyebrow raised. His gaze is challenging, sceptical, clever, a trifle haughty. His bearing is still militarily upright. Isabella wears a more resigned expression. Although still beautiful, her hair under her lace bonnet dark, her nose perfectly straight, her large gentle eyes set wide apart, her forehead high, her brow is furrowed and as she leans her head in her hand she looks worn out. As if to convince the viewer of her tireless work as a wife and mother, she holds some knitting.

Fred had not been home since June 1863, after he lost his gold. He did not share his parents' religious extremism, but that did not stop him from missing them. He had failed to visit partly because he had been swept up in war, but also because absence from the army would place him on half-pay, leaving him too poor to make the journey south. Fred was a professional militia officer, not a colonist, but part of his payment included the offer of land. In November 1869 he wrote to

338

McLean to beg him to 'take such steps as you deem advisable' to cause confiscated Maori land at Poverty Bay to be allotted to him.* If he was given his allotment papers, he could use them to raise a loan.

Nothing happened for two and a half years. McLean's policy was to stop all settlement on confiscated land. Nevertheless commitments had been made, and in 1872 Fred was at last able to write to thank McLean for fifty acres in Hawke's Bay. Although not much, and not exactly what he had wanted, Fred could now raise a mortgage to pay for him to go to Pangatotara. He had not seen his parents for nine years.

He left it too late. On 5 September of the same year Charles, aged sixty-six, died.

Isabella, with her eldest son at her side, joined the rest of the family in the parlour at the Bungalow for executors John and Frederick Greenwood to read out Charles's last will and testament. Isabella had rejoiced in her reconciliation with her husband. Now she discovered that he had betrayed her after all.

Province of Nelson, New Zealand, 7th of January 1866.
I, Charles Manners Gascoyne, do hereby will and bequeath to Amelia Sutherland the whole of my flock of sheep (at this time in charge of Henry Williams and George Williams, brothers) to retain or sell or otherwise dispose of, in any manner she, the

---

* He was keen to be stationed at Poverty Bay not only because he knew the area and its natives so well, but also because part of his division was already there. Furthermore, his knee had never recovered from his injury while tracking Te Kooti, and he found marching and rough work very painful, but on the plains of Poverty Bay he could do all his soldiering and farming on horseback. He did not mention the delightful young Marion Carr, who lived nearby and had been the object of his attentions for several years.

aforesaid Amelia Sutherland pleases. I likewise bequeath to the said Amelia Sutherland my filly named 'Shade'. Also to the said Amelia Sutherland I bequeath the books, furniture, prints, clock and all other articles, heretofore my property, which may be found in her apartment at the hour of my death.

There was a further request, which would have tested the strength of even Isabella's devotion to duty.

It is my hope that my sons may be led to remain on the estate with their mother and sisters to cultivate and improve it – and that Amelia Sutherland may be led by the deep affection and respect of the whole family to remain with them as heretofore, a member of the family, residing with them as in her own home.

This seemed, at last, to offer proof of Charles's love for the governess. However, after making his will, Charles had time to reflect on the effect these words might have on his family and his reputation.

It has pleased my heavenly father to prolong my life another year, during which events have occurred to induce me to add a codicil to my last will and testament as this.

To lessen any surprise that might possibly be felt or expressed at my leaving my flock of sheep to Amelia Sutherland, I hereby declare that I owe the said Amelia Sutherland more than the full value of the said flock as her salary, which owing to her friendly generosity and my straitened circumstances was always greatly in arrears. But while this my bequest will, I trust, render my beloved friend independent of others, I still indulge the hope that my widow with all my sons and daughters will each and all ever regard her not only as a member of the family, but its best friend.

So even now the precise nature of Charles's relationship with Amelia was in doubt. Were they adulterous lovers, or was that simply a figment of Isabella's post-natally warped imagination? What did the words 'beloved friend' actually mean?

It no longer mattered. Charles need not have worried about Amelia, nor whether Isabella would be able to treat her as her 'best friend', because by the time the will was read Miss Sutherland, at the age of fifty-four, had succumbed to typhoid followed by 'a softening of the brain', and had been dead for four years. Charles was buried beside her in Pangatotara cemetery, where Isabella did not join them.

In a letter to McLean – black-bordered, so observing the etiquette – Isabella did not mention Charles or her grief at losing him. Instead she rallied.

The Bungalow
Dec. 4th 1872

My dear Cousin,
Although long years have passed since I have heard from you
– I know that your time and thoughts are occupied by public
matters – that I am not surprised at your curtailing an
unnecessary correspondence. I have taken great interest in
your public career, and always feel a personal pride in your
success.

My daughter Mary wishes to join me in receiving a few
young ladies to educate, and as I know of no one who has a
more extensive acquaintance than you, I enclose a
'prospectus', and will feel indebted to your distributing them
among any friends you think likely to send as pupils.

I have long expected a visit from Douglas, but fear he has

not the same warm remembrance of his childish affection,
that I have. If with you, pray give him my love.

Fred in his last letter tells me that he had paid a visit to
your brother Alick, who with Mrs Captain McLean were
delighted to see him, and much pleased to hear of his
engagement to Marion Carr, whose father was an old friend.

Do write me a line if you can spare the time, and with
my daughters' kind regards added to mine, believe me,
    Your affectionate cousin,
    Isa. Gascoyne
    Accept all the compts. of the season

PROSPECTUS
Mrs Gascoyne, aided by her daughters, will be willing to
receive a few young ladies under 14 years of age as Boarders,
after Easter next. Terms 50 guineas per annum including all
Extras save medical aid when required.

The instruction will comprise French, Music and the
usual branches of a thoroughly good English education,
Dancing and Drawing if required.

The situation is remarkably healthy.

The situation, however, was not healthy. That very year the
Motueka River had risen and poured across the valley into the
house. Much of Isabella's furniture, including the piano, was
wrecked, while the road was washed away. Even so, Isabella
struggled on at Pangatotara for another five years.

In 1877 her letters ceased when McLean, aged only fifty-six,
was felled by a combination of rheumatism and dropsy. Isabella
must have been devastated; their correspondence had lasted
more than two decades. Recently they had drifted apart –
McLean was being feted on a tour of south-east Australia, and

in 1874 being knighted for his role as architect of peace, and Isabella no longer relied on his emotional or material support – but he was still her greatest friend. In their last photographs she and Charles each had something on the table beside them, like a saint's emblem providing the clues to their personalities or to their martyrdom – St Peter with his keys, St Lawrence with his rack of coals. For Charles it was a pile of books, for Isabella a photograph of a child. One the intellect, the other the heart. The photograph was not of one of her own children, although her love of children was a key to her character and a source of pain, but was of an infant Donald McLean. She seemed to be saying that it was McLean she cared about most in the world.

Thousands of Maori attended McLean's Gaelic–Maori funeral in Napier, and those who could not attend held korero around the country in memory of Te Makarini, and although he is remembered by the Ringatu church as 'Pharoah' who held Te Kooti and his followers in bondage and stole their lands, and although he was criticized for sparking the Taranaki War, for failing to open up the King Country for settlement, and by some Maori chiefs for putting undue pressure on them to sell, mostly effusive tributes from Maori chiefs rolled in.

It was a disastrous year for Isabella, a year of endings. Not only did she lose her most loved and admired confidant, but on 6 February 1877 she lost her home.

It was midsummer, after a long spell of sultry weather. The air was stagnant and many people sensed something terrible approaching. They expected an earthquake. Then heavy clouds massed on the hills, so swollen with rain that they seemed to rest on the summits for support. When sheets of blue lightning rent the black clouds, the deluge began. Throughout the night the earth seemed to moan in protest. Every little rivulet became a torrent, gouging out rocks and soil and uprooting trees. The soil had been loosened by the bush-felling by farmers and gold miners, like Fred. The debris was shot downstream into larger tributaries and valleys where it collected in gully mouths to form dams, which became a series of lakes. These lakes swelled in the Baton River, and the Clarke, Wangapeka and Stanley Brook rivers. The following day almost simultaneously they burst, sending rocks and trees and water into the Motueka River, whose height suddenly leapt in a way never seen before.

When those indoors saw water seeping into their houses, most gathered what provisions they could carry and fled to barns on higher ground. As the water followed them there, they struggled to drag horses and cows and calves and dogs up onto the relative safety of piles of grain. By morning they were surrounded by three feet of swirling mud-brown water. Outside, entire haystacks were seen shooting past, then their neighbours' cowsheds, fowl houses and pigsties. A settler described watching horrified as cattle struggled for their lives, only to be sucked under; he saw a goose going by, honking defiantly on a log.

The force of the flow with its mountain of timber and stones shattered everything in its path and drove the detritus ahead of it. The bridge at Pangatotara was swept away and left sprawling on the bank. Earth and sand and rocks and tree trunks and remains of fencing and barns and ploughs and carts and horses thundered past the Bungalow. One family had left their house twenty minutes before the house itself was washed away, and it fetched up with the remains of its contents on Isabella's field.

As always Mr Jennings was keen to help. He and his son risked their lives by saving their boat and using it to rescue their neighbours. Some of those they failed to reach were forced to take refuge on logs, where they remained for twenty-four hours. It was a miracle that no one drowned.

The floodwaters filled the valley from hill to hill, and when they receded they left behind a scene of desolation. The valley, as Isabella had known it, was gone. She knew it would never recover its pristine beauty. The road was destroyed. Orchards were so drowned in mud that only their tops were visible, and rocks that must have weighed over fifty tons were strewn across paddocks. Some people could barely tell where their homes had once been. Of all the farms, the Gascoynes' was the worst. Not a single crop or even a blade of grass was left standing.

The Motueka River had ferried the family upstream, given them life in the form of water, food and gold, and spiritually borne them into a new life in Christ. Now this river took everything back. The Gascoynes' debt was repaid with interest, first with Fred's gold, then with the farm, Isabella's school, the meeting house, even the actual land because the river changed course, and much of Isabella's property now lay on the other bank.

Not content with sweeping away the life of the living, the river swept away the dead too. The cemetery at Pangatotara was swamped. Charles's headstone was sluiced out into Blind Bay and beyond, along with Miss Sutherland's, neither of them ever to be seen again.

Epilogue

In Napier on Christmas Day 1872, with peace assured at last, the Bishop of Waiapu married Fred to Marion Carr. Now with the stalwart Marion at his side, Fred continued his snakes-and-ladders rise up the military hierarchy, suffering many a career setback along the way. On the positive side Fred felt he had the ability to act quickly on his own initiative, while his experience of the Maori and knowledge of their language enabled him to recognize when there might be genuine cause for alarm. But he had no time for diplomacy. He was twice arrested for insubordination, and he had more rows with the hated Whitmore. Fred also failed to conceal his contempt for the lack of patriotism and common sense that he perceived to be the main traits of the Liberals who ran the government.

In 1863 Fred was commanding Alexandra, a strategically important redoubt cresting a 300ft crag much like that at Pukearuhe, on the northern boundary of the King Country. Relations with the Kingites had improved, but when two pakeha and a 'friendly' chief attempted to cross the King Country to go south to Mokau they were turned back. One was a government surveyor attempting to prospect for the North

Island railway to continue its journey south from Auckland across the King Country, to which many Kingites objected. Fred urgently summoned the Defence Minister, John Bryce,* to arrange for these travellers to be given a safe passage, and the group left again, this time under the protection of a strong party of Ngati Maniapoto. But they were captured, bound with bullock chains and thrown to the ground in an open shed.† Three pigs were named after each of the prisoners, and they were then eaten in a symbolic act of cannibalism that destroyed the captives' mana. Fred immediately called for reinforcements to help him rescue the prisoners by force.

It transpired that the surveyor was Captain Charles Wilson Hursthouse, son of one Charles Flinders Hursthouse, author of *Hursthouse's New Zealand*, the very book that had lured the Gascoynes to New Zealand in the first place. His companion was the man who had killed the dream, none other than Wetere himself. Wetere was never punished and – to Isabella's outrage – he was exonerated that same year.

In a further twist, to Fred's astonishment, he was beaten to their rescue. Their saviour was the very man who had been Fred's quarry for so long. The prisoners had heard a voice calling through the walls of the slab hut of their incarceration, 'It is I! It is I! my children.' When the hut door was forced open they must have been terrified to find themselves face to face with

---

* It was John Bryce who led Captain Newland's cavalry into the fray at Handley's Woolshed when the Maori children were massacred, and for which the Gascoyne children's murder may have been revenge.

† The surveyor's presence was particularly objectionable because he surveyed confiscated land for settlement. He had surveyed the Waitara block in 1860, which sparked the Taranaki War.

Te Kooti. Instead of murdering them on the spot, he escorted them to safety. A month earlier Te Kooti, now living in the King Country across the river from Fred's redoubt, had been promised an amnesty for past crimes on condition of good behaviour, and this rescue was a demonstration of his change of heart. To thank him personally for his help, the Defence Minister invited Te Kooti to Alexandra, so Fred met his elusive enemy at last. He watched Te Kooti arrive with forty followers, and get blind drunk. His companions, who remained sober, escorted him home the next day.

Isabella was disgusted that not only was Wetere pardoned, but in 1884 the Royal Humane Society of Australia awarded him a medal. This was for rescuing a man from drowning. Wetere became a minor celebrity, and a photograph of him with his wife and son was used as a postcard and bought by tourists. It showed his wife in a handsome flax cloak, and his son in a smart hat and coat. Isabella might have felt a pang when she looked at the boy; he was just a little older than baby Cecil when Wetere tomahawked him. Isabella may even have recognized the fob watch strung proudly across Wetere's broad belly, and possibly the greatcoat.

And the story of Wetere's heroic deed? A surveyor taking soundings off the Mokau bar in 1884 capsized and would have drowned but for Wetere climbing into a canoe and, endangering his own life, hauling the man out of the surf. The drowning man was the accident-prone surveyor Charles W. Hursthouse.

Te Kooti was not the only great Maori leader who Fred encountered at Alexandra. In October 1882 Fred was asked to help arrange a meeting between the Defence Minister and King Tawhiao along with six hundred of his people at the King's town of Whatiwhatihoe, just across the Waipa River from Fred's redoubt. The government hoped to increase security for the isolated farmers and townships still under threat from the Ngati Maniapoto, and also to push through the railway line. In return for opening up the King Country, the Kingites sought a pardon for all offenders including Te Kooti, and legal title for their lands. During the six weeks of negotiations King Tawhiao became an almost permanent fixture in the Gascoyne home. Fred found him 'a curious mixture of cunning and childish greed and self-importance'. King Tawhiao liked to help himself to anything in the house that took his fancy; he seldom spoke but would indicate what he wanted to a chief (probably Rewi Maniapoto). Although Fred and his wife Marion did not want to offend the King, when word came that he was on his way, Marion would quickly hide their favourite ornaments. Perhaps Tawhiao was making a subtle comment on the humiliating hand-outs the government was offering in exchange for peace: a new (British-style) house, an annual pension of £300 (£14,000 today) and a free pass for the railway which, the government hoped, would soon probe into the King Country, destroying its independence for ever. Warned by his chiefs that this was an attempt to divide the King movement, King Tawhiao turned down all but the pass and went to England to petition Queen Victoria for the return of confiscated Waikato land.

As for Te Kooti, in 1889 the government gave him a grant of land in Poverty Bay, but such was the strength of the settlers' opposition to his return, led by Charles (now Major) Westrupp, that he never took it up and remained in the King Country. His Ringatu faith lives on to this day.

Epilogue

The Armed Constabulary was disbanded in 1885 and Fred moved to Auckland, where he became sheriff. He enjoyed his stint there, largely because of the delightful parties at Government House to which he and Marion were invited thanks to a memo from Lord Salisbury to the Governor, Lord Onslow. But Fred, unable to resist offending his commanding officers, was eventually sacked.

When offered a post in the middle of nowhere with a miserable salary, he had no choice but to accept. He was to be resident magistrate of the Chatham Islands. It was the final twist: exile to the very islands on which his enemy had been imprisoned twenty-five years earlier. Like Te Kooti, Fred was promised that his banishment would be brief. He was to stay just long enough for him to quell some trouble brewing between the Maori, whereupon he would be transferred back to the mainland.

In September 1891 Major and Mrs Gascoyne boarded the government steamer to travel five hundred sick-making miles from Napier to Waitangi – Weeping Water. Most of the inhabitants came to inspect the man who would be running the place for the next few years. The arrival of ships with mail and goods every three or four months was the major event of the social calendar, not least because in the absence of a dock passengers had to be ferried ashore on dinghies which were liable to overturn in the surf.

The Residency stood on a deforested plateau overlooking the bay from which Te Kooti had escaped.

Since childhood Fred's world had been shrinking. The limitless Indian plains and soaring Himalayas had dwindled to a skein of an island in the middle of the south Pacific.

Chatham was nothing more than strands of land holding together dozens of lakes and a shallow lagoon that stretched over a hundred square miles. Of the thirteen islands, only two were inhabited, Pitt by just a handful of solitary pioneers, and Chatham by five hundred pakeha and Maori, who clustered in two villages. Waitangi, the capital, consisted of one store, one pub, a courthouse and post office, and a lock-up.*

Fred's first move was to call on the Maori chiefs. Paina te Poki was surly and aloof; all the Chatham Maori had come from Taranaki in 1831,† and were mostly supporters of Titokowaru and Te Whiti. Fred realized he needed tact and patience to win him over. One night he was woken by a shuffling sound outside the house. Telling Marion to stay in bed, Fred put on his dressing gown and gingerly opened the front door. Faced with a crowd of armed Maori, perhaps Reginald Biggs and Bamber flashed into his mind. He asked what they wanted. Paina Te Poki replied that they had come to make sure he would treat the Maori justly, both in court and out, and no differently from the pakeha. Fred was very moved, and

---

* The Maori lived by fishing and whaling, and at the end of each nesting season they went on birding expeditions to outlying islands, where they scaled the cliffs to capture hundreds of albatross as they reached the cliff edge just before taking flight. They ate the meat and decorated their cloaks with the feathers, and made their feet into little purses. They boiled the rest and shipped them over to the Maori in Taranaki. Most of the pakeha were sheep-farmers, none of them successful.

† On landing, the Taranaki Maori (armed and shipped over by the British) had wiped out the entire population of the pacifist Morori who (it is thought) had left New Zealand for the Chathams in the fifteenth century.

Epilogue

assured them he would be their friend, and considered pakeha and Maori to be equal.

Fred and Marion had shipped over their possessions, little realizing the destructive power of the damp. Moth and mould ate the carpets, the silver turned black and the piano was muffled. The damp laid Fred low with mare-mare, a congestion of the lungs that had bedevilled Te Kooti. Marion, on the other hand, who had been diagnosed with Addison's disease, regained her strength and got busy with her vegetables and farmyard and (because there was not a single road) with riding around the island organizing fund-raising events and parties. When people joked about 'the Major' they did not mean Fred.

Besides being resident magistrate, Fred quickly discovered that he was also postmaster, collector of customs, registrar of births, marriages and deaths, receiver of wrecks (of which there were several), licensing officer, paymaster, chief doctor (homoeopathic and allopathic) and arbitrator of connubial quarrels. When he was well enough, Fred enjoyed boating and fishing, and with the help of a book of Canadian designs built two flat-bottomed fishing boats, a whaler and (this was a three-month job) a 22ft yacht. He burst with schemes to improve the Chathams, and built a road bridge and the first dock.

Nevertheless, he chafed to be transferred back to the mainland. He bitterly resented his exile. His salary was so small he could barely live, and so long as he remained on the Chathams he would never shake off the mare-mare. But he was a victim of his success, and his stay was endlessly prolonged. The Prime Minister, John Ballance, had promised Fred that he would soon come home, and Fred considered Mr Ballance an honest man even if he was 'handicapped by humanitarian ideas', but

353

Ballance died in 1893 and his promise was buried with him, leaving Fred trapped on the Chathams for a biblical seven years. Like Te Kooti, Fred railed at the broken promises, the hope deferred, but unlike Te Kooti he had no Old Testament revelations, no visits from God to help set him free. Since the government had never heard of unpaid sick leave, the only way for Fred to escape was by retiring altogether.

Major Fred eked out the rest of his days on his Hawke's Bay plot.

Isabella had sold what remained of the farm for a pittance, and was living in straitened circumstances with Caroline and Charlotte – who both remained unmarried – in Nelson. Mary and Charlie also moved to Nelson, Mary as a teacher and eventually headmistress, Charlie as a wheelwright and inventor. His only son, Archie, a cousin of marquesses and generals, was a midget – though much loved in Nelson where he was seen about town playing in a brass band and delivering logs in a hand cart. Izzy and John Greenwood moved with their five children to Greymouth where John worked as a dentist and Native Commissioner, responsible for the affairs of the local chief, Tainui.

Amy secretly longed to go on the stage, but this was out of the question for one from her background. Instead, she had a 'sentimental friendship' with the frail but still charming Edward Gibbon Wakefield. Founder of the New Zealand Company, one of the architects of the colony, his early prediction that the Maori would succumb to 'wonderful peaceful conquest' may have sounded hollow to Gascoyne ears. Her engagement to Frederick Greenwood broken off, Amy married her cousin Henry Gascoyne, Bamber's younger brother. Perhaps, even now, the taint of family scandal narrowed her choice to these two families. Henry Gascoyne had a business selling wine and spirits in Waimate, South Canterbury. Amy, who despised 'trade', persuaded him to sell up and buy a farm, but while the liquor business thrived, his farm did not.

Isabella had lost her capital, and her savings in India had vanished too. She had suffered war, bereavement, earthquakes, massacre, fire, poverty and – perhaps worst of all – the loss of love, but Isabella never lost her faith. When she wrote her memoirs in 1888, she quoted bravely from Psalm 23 that 'goodness and mercy have followed me all my days from childhood to old age.' She was, she declared, ready to depart and join those loved ones gone before – her parents, all her brothers, Charles, their two babies and Bamber and his family. In fact Isabella would live another fifteen years to die in 1903 at the venerable age of ninety-two.

Mary moved north to Hastings to look after her brother after Marion died. Like Isabella and Izzy, Fred busied himself with his memoirs, which he dedicated to 'dear little Dougie' McLean, now the sixty-four-year-old owner of the vast and hugely profitable Maraekakaho estate. Fred had little else to interest him other than the 'irksome endeavour' to pay the butcher and grocer from his meagre army pension, with the unpleasant reminder as his old friends departed that he too would soon hear the Last Post.

Letter from Cecil Gascoigne to his father Clifton Gascoyne
(General Isaac's grandson), 3 January 1897*

c/o E C Studholme esq,
Waimate,
Canterbury
NZ

My dearest Father,
I've got a wonderful story for you now. In the township here
there is a certain Mrs Gascoyne [Amy], who says she's a
relation of Lord Salisbury's. She's a most worthy woman,
very clever, but has evidently had very bad luck in every way,
which has reduced her to a sad state of poverty. I don't
know her yet, but I'm in no hurry to because, worthy as she
is, she's a bit of a bore I believe. She's already found me out
and come to call with the intention of seeing me. I found out
that she must be some connection of ours somehow. She
knew all about the row between your father and some one
else re money, and his changing his name to Gascoigne.† She
married a cousin who was also GasCOYNE [Henry]. She's
so poor that she lives in a very small cottage in Waimate and
is obliged to associate with the poorer classes. But people
round here seem to be very kind to her and ask her into
society as much as possible. Her brother, a Major G, is

---

* As a young man Cecil laboured on the Studholmes' farm in Waimate before
going on to fight in the Boer War and thence returning home to Scotland.
† It is thought that Frederick, Isaac's son and Charles's first cousin, reverted
to the earlier spelling in an attempt to dissociate his branch of the family from
the Gascoyne-Cecils because he was disgusted that all the family fortune had
been left to his daughter Fanny, and thence to Lord Salisbury.

Epilogue

Resident Magistrate of the Chatham Islands, some 400 miles west of NZ.

No more news for you today.
My best love
Yr most affectionate son
Cecil

Letter from Cecil to his sister Ida Gascoigne, 23 February 1897

c/o E C Studholme esq,
The Waimate
Canterbury
NZ

My dear old Girl,
Many thanks for yours of a few days ago. I just wanted to tell you I went over to see Mrs Gascoyne on Sunday. The family consists firstly of Mrs G, who is nice I think, evidently very clever and well up both in things that happen every day, and in her family pedigree. I'm sorry to say I didn't know enough of my own family to find out exactly how we were connected. We are evidently not only connected but related. They have the same crest & the same motto with the word 'mon' put in. Raison pour mon guide. Wasn't Isaac Gascoigne the MP for Liverpool who was given that huge great silver thing with the engine on it. She was the daughter of a Major G in India. (Mrs & Mr G are first cousins.) They knew all about this Isaac G and we're pretty closely related.*
Mr G is a good old sort of chap. The world has evidently

---

* Cecil was a second cousin once removed of both Amy and Henry.

used him very roughly and consequently he *is a bit rough.*
They are wretchedly poor and live in a wretched little
unpainted wooden house. There are 2 sons and 3 daughters.
The two sons are very rough indeed. The two daughters very
shy, but otherwise rather nice. The 3rd daughter I have not
yet seen. She is in the Chatham Islands with her uncle,
another Major G, but only Major in the Colonial forces.
Now here's something rather funny. You remember a Dr
Hiddough of Bognor who either got DT or went off his dot
or something. Well his wife is this Mr G's youngest sister,
Annie.

   Mr G is second cousin to Lord Salisbury and knew him
when he was out here.*

   'Humping your bluey.' This is a NZ expression. It means
slinging your belongings over your back and marching. Lord
Salisbury 'humped his bluey' pretty well right through the N
Island when he was out here.

   Goodbye old girl. Much love from
   Your affectionate brother
   Cecil
   PS I told old G that there was a baronetcy somewhere
   about & he said if it was ever found it would come to
   him. Why? I don't know.

---

* This wasn't true. Perhaps Henry was trying to impress his smarter cousin.
Lord Salisbury was in New Zealand in 1852, seven years before Henry arrived
in the *Golconda* from London in 1859.

Epilogue

Letter from Marion (a.k.a. June) Gascoigne to her father Cecil Gascoigne, 14 April 1929*

Timaru
New Zealand

Dearest Dad
I met a darling old bird at tea called Mrs Gascoigne (aged 88) [Amy] who fell on my neck and said I was a dear child and she felt she'd known me all her life (very good method with the aged I have!) She produced a letter from you, written during the Boer War, which she presented to me. She had evidently treasured that for years. She was rather a pious old thing and we had a long conversation about religion. She's rather like you in that she doesn't approve of foreign missions. She said that before your father died he promised to ask you to draw a Gascoigne coat of arms for her. She apparently collects these things, so what could I say but that I'd ask you to do one for her now. Whereupon she nearly wept with excitement, so do draw one Dad. As Mummy would say, 'You're so good at doing things like that!' I don't know if a coat of arms just means the pike's head and crown, or is it something more? The old lady said you knew her address.

> *Your loving*
> *June*
> P.S. Don't forget the coat of arms for the old trout.

---

* On his return from the Boer War, Cecil had married a Miss Munro of Foulis, a distant cousin of Isabella's, so although she did not know it, Marion was related to Amy twice over. Marion was in New Zealand on holiday, visiting her father's old friends and haunts.

359

Postscript

Strangerland began with Sir George Bowen, who was my great-great-grandfather. Bowen was a professional imperial governor. For over twenty-eight years he governed more British colonies than anyone before or since, moving with his family from the Ionian Islands, where he was President of the Ionian University and then Secretary of the Ionian Islands Government, to Government Houses in Queensland (1859–68), New Zealand (1868–73), Victoria (1873–79), Mauritius (1879–83) and Hong Kong (1883–7).

Throughout his career he kept huge scrapbooks. These are pasted with cuttings about his vice-regal peregrinations around the country, and copies of his voluminous speeches. They include the full texts of Addresses and Replies, detailed descriptions of balls and eulogies to every visible garment worn by the stylish Lady Bowen at every ball. There are cartoons from *Punch*, military dispatches, verses of welcome and excerpts from trials and debates in parliament.

The New Zealand scrapbook is the bulkiest of the collection, and in the worst condition. The leather binding has flaked and the spine broken; the ink has faded and the paper curled at the edges. Perhaps this is because late in life, when my great-great-grandfather had retired to a country house in England

and was seated by the fire, this volume was the one he opened most frequently. Of all the countries he governed, New Zealand interested him most, largely because his years there coincided with the Maori Wars (now known as the New Zealand Land Wars). His role as Governor included direct responsibility for Native Affairs, which enabled him to play his part in the attempt to make peace. He was also charmed by the Maori themselves – their rhetoric, their chivalry, their elaborate courtesy, their clannish customs.

The Maori Wars have barely been heard of outside New Zealand. As I discovered while poring over these papers, the image of New Zealand as being peaceably settled, with the sophisticated Maori accepting and even welcoming the protection of the British crown, is completely false. The Maori were fierce and clever warriors, and the British defeated them largely because they played on their tribal loyalties to divide and rule, and persuaded a sufficient number of Maori to fight on their side. The image of white New Zealand as a blandly decent society is equally wrong: the settlers wanted that land, and were going to get it by fair means or foul, even if that meant a fight to the death.

Another revelation was how reluctant the British government was to colonize New Zealand. Far from orchestrating the empire-building from Whitehall, many in the British government saw their involvement with these far-flung islands as financially draining and pointless. Many statesmen of the day, including even some in the Colonial Office, talked eagerly of the day when Canada, Australasia and South Africa would govern themselves so responsibly that they could shake off the parental yoke. Bowen was an early and enthusiastic voice in the pro-imperial lobby. His was a dream of harmony and equality, a precursor to modern dreams about Europe. When Bowen was governing New Zealand, this dream was not widely shared; in fact it was not until twenty years later with the Colonial and Indian Exhibition of 1886 and the Colonial Conference of 1887 that the general public became convinced that, in Bowen's words, 'trade followed the flag'.

Bowen also enjoyed New Zealand because his tenure coincided with the visits of Prince Alfred in 1869 and 1870. Press cuttings in his scrapbook describe the Queen's birthday ball in the Prince's presence as the most fabulous ever. Carriage after carriage rolled up the avenue to Auckland's Government House where guests were introduced to the Governor and his wife, Diamantina, a handsome Greek-Italian contessa from the Ionian island of Zante. Some of the Maori chiefs and their wives appeared dazzled by the brilliancy of the light and the setting, but after some diffidence were put at ease by Lady Bowen. They studied a tasteful table arrangement of Turkish weapons, and an interesting collection of silver trowels with which Sir George had been presented on opening railways in Queensland. The band of the *Galatea* struck up the first set of quadrilles, and Prince Alfred swept Lady Bowen into the ballroom, which had been built especially in his honour. Beneath the brilliantly lighted gas chandeliers, the assemblage of the elite of Auckland was as animated and festive as possible, the dresses and scarlet uniforms and feathered flax cloaks vivid against the sober black frock coats of the civilians.

The Sailor Prince was a guest of the Bowens in Auckland when my great-grandmother was born there in 1869. The Prince became her godfather and gave her a beautiful diamond ring, which I have. He also gave her all his names: Alfreda Ernestine Albertha, known as Affie – as was he.

I had planned to write about the Bowens, but was distracted by a newspaper cutting in the scrapbook, 'FURTHER PARTICU-LARS OF THE MASSACRE OF SETTLERS AT WHITE CLIFFS'. The article described the murder of a Bamber Gascoyne/Gascoigne and his wife and three children near New Plymouth in 1869. This unusual name (each spelling was used) happens to be that of my cousin, the celebrated writer and quizmaster. The murdered pioneer had to be a relation, since Bamber is an old family name, inherited from a Miss Margaret Bamber, an eighteenth-century heiress who married Sir Crisp Gascoyne, a brewer who became Lord Mayor of London, and my great x 6 grandfather. When Sir George Bowen's secretary pasted the story into His Excellency's scrapbook he had no idea that baby Affie's daughter would marry a Gascoigne and thus unite the two families. They became my grandparents.

It transpired that three of the murdered Bamber's relatives had written memoirs of those difficult times. A descendant had transcribed them and added memoirs of her own, and after seeing Bamber Gascoigne on TV during the 1970s had sent him copies. I contacted him, and a bundle of papers, typed on an ancient typewriter with hand-corrected errors, soon landed on my doormat. The earliest and most substantial memoir was written by Isabella in 1888. She apologized for writing her narrative 'straight off, without a copy', and added that 'if there are errors, please excuse them, as I am now seventy-eight years old.' There *are* a few errors of dates and names, and the story is related in a confusing to-and-fro manner, but on the whole it is astonishing for its detail. It was never intended to be published. She introduced it as a 'letter' to be read by her children and grandchildren who, she wrote fastidiously, 'from being brought up in this colony know little or nothing of their family history'. She dwelt lovingly on their ancestry. This not only informed them of their past, but fixed them in the migratory whirl, gave them their still point.

Then she related the story of her own eventful life. I was intrigued by her twenty years in India not only because of the almost unimaginable way of life that she described, but because they were balanced on a fulcrum of change: Charles's attitudes towards Indian customs and morality were positioned to one side at the end of the old India, and Isabella's new Nonconformist sobriety on the other side at the start of the new. Charles was no swashbuckling William Hickey or orientalist-turned-native with hordes of concubines – those days were largely gone – but he was also not as moralistic, pompous or intolerant as younger men would become over the next few decades. He was something in between. During the 1820s and 30s it was still common for men like Charles to treat the Indians with consideration and good manners; a minority openly criticized the entire concept of colonialism. Charles did not see British rule in India as God-given, as would be the case by the 1840s and 50s.

After the excitement of India, Isabella found New Zealand 'a new world, in a very painful sense, and there we were buried alive for twenty years.' Their capital was partly invested in sheep, the rest in land. 'We finally lost both, and all our savings in India vanished too.'

Here, abruptly and tantalizingly, her story ended. She mentioned Bamber's murder, but about New Zealand itself, nothing. I longed to know what happened next. How did Isabella cope with pioneer life? Why did they lose everything? *There I found a new world, in a very painful sense.* What was so painful? What did that thin-lipped sentence mean? There was no answer. The memoirs petered out.

Isabella's reticence was compounded by the lack of any reference to the Gascoynes in contemporary diaries or letters home. Mary Hobhouse, the prolifically epistolary wife of the first Bishop of Nelson, who spent four hours a day communicating with Home – to the extent that her first child nearly died from neglect – made no mention of the Gascoynes, even though she met Isabella. Motueka commemorates its early inhabitants in its street names. There is a Fearon Street and a Greenwood Street, a Hursthouse Street, but is there a Gascoyne Street? Of course not. They withered away so completely that their branch vanished from my own family tree. In one published family history Charles Gascoyne's name has been added in pencil by some diligent genealogist with the query 'illegitimate???' alongside. It was as if he had gone to the bottom of the world and vanished into the Long White Cloud. He had become nothing but a rumour.

The second, briefer memoir by Izzy covered the same ground. Then came a chapter by a Constance Miller, granddaughter of Amy, great-granddaughter of Isabella. This included family stories passed down by her mother, Caroline Gascoigne, but was mainly about the remarkable pioneer life of Fred, her great-uncle, and much of it quoted from his autobiography, *Soldiering in New Zealand.*

Disloyally deserting the Bowens for these more intriguing relatives, I had the skeleton of a wonderful family saga. But I needed more. I had been introduced to the Gascoynes, but didn't have enough material to get to know them. I wanted to steep myself in their world, but I didn't even know what they looked like. Isabella mentioned having family miniatures painted in Clifton, Bristol, by a reputed artist named James Fisher, who had painted the young Queen Victoria. These portraits meant a lot to the family: when they were escaping from bandits during the Sikh Wars, they were one thing they sought to preserve. I had no idea how to trace them.

I could begin with Constance Miller, but she described her father as having fought in the Boer War, so there was little chance of her being alive. But I wrote to her anyway. At the same time, on the advice of a historian from New Zealand's Ministry for Culture and Heritage, I posted a message on a website called history.nz, asking if anyone had ever heard of Frederick Gascoyne. Astonishingly, I had an immediate reply both to the letter and the web message from Constance's brother – great-nephew of both Fred and Bamber – saying that although the surname had died out in New Zealand, Isabella's descendants were still going strong. With typical Kiwi friendliness, he invited me and my family to join them for Christmas.

We met in a beautiful garden outside Hastings, on the east coast of the North Island. Constance Miller had inherited Isabella's longevity and at the age of ninety-three was still refined, and neat as a little bird, though reluctantly poised to move into a retirement home. The garden belonged to her brother, who embodied their great uncle in his splendid name: Gascoyne Francis Bamber Miller (although with typical Kiwi prosaicism, he was known as Jim). We were, we established, fourth cousins twice removed. Hanging on Jim's sitting-room wall were the family miniatures, so here at last was the young

Isabella: a beauty, and the dashing curly-haired Charles. Even more special was the gift of a copy of the photograph of Charles and Isabella standing in front of their house at Lohughat, almost in the flesh.

Although I now knew what Isabella and Charles looked like – and that was a huge step forward – I still had only the Indian half of their story. The following fifty years had vanished. I was condemned to relying on other people's memoirs and clotting the prose with the weasel words 'would have' and 'might have been', 'doubtless' and 'probably'. I didn't want to cloud the story with these uncertainties. I wanted the truth.

Browsing in a bookshop in Nelson, I came across a novel called *Season of the Jew* by Maurice Shadbolt, one of New Zealand's best-known writers. As I read, I realized that I knew this story. It was Fred's. I wrote to Maurice Shadbolt to ask if we could meet and also if he knew where I could get hold of Fred's autobiography, which I had failed to find in the British Library or on the Internet.

From: David Ling
To: Helena Drysdale
Subject: Maurice Shadbolt

Dear Helena Drysdale
Thanks for your letter to Maurice Shadbolt which I took the liberty of opening. Maurice was diagnosed with Alzheimer's a couple of years ago and has deteriorated over the last 12 months to the point where he is now in a rest home and incapable of dealing with any correspondence. He remembers that he is a writer but not much more than that. It is quite tragic for someone whose mind was so much sharper than

most. I know that he would have enjoyed meeting you and would have given any assistance that he could.

Season of the Jew *was of course written in the 1980s and I don't know how I could find out just what he read and who he spoke to. I do know though that he spent a considerable amount of time in the Gisborne Public Library poring over old newspapers and documents as well as tramping the bush himself. He also spent quite a lot of time in the National Library in Wellington.*

I'm sorry that I can't be of more help.

With best wishes,

David Ling

I too combed the records in the National Library, the superb Alexander Turnbull Library in Wellington. I was still looking for Bowen material but I was also intrigued by his Native and Defence Minister, Sir Donald McLean, who was Bowen's main link with the Maori, and who Bowen clearly admired. McLean's career covered the whole history of pioneering in New Zealand; he was in many ways the most impressive figure of the day. Since the Governor had retained control over Native Affairs, and since the Maori Wars were at their height and therefore Native Affairs of paramount importance, both Bowen and McLean played major roles at this time. There were collections of documents about their combined attempts to end the Maori Wars, their trips up rivers into the heart of Maoridom to nego-tiate with Maori chiefs at vast koreros attended by over a thousand warriors. When Bowen died in 1899, his obituary in *The Times* lauded the firmness and justice with which he dealt with war in New Zealand, but it seemed that his pomposity had often disguised his intelligence and energy, and as a result he had not been given the credit he deserved.

While scrolling through the McLean catalogue, I stumbled on a correspondence with Isabella Gascoyne. The letters had been preserved by chance, simply because they were among the papers bequeathed to the library by McLean's estate. None of Isabella's descendants had any idea that they existed.

At first I simply stared. Here in front of me was what I had been looking for. Here was what happened next. And here at last was Isabella herself. Although I was seeing her handwriting through the medium of microfilm, her letters brought me into closer contact with her than any miniature or photograph. They were static; the letters moved and changed with each day that she wrote, with her mood. They bore the imprint of her actual hand, and gave me a peculiar feeling of almost getting inside her body, looking out through her eyes.

In fact the letters were difficult to read. Isabella's flowing copperplate was striped with lots of underlining for emphasis, and dashes used not as parentheses but in place of full stops. The paper was thin and sometimes the ink showed messily through from the other side, blurring her words. There were blots and smudges, and times when her quill had needed sharpening. To save paper and postage she often frugally over-wrote at ninety degrees across paper she had already written on. The warp and weft of her words wove unintelligible hieroglyphics.

After endless reading and re-reading, my eyes adjusted. But I was still confused. This was partly because the letters were mixed up, out of date order. It was also because I was piecing together a version of events that made no sense. The memoirs presented one story, but these letters suggested its opposite, almost a positive and negative. The letters appeared to present the truth as Isabella saw it, the memoirs another kind of truth – as she would have liked it to have been. As she wrote to McLean, 'We might hope, with God's blessing, to obliterate the past from our children's and our own minds.'

Just as I was beginning to take it all in, the archives closed. I had a ferry booked that night for the South Island and no plans to return to Wellington. Photocopies could be sent to my home in London, but that meant waiting weeks before I discovered the outcome of the story.

I visited Pangatotara and was surprised by its beleaguered feel. The poplars looked diseased, the plantations thin. Sheep foraged amongst reeds and thistles in the plains beside each riverbank. Despite the roads and bridges, few of which existed in Isabella's day, this valley felt abandoned, a forgotten backwater. Farmers blame it on the 1877 flood, which destroyed the Gascoynes' land and dumped silt all over the valley.

The scattered houses were too modern to have been the Bungalow. The only possible contender was a clapboard cottage on the east bank but its elderly owner had never heard of the Gascoynes. I chatted to her through her open kitchen window. She was tucking a cosy over her teapot. 'I should think about the present,' she advised me with typical Kiwi practicality. 'I wouldn't waste your time fussing about what's dead and gone.'

Ignoring her, I immersed myself in pioneer life. I visited private museums in Nissen huts filled with camp ovens and butter churns, flat irons and, for the most sophisticated settler, an OK Washing Machine made in 1888 which was rotated by hand. I also tried my hand at gold panning near Collingwood. What in Fred's day was a thriving town of stick-and-canvas dwellings

has today almost dwindled away, with just a few souvenir shops
and a museum on a silent street that peters out into nowhere.
Like Maurice Shadbolt I tramped the bush in the Urewera. The
settlers never managed to penetrate the Urewera, and even
today the Tuhoe tribe who live there expect to be asked permission for aircraft to fly over. I flew four hundred miles into
the Pacific to visit the Chatham Islands, a tropical Falklands –
sheep grazing under palm trees. I stayed with someone who
longed for one thing in life: to browse in a supermarket and
pluck what she wanted from the shelves; instead everything had
to be ordered from catalogues, and took months to be shipped
from the mainland. It was easy to imagine how isolated it was
a century earlier.

In Auckland I explored the old Government House (one of
the oldest secular public buildings in New Zealand), where
Affie Bowen was born. It was still surrounded by magnificent
trees and the lawn on which Diamantina Bowen practised
archery. With its pediments and architraves and cornices it
looked like a classic Georgian mansion, but in fact it was not
built until 1856, and not of stone, but of wood disguised as
stone: wood was the local material, and could best withstand
the earthquakes. I was shown around by Denys Oldham,
the architect who remodelled it for its present use as a staff
common room for Auckland University. The reception rooms
that once thronged with Auckland's grandees was now clumped
with modern wooden-framed armchairs at one end, and a cafe
at the other, and the walls were hung with abstract paintings.
The Bowens might have flinched at seeing modern academic
taste displacing their own elegance, but they might also have

been thankful that the house was there at all, defying repeated bureaucratic attempts to demolish it.

The ballroom was a barn-like structure painted pink and tacked onto the back, one entrance now blocked to make a bar. It housed lecture equipment and stacks of chairs. Denys Oldham explained that it had been built as a bribe by Governor Sir George Grey to tempt Prince Alfred to visit New Zealand. If you come, Grey promised, I'll build you a ballroom. By the time he arrived, Grey had been sacked and replaced by Bowen, but the ballroom was ready. Even in its state of unaesthetic academia it was not hard to envisage the swirl of ball gowns, the twinkling quadrilles, Diamantina in her tiara.

I went to New Plymouth, a scruffy town at the end of the road in Taranaki; the museum was closed for renovations. But on the outskirts rose the beautifully tended Te Henui cemetery and at its summit beneath the shade of a pohutukawa tree in full red bloom, overlooking the town and a turquoise sea, the victims of the White Cliffs massacre were buried beneath a commemorative obelisk. Thirty miles north, in country that grew wilder by the mile, I reached Pukearuhe, the scene of their deaths. I'd imagined it in a deep dark forested dell, but in fact they were killed in broad daylight, on an open sunny cliff top. A few grassy mounds and a fireplace are all that remain of the blockhouse of Bamber's redoubt.

Photocopies of Isabella's letters arrived in London. They described scenes from another era, of Stone Age primitiveness, even though Isabella died in 1903 – only just beyond living memory. What was equally striking was that the story itself was as modern as the world in which it took place was remote. Isabella's bewilderment at Charles's treatment of her made this a human story that could not fail to move anyone, at any time or place. I tried to remain detached, but I couldn't help sharing her rage and grief. What was most touching, and perhaps surprising given the distance between most Victorian women of Isabella's class and their children, was her desperate need for those children.

The letters did not reveal everything. There were still gaping holes. Many were filled both by my own travels in Bengal and the Himalayas and during the months that I combed the records of the East India Company, now housed in the climatically controlled top floor of the British Library. Sitting beside bearded sadhus in saffron robes, I turned the wheels of microfilms, pored over maps, flicked through card indexes. As a cavalry officer, Charles's every professional move during twenty years of service was noted in his military records.

Other facts were verified by the essential handbook, *The Bengal Directory and Annual Register*. Its scope was huge. It listed every regiment, with every officer, his rank, and whether or not he was on furlough/sick certificate/visiting the hills. It listed the date he was commissioned, when he attained his present rank, when he was invalided. It listed his salaries when in camp, in the cantonment, in the field or on furlough. Thus young ladies more materialistic than Isabella could use the *Register* to work out exactly what everyone earned, and choose a husband accordingly. The *Register* also listed the huge number of civilians employed as writers or in public offices – Lottery Offices, Military Board Offices, Adjutant General's Office, Surveyor General's Office, Salt Office and Opium Office. It was a heroic and yet somehow ludicrous attempt to make order from the chaos of India, to get it under control. Being an Anglo-Indian in Bengal was like being part of a huge club, which teetered on the edge of anarchy and had to be kept in line through strict adherence to its infinite rules and regulations.

The *Bengal Register* also contained a section headed 'shipping news' and there, month by month, were listed all ships arriving and departing, and all passengers.

The *Register* provided the outline, and ships' logs could colour the picture in. After 1833 the East India Company lost its monopoly of trade with India and abandoned strict record-keeping. In an act of bureaucratic vandalism, hundreds of ships' logs and ledgers were simply thrown away. But amongst the surviving records is the log of the *Sovereign*, which carried the baby Isabella back from India to England in 1811. I lifted it gingerly out of its conservation-grade cardboard box, and laid it across the v-shaped cushion designed to protect its spine, leaving behind shreds of paper that had disintegrated into the box. Like all early Company logs, it was bound in red leather; some of the logs have suffered water damage, suggesting some sort of accident at sea, but Captain Campbell's pages are in pristine condition, as if barely looked at since he wrote them. In calm copperplate he provided a glimpse of the drama of the high seas.

It was harder to track down the story of Isabella's journey to New Zealand, for her memoirs and letters left out a crucial detail: the ship's name. Without that, or a New Zealand equivalent of the *Bengal Register*, I could discover nothing about the journey even though it occupied six months of her life, and was of huge importance to her. Her failure to record the name was unusual since she was otherwise precise about tonnages, captains and so on, but an explanation may be that once people landed in New Zealand the journey there quickly became a subject for bores: everyone had done it, there was nothing new to say. It was thought better to forget the past and get on with the new life. Isabella's silence may also have been because she was so distressed by what the journey led to that she couldn't bear to think about it.

The trail went cold. At the Public Record Office in London a discouraging librarian said that no passenger lists were kept before the 1890s. Isabella had left for New Zealand in 1853. I sat disconsolately in the PRO cafe, briefly diverted by the time-warping sight of a man outside stalking around the lakes in pursuit of pigeons with a falcon on his shoulder. Then I squeezed back through the security barriers and tried again. I read the New Zealand Governors' dispatches to the Colonial Office, their brief mentions of Maori unrest and of outbreaks of smallpox and the need to quarantine the immigrants. It was a few days before I discovered that the PRO held a small collection of bound copies of the biweekly *Wellington Independent*, covering the early 1850s. I carried them from the delivery desk in huge cardboard folders tied up with ribbons. I prepared to wade through every edition in the hope of finding some passing reference to some ship that might have carried Isabella and little Charlie. I lifted out one volume and opened it at random. 10 May 1854. There, under the heading 'shipping intelligence', was a note of the arrival three days earlier of the barque *Balnaguith*, 453 tons, under Captain A. Smith from London via Lyttelton. The passenger list included a Mrs Gas-

Postscript

coigne (sic) and a Master Gascoigne. I could barely restrain my yelp of excitement.

During the early 1850s arrivals from England were still so eagerly anticipated, and so rare, that the *Wellington Independent* also carried a long description of the voyage. I had what I needed.

Family members dug out old letters and photographs, and more connections arrived through the Internet. The Nelson Provincial Museum revealed that someone else was researching the Gascoynes in New Zealand, and some detective work led to a retired psychiatrist living outside Bristol. When we spoke on the phone I found it hard to place his lilting accent. I thought it might be Welsh. Only gradually did it emerge that he was Indian, born in Calcutta, and a great-grandson of Isabella's brother Archy and the half-Indian Emily Payter. Here was a living link to that fateful journey to Cape Town, and to the widowed Emily's decision to return to India with her children.

In the Royal Commonwealth Society Collection in Cambridge University Library, I tracked down one of the UK's two known copies of *Soldiering in New Zealand*. It must have been years since anyone had bothered to pluck Fred's autobiography from the shelf and blow away the dust. Fred was no writer, but his story was a splendid adventure. His quarry, Te Kooti, a brilliant leader and master of guerrilla warfare, remained a source of terror for decades. He was New Zealand's Boney: the mere mention of Te Kooti's name was enough to persuade naughty children to be good. He assumed almost satanic status, partly because of his ability to pounce out of nowhere, but also because he could melt elusively away. In his ability to escape, in the absolute power over his followers that arose from his

377

religious fanaticism, in his willingness to massacre large numbers of people, in the ruthlessness of his leadership and in the extent of the fear he generated, he resembled not Napoleon so much as a modern terrorist, a Maori bin Laden.

Fred's career brought him into contact with two of the other greatest Maori leaders of all time, Titokowaru and King Tawhiao, both of whom were indirectly responsible for Bamber's death.

So here were two generations of one family who traversed oceans and continents to reach three corners of the empire at a time when that empire was taking shape. The Gascoynes were involved physically and emotionally in the First Afghan War, the First Sikh War, the Indian Mutiny and the Maori Wars – all great public events that transformed the way the empire developed.

The main protagonists responded to these events in unconventional ways. They did not share the casual racism of many of their peers. They were more complex in their attitudes, full of paradoxes. Fred, McLean and Bowen admired and even loved the Maori, but devoted their careers to – in effect – wiping out Maoridom. Their desire for the spread of civilization was criticized by Lord Salisbury as a cover for racial arrogance. Like Victorian butterfly hunters, they killed what they loved.

Their stories, as I unravelled and put them together again, raised intriguing questions of race, Britishness, empire, religion and politics. But what made them so special were the intimate revelations of their familiar human concerns – love, loss, marriage, betrayal, grief, faith, ambition, endurance and (possibly) reconciliation. In many ways the private story reflected the public one.

Postscript

Public events did not turn out as expected. It was thought that the Maori would soon be gone, like the moa, the huge flightless bird that they had eaten to extinction. But instead they are rediscovering themselves and fighting back. The 1840 Treaty of Waitangi is as important today as it ever was, now that the Maori have persuaded the New Zealand Government to look again at its provisions, to redefine the promises made beside that weeping waterfall, and to fulfil them. At Pukearuhe there stands a stone memorial to Reverend Whiteley. As part of the ongoing cultural redress that has emerged from the Waitangi Treaty settlement, the 4.3 hectares of the Pukearuhe site have been returned to the Ngati Tama iwi, from whom they were confiscated in the 1860s. The Ngati Tama say they were not involved in any fighting and want the land back in the same state as when it was taken in 1865. This means that the Whiteley memorial is to be removed. When Constance and Gascoyne Miller are no longer with us, few will remember what happened on the crest of those White Cliffs one sunny day in 1869, and little will remain to remind them – except perhaps, dear reader, this book.

INDIA

amir – ruler

Anglo-Indian – in East India Company context not a person of mixed blood, but a British person who had lived in India

arrack – native alcohol

ayah – nanny or maid

badmash - rogue

bibi-ghar – woman's house

bihishti – water carrier

cantonment – Anglo-Indian standing camp or military quarter of a *station*

charpoy – light wooden string bed

civilian – in Anglo-Indian context an administrative officer of the East India Company

collector – an administrative officer of the East India Company who collected taxes, usually in some remote outpost

coolie – worker

dak/dawk – post, or transport by relays of men and horses

dak bungalow – house for travellers at rest stop

darzee – tailor

dhobi – laundryman

dooli – covered litter

granthi – learned Sikh scholar or priest

furlough - leave

hookah – water pipe or hubble-bubble

jhampan – open litter

khalsa dal – Sikh army

khansaman – butler or cook

khitmagar – in charge of plate, and waiting at table

khus-khus – odiferous tall jungle grass used to make *tatties*

maidan – open meadow or plain, in Anglo-India often in front of the *cantonment*

manji – captain of a boat

maulvi – Muslim priest or learned scholar

memsahib – wife of a *sahib*, lady

munshee – language teacher

nabob – English corruption of Hindustani 'nawab', meaning Mogul governor. It became a word for an old India hand, usually hugely rich

nautch girls – Indian dancers

palanquin – enclosed Indian litter, about three foot high, carried on protruding poles

palque-gharri – horse cart

pandit – Hindu priest or learned scholar

peg – drink, especially of brandy and soda

piquet – sentinel

punkah – cloth fan, usually suspended from the ceiling and pulled by hand by a punkah wallah

Punjab – Five Rivers, i.e. land of the five rivers between the Indus and the Sutlej

sabre – cavalry sword with a curved blade especially adapted for cutting

sabretache – leather satchel containing a sabre suspended from the swordbelt of a cavalry officer

sadhu – Hindu who has renounced worldly possessions

sahib – Sir/Mr/Master

salaam – Indian salutation

sepoy – native foot soldier

shah – king

shikari – huntsman

sirdar – chief

solar topee – hard hat worn by British against the sun

sowar – native cavalry trooper

station – in Anglo-Indian context a place where British officials lived and worked

subedar – chief native officer of a company of native troops

suttee – traditional practice of immolation of widows

syce – groom

tatties – screens of woven *khus-khus*, on which water was thrown to cool rooms

tulwar – curved sabre

NEW ZEALAND

haka – challenging dance, often preceding battle

hapu – sub-tribe or clan

Hau-hau – follower of the Pai Marire movement

iwi – tribe

kainga – unfortified village

kahikatea – native white pine (*Dacrycarpus dacrydioides*)

kauri – native pine (*Agathis australis*)

kokiri – attacking party

korero – discussion, dialogue
kumara – sweet potato
kupapa – pro-government Maori
mana – power, prestige, face
manuka – tea tree, a scrubby
    native shrub (*Leptospermum*
    scoparium)
mare-mare – congestion of the
    lungs familiar on the Chatham
    Islands
moa – flightless ostrich-like bird,
    now extinct
Moriori – pacifist Polynesian
    people who possibly left New
    Zealand in the fifteenth century
    to settle on the Chatham Islands
ngati – the many of (often precedes
    name of *iwi*)
nikau – indigenous palm
    (*Rhopalostylis sapida*)
niu – great mast or flagpole used at
    the centre of worship by the *Pai*
    Marire
pa – Maori fort, or fortified village
Pai Marire – Maori spiritual
    movement
pakeha – foreigner, especially
    European

podocarps – family of native trees
ponga – silver fern, a native tree
    fern (*Cythea dealbata*)
pohutukawa – red-flowered native
    tree (*Metrosideros excelsa*)
poro poro – openly branching
    shrubs or small trees (*Solanum*
    laciniatum)
rama-rama – torches or flares
raupo – bulrush (*Typha*
    augustifolia)
rimu – red pine (*Dacrydium*
    cupressinum)
tapu – forbidden, taboo, holy
taua – war party
totara – large forest tree
    (*Podocarpus totara*)
tui – songbird
tutu – shrub with poisonous seeds
    (*Coriaria ruscifolia*)
utu – payment, reciprocity
weka – small flightless bird
wahine – girl
whare – house
whati – mass panic

UNPUBLISHED SOURCES

Miller, Constance, *The Gascoyne Story*, including memoirs by Isabella Gascoyne and Isabelle Greenwood

Alexander Turnbull Library, National Library of New Zealand: Te Puna Matauranga O Aotearoa

Inward letters – Charles & Isabella Gascoyne, FJW Gascoyne, 1858–1872 in MS-Papers-0032-0287, McLean, Donald (Sir), 1820–1877: Papers
Gascoyne, Frederick. Papers. MS-Papers-2/16.
Greenwood family 1791–1951. Papers. MS-Papers-0098-6; MS-Papers-0098-10
Hooker, William, Letters 1868–1870, qMS-0096

Bank of England

Equivalent contemporary values of the pound

Hocken Library

Whiteman, George. Diary. MS-0511

John Oxley Library, Queensland

Bowen, Lady Diamantina. Papers

Bibliography

Queensland Women's Historical Association

Papers.

National Archives: Public Record Office, London

Colonial Office. Despatches to the Secretary of State, 1845–6, CO/209/134–6

New Zealand Company. Surgeon's Log of barque *Birman*

Note in correspondence register of Colonial Office re establishment in hill stations of convalescent homes for soldiers WO 43/475

Wellington Independent 1854 CO/213/24

Oriental and India Office Collection, British Library

Charles Gascoyne's service records: L/MIL/10/28/7 (microfilm); L/MIL/10/38/255; L/MIL/10/40/255; L/MIL/10/42/255; L/MIL/10/44/255; L/MIL/9/163 – pp. 174–7; L/MIL/5/12/185

East India Company records of Gascoyne and Campbell births, marriages and deaths: N/1/42/27; N/1/89; N/1/44/27; N/1/50/125; N/1/56/32; N/2/6/154 (microfilm); N/2/3/258; N/2/3/68; N/2/4/50

Shipping

L/MAR/B/195/G–I: log of *Sovereign* 1810–11

L/MAR/B/195H: logs of *Sovereign* 1808–12

L/MAR/B/195L: ledger & pay book of *Sovereign* 1806–7

Maps

Y/104/62C Map of Luhooghat and Champawat, 1932, scale 1 inch = 4 miles

Y/101/62C Luhooghat and Champawat, scale 1 inch = 2 miles

X/1491/EI 21 – Relief map of entire area of Kumaon & British Gurwhal, 1849, scale 12 inch = 8 miles

X/1493/1/24 – topographical map of Almora and district incl. Luhooghat, scale 1 inch = 1 mile; X/1493/1/25 topographical map of Almora and district incl. Luhooghat; X/1493/1/33 topographical map of Almora and district incl. Luhooghat – all 1868–1872

Photographs, paintings and drawings
Volumes of 'conveyances' – paintings, drawings and photographs, vol. 51
    4851–4890; 4852
Early photographs taken in India: Photo 835/(325); 409; 682 (102–116);
    682 (96–101); 247/3; 247/4
Paintings and drawings: views of Almorah by J. Manson, 1827 (WD 543)
Paintings of 1st Sikh Wars P894; P895(F472)

Private archives

Bowen papers, Devon
Gascoigne and Munro papers, Ross-shire
Gascoyne letters, Hatfield House, Herts

Puke Ariki and District Libraries, New Plymouth

Whiteley, John. Inquest proceedings on those murdered at the White
    Cliffs, February 1869. ARC 2004–208

Royal Commonwealth Society collection

Thornhill family. Letters 1862–1919
New Zealand immigration news cuttings

PUBLISHED SOURCES

India

Allen, Charles, *Soldier Sahibs, the Men Who Made the North-West Fron-
    tier*, John Murray, London, 2000
Atkinson, G. F., *Curry and Rice, or The Ingredients of Social Life at 'our'
    Station in India*, W. Thacker & Co., London, 1911 (5th edition)
Bengal and Calcutta Directories 1817–1853
Carman, W. Y., *Indian Army Uniforms under the British from the 18th
    Century to 1947*, Cavalry volume, Morgan-Grampian, London, 1961
Corbett, Jim, *Man-Eaters of Kumaon*, Oxford University Press, London,
    1946

Bibliography

Diver, Maud, *Honoria Lawrence: A fragment of Indian History*, John Murray, London, 1936

Eden, Emily, *Up the Country*, np, 1866

Farrington, Anthony, *A Biographical Index of East India Company Maritime Service Officers 1600–1834*, British Library, London, 1999

Farrington, Anthony, *Catalogue of East India Company Ships' Journals 1600–1834*, British Library, London, 1999

Farwell, Byron, *Armies of the Raj*, Viking, London, 1989

Guy, Alan J., and Boyden, Peter, *Soldiers of the Raj: The Indian Army 1600–1947*, National Army Museum, London, 1998

Heber, Reginald, *A narrative of a journey through the Upper Provinces of India from Calcutta to Bombay 1824–1825* (3 vols), London, 1827

Hickey, William (ed. Alfred Spencer), *The Memoirs of William Hickey*, 4 vols, London, 1925

Hodson, Major V. C., *List of the Officers of the Bengal Army, 1758–1843*, Constable, London, 1928

Hudson, Roger (ed.), *The Raj: An eye-witness history of the British in India*, Folio Society, London, 1999

Kaye, M. M., *The Sun in the Morning*, Viking, London, 1990

– *Golden Afternoon*, Viking, London, 1997

Kincaid, Dennis, *British Social Life in India*, George Routledge & Sons, London, 1938

Kipling, Rudyard, *Kim*, Bernard Tachnitz, Leipzig, 1901

Mackenzie, Alexander, *A History of the Munros of Fowlis*, A. & W. Mackenzie, Inverness, 1898

Mason, Philip (as Woodruff, Philip), *The Men Who Ruled India*, Jonathan Cape, London, 1953

Moore, Surgeon-General Sir William, *A Manual of Family Medicine and Hygiene for India*, Churchill, London, 1872

Newby, Eric, *Slowly down the Ganges*, Hodder & Stoughton, London, 1966

Parkes, Fanny, *Wanderings of a Pilgrim in Search of the Picturesque, during four-and-twenty years in the East*, Pelham Richardson, London, 1850

Pinney, Thomas (ed.), *Selected letters of Thomas Babington Macaulay*, Cambridge University Press, London, 1982

Walton, E. G., *Almorah, District Gazetteer of the United Provinces*, vol. XXXV, Allahabad, 1911

Yule, Henry & Burnell, A. C., *Hobson-Jobson: A Glossary of Colloquial Anglo-Indian Words and Phrases*, John Murray, London, 1903

New Zealand

Allen, Ruth, *History of Port Nelson*, Wellington, 1954

- *Nelson, A History of Early Settlement*, A. H. & A. W. Reed, Wellington, 1965

Barker, Lady Mary, *Station Life in New Zealand*, np, London, 1874

Barraud, Charles D, *New Zealand, Graphic and Descriptive*, Sampson Low, London, 1877

Beatson, Kath & Whelan, Helen, *The River Flows on – Ngatimoti through Flood and Fortune*, np, Motueka, 1993

Beaufoy, Betty, *Emma of the Hill Country*, Dorset Enterprises, Wellington, 1997

Belich, James, *The New Zealand Wars, and the Victorian Interpretation of Racial Conflict*, Auckland University Press, Auckland, 1986

- *I shall not Die, Titokowaru's War, New Zealand 1868–1869*, Allen & Unwin New Zealand with Port Nicholson Press, Wellington, 1989

Binney, Judith, *Redemption Songs, A life of Te Kooti Arikirangi Te Turuki*, Auckland University Press & Bridget Williams Books, Auckland, 1995

Bowen, Sir George, *Overland Journey of the Governor of New Zealand, notes of the journey of Sir George F Bowen, GCMG, in April 1872 from Wellington to Auckland across the centre of the North Island*, G. Street, London, 1872

Bradley, Ian, *Abide With Me, the World of Victorian Hymns*, SCM Press, London, 1997

Bridge Brereton, Lt Col. Cyprian, *No Roll of Drums*, A. H. & A. W. Reed, Dunedin, 1847

Butler, Samuel, *A First Year in a Canterbury Settlement*, Longman, London, 1863

Bibliography

Canton, J. R., *Pioneers of the Valleys*, Motueka and District Historical Society, Motueka, 1984

Cornwall, E. E., *Songs of Pilgrimage and Glory, Notes on the hymns of certain hymn writers*, The Central Bible Truth Depot, London, 1932

Cowan, James, *Sir Donald Maclean, the story of a New Zealand Statesman*, A. H. & A. W. Reed, Wellington, 1940

– *The New Zealand Wars, A History of the Maori Campaigns and the Pioneering Period* (2 vols), R. E. Owen, Wellington, 1956

Dalton, B. J., 'Browne, Thomas Robert Gore 1807–1887', *Dictionary of New Zealand Biography*, vol. I (1769–1869), Ministry for Culture and Heritage, Wellington, 1990

– *War and Politics In New Zealand 1855–70*, Sydney University Press, Sydney, 1967

Dashwood, Frances, *The Dashwoods of West Wycombe*, Aurum Press, London, 1987

Dawber, Carol, *Bainham, a History*, River Press, New Zealand, 1997

Dawson, Bee, *Lady Travellers, the Tourists of early New Zealand*, Penguin, Auckland, 2001

Deck, James, *Joy in Departing: a memoir of the conversion and last days of Augustus James Clarke*, Hamilton, Adams, London, 1847

– *Hymns and Sacred Poems*, W. H. Broom & Rouse, London, 1889

Donne, T. E., *The T. E. Donne collection of New Zealand watercolours*, Sotheby & Co., London, 1973

Fairburn, Miles, *The Ideal Society and its enemies, the foundation of Modern New Zealand society 1850–1900*, Auckland University Press, Auckland, 1989

Fell, Alfred, *A Colonist's Voyage to New Zealand under Sail in the Early Forties*, London, nd

Gascoyne, F. J. W., *Soldiering in New Zealand: being reminiscences of a Veteran*, with an appendix, *Pursuit of Te Kooti though Urewera Country* by G. A. Preece, T. J. S. Guilford, London, 1916

Gibson, Tom, *The Maori Wars: the British Army in New Zealand, 1840–1972*, L. Cooper, London, 1974

W. P. Morrell (ed.), *Narrative of the Waitara Purchase and the Taranaki*

War, by Harriet Gore-Browne, 1861, University of Otago Press, Dunedin, 1965

Gudgeon, T. W., *The Defenders of New Zealand*, Auckland, 1887

Hale, John (edited and introduced by), *Settlers, being extracts from the journals and letters of early colonists in Canada, Australia, South Africa and New Zealand*, Faber, London, 1950

Hassam, A. (ed.), *Sailing to Australia: shipboard diaries by 19th century British immigrants*, Manchester, 1994

Hursthouse, Charles, *New Zealand, or Zealandia, the Britain of the South*, 2 vols, Stanford, London, 1852

Kumar, R. & Brockington, I. F. (eds), *Motherhood and Mental Illness 2*, Butterworth, London, 1988

Lambert, Gail & Ron, *An Illustrated History of Taranaki*, Dunmore Press, Palmerston North, 1983

Lane-Poole, Stanley, *Thirty Years of Colonial Government, a selection from the despatches and letters of the Right Hon Sir George Ferguson Bowen* (2 vols), Longmans, Green & co., London, 1889

Lash, Max D., *Nelson Notables 1840–1940*, Nelson Historical Society, Nelson, 1992

Lineham, Peter J., 'Deck, James George 1807–1884', *Dictionary of New Zealand Biography*, vol. I, Ministry for Culture and Heritage, Wellington, 1990

Lloyd's Register of Shipping

Macgregor, Miriam, *Early Stations of Hawke's Bay*, A. H. & A. W. Reed, Wellington, 1970

– *Petticoat Pioneers, North Island Women of the colonial era*, A. H. & A. W. Reed, Wellington, 1973

McCaughey, Davis; Perkins, Naomi; Trimble, Angus, *Victoria's Colonial Governors 1839–1900*, Melbourne University Press, Melbourne, 1993

Maning, Frederick (as 'A Pakeha Maori'), *Old New Zealand and War in the North, A Tale of the Good Old Times*, Robert Creighton & Alfred Scales, Auckland, 1863

Miller, F. W. G., *Gold in the River*, A. H. & A. W. Reed, Wellington, 1946

Motueka and District Historical Society, . . . *and so it began*, Motueka, 1982

Neale, June E., *The Greenwoods*, General Printing Services, Nelson, 1984

Nolan, Tony, *Historic Gold Trails of Nelson and Marlborough*, A. H. & A. W. Reed, Wellington, 1976

Paul, Janet, 'Greenwood, Sarah 1809?–89', *Dictionary of New Zealand Biography*, vol. I (1769–1869), Ministry for Culture and Heritage, Wellington, 1990

Pickering, H. Y., *Chief Men among the Brethren, 100 Records and Photos of Brethren Beloved*, Pickering & Inglis, London, nd

Renton, Alice, *Tyrant or Victim, A History of the British Governess*, Weidenfeld & Nicolson, London, 1991

Rienits, Rex & Thea, *The Voyages of Captain Cook*, Paul Hamlyn, London, 1968

Salmon, J. T., *Native Trees of New Zealand*, 2 vols, Reed, Auckland, 1998

Salmond, Jeremy, *Old New Zealand Houses 1800–1940*, Reed, Auckland, 1986

Shadbolt, Maurice, *Season of the Jew*, David Ling, Auckland, 1986

Simpson, Helen, *The Women of New Zealand*, Allen & Unwin, London, 1940

Simpson, Tony, *The Immigrants, the great migration from Britain to New Zealand 1830–1890*, Godwit, Auckland, 1997

Sinclair, Keith, *The Origins of the Maori wars*, New Zealand University Press, Wellington, 1957

– 'Grey, George 1812–1898', *Dictionary of New Zealand Biography*, vol. I (1769–1869), Ministry for Culture and Heritage, Wellington, 1990

– (ed.), *Oxford Illustrated History of New Zealand*, Oxford University Press, Auckland, 1996

Stone (ed.), *Verdict on New Zealand*, A.H. & A.W. Reed, Wellington, 1959

Thomson, Jane (ed.), *Southern People: a dictionary of Otago Southland biography*, Longacre Press, Dunedin, 1998

Thwaite, Ann, *Glimpses of the Wonderful: the Life of Philip Henry Gosse 1810–1888*, Faber, London, 2002

Tunnicliff, Shirley (ed.), *The Selected Letters of Mary Hobhouse*, Daphne Brasell Associates, Wellington, 1992

Tyler, W. P. N., 'Bowen, George Ferguson 1821–1899', *Dictionary of New Zealand Biography*, vol. I (1769–1869), Ministry for Culture and Heritage, Wellington, 1990

Wakefield, E. Jerningham, *Adventure in New Zealand from 1839–1844*, vol. I, London, 1845

Walker, Peter, *The Fox Boy, The Story of an Abducted Child*, Bloomsbury, London, 2001

Ward, Alan, 'McLean, Donald 1820–1877', *Dictionary of New Zealand Biography*, vol. I (1769–1869), Ministry for Culture and Heritage, Wellington, 1990

Washbourne, H. P., *Further Reminiscences of Early Days*, np, Nelson c. 1925

Wells, B., *The History of Taranaki*, Edmonson & Avery, Taranaki News Office, New Plymouth, 1878

Who's Who in New Zealand and the Western Pacific, Gordon & Gotch, Wellington, 1908

Wood, G.A., *The Governor and his Northern House*, Auckland University Press, Auckland, 1975

Woodhouse, A. E., *Tales of Pioneer Women*, collected by Women's Institutes of New Zealand, nd

Wright, Shona, *Clifton, A Centennial History of Clifton County*, Clifton County Council, Waitara, 1989

General

Brander, Michael, *The Victorian Gentleman*, Gordon Cremonesi, London, 1975

Morris, Jan (as Morris, James), *Pax Britannica, the Climax of an Empire*, Faber & Faber, London, 1968

– *Heaven's Command, An Imperial Progress*, Faber & Faber, London, 1973

– *Farewell the Trumpets, An Imperial Retreat*, Faber & Faber London, 1978

Bibliography

Oman, Carola, *The Gascoyne heiress, the Life and Diaries of Frances Mary Gascoyne-Cecil 1802–1839*, Hodder & Stoughton, London, 1968

Quennell, Peter, *Victorian Panorama*, Batsford, London, 1937

Roberts, Andrew, *Salisbury, Victorian Titan*, Weidenfeld & Nicolson, London, 1999

Wilson, A. N., *The Victorians*, Hutchinson, London, 2002

Newspapers

Auckland Provincial Government Gazette

Daily News

Hawke's Bay Herald

Nelson Colonist & Nelson Examiner

Nelson Evening Mail

Punch, or the Wellington Charivari

Taranaki Daily News

Taranaki Herald

The Daily Southern Cross

The Evening Herald

The Evening Post

The Evening Star

The New Zealand Advertiser

The New Zealand Herald

The Otago Daily Times

The Press

The Saturday Review

The Wanganui Chronicle

The Westland Observer

Weekly Herald, Auckland

Wellington Independent

Picture credits

Jacket (front)

1 Private collection
2 Private collection
3 Private collection
4 Tyree Studio Collection, ref. 179311/3, Tasman Bays Heritage Trust/Nelson Provincial Museum

(back)

1 Puke Ariki
2 Hocken Collection, Otago

Colour

1 Private collection
2 Private collection
3 Private collection
4 Private collection
5 Private collection
6 Private collection
7 Sir Donald McLean papers, ref. MS-Papers-0032-0287-003, Alexander Turnbull Library
8 Private collection
9 *View at the Rangitaiki River* by Thomas Ryan, 1891, ref. B-159-008-1, Alexander Turnbull Library, Wellington, NZ
10 Sir Donald McLean Papers, ref. MS-Papers-003200287-004, Alexander Turnbull Library
11 Chromolithograph, 1877, from painting by John Gully, 1875, ref. PUBL-0010-10, Alexander Turnbull Library

Strangerland

16 Photograph by Holby, ref. P.3.76, Puke Ariki
17 Copyright Chapter Two
18 S. Carnell Collection, ref. G-22027-1/4, Alexander Turnbull Library